The Impact of Formal and Informal Institutions on Economic Growth

Hohenheimer Volkswirtschaftliche Schriften

Band 65

PETER LANG
Frankfurt am Main · Berlin · Bern · Bruxelles · New York · Oxford · Wien

Constanze Dobler

The Impact of Formal and Informal Institutions on Economic Growth

A Case Study on the MENA Region

PETER LANG
Frankfurt am Main · Berlin · Bern · Bruxelles · New York · Oxford · Wien

Bibliografische Information der Deutschen Nationalbibliothek
Die Deutsche Nationalbibliothek verzeichnet diese Publikation in der Deutschen Nationalbibliografie; detaillierte bibliografische Daten sind im Internet über http://dnb.d-nb.de abrufbar.

Zugl.: Hohenheim, Univ., Diss., 2011

D 100
ISSN 0721-3085
ISBN 978-3-631-61616-1

Internationaler Verlag der Wissenschaften
Frankfurt am Main 2011

www.peterlang.de

To my parents

Acknowledgements

The present work was approved by the Faculty of Business, Economics and Social Sciences at the University of Hohenheim as a dissertation in February 2011.

I am especially grateful to my supervisor Professor Dr. Harald Hagemann for his advice and support, his encouragement and for the freedom I was granted during my time as doctoral student and research assistant at his chair.

Furthermore, I want to thank the second referee Professor Dr. Jochen Streb for his second opinion, as well as Professor Dr. Michael Schramm for his interest and his participation in the oral doctoral examination.

I am grateful to my colleagues at the chair of economic theory for their encouragement and support, as well as their help and friendship. The many coffee and lunch breaks, seminars and other meetings induced the cooperative and inspiring atmosphere that contributed to the successful finish of the dissertation project.

My greatest thanks, however, go to my mother, who sadly passed away in 2010, and to my father.

Stuttgart-Hohenheim, March 2011 Constanze Dobler

Contents

Figures ... XI
Tables ... XIII
Abbreviations and variables ... XIV
1. Introduction ... 1
2. Institutions – a theoretical approach ... 10
2.1 Introduction ... 10
2.2 Formal and informal institutions ... 15
2.3 Growth-supporting institutions ... 18
2.4 Transaction costs ... 20
2.5 Institutional change and transplantation ... 21
2.6 Institutions and technology ... 28
2.7 Equilibrium view of institutions ... 33
2.7.1 General remarks ... 33
2.7.2 Shared-beliefs cum equilibrium-summary-representation approach ... 35
2.7.2.1 Model I ... 38
2.8 The form of societal organization ... 47
2.8.1 Model II ... 48
2.8.1.1 Horizontal and vertical societal structures ... 55
3. Institutions – an empirical approach ... 61
3.1 Informal institutions ... 61
3.1.1 Trust ... 63
3.1.2 Limited and generalized morality ... 64
3.1.3 Beliefs that encourage the accumulation of physical and human capital ... 67
3.1.3.1 Destiny ... 67
3.1.3.2 Life after death ... 68
3.2 Formal institutions ... 69
3.2.1 Property rights ... 69
3.2.2 Legal system – the rule of law ... 71
3.2.3 Form of government – democracy ... 73
3.3 Measuring institutions – a literature review ... 75
3.4 Endogeneity ... 83
3.5 Deep determinants of growth ... 86
3.6 Methodical issues ... 88
3.6.1 Two stage least squares ... 89
3.7 Religion as an instrumental variable for institutions ... 92
3.8 Regression analysis: the impact of formal and informal institutions on per capita income ... 101
3.8.1 Data ... 101
3.8.2 Regression approach ... 106
3.8.3 Regression results ... 108

4. Institutions and economic development in the MENA region 123
4.1 Introduction 123
4.2 Arab economic performance 126
4.3 Economic development in the second half of the 20th century 129
4.4 Total factor productivity 132
4.5 Investment 133
4.6 Public sector 136
4.7 Demography and education 138
4.8 Business environment 140
4.9 Financial sector 143
4.10 Trade 147
4.11 Corruption and red tape 148
4.12 Political and legal Institutions 150
4.12.1 Property rights 151
4.12.2 Constraints on the executive and democracy 152
4.12.3 Good governance 157
4.13 Informal institutions 165
4.13.1 Trust 165
4.13.2 Control 166
4.13.3 Respect and obedience 167
5. Differences in early institutional development 176
5.1 Introduction 176
5.2 The emergence of state and religion 179
5.3 The acceptance of Islamic occasionalism and the role of foreign sciences 182
5.4 Law 190
5.5 Corporate institutions 194
5.6 Education 196
5.7 The *waqf* 198
5.8 Foreign rule and historical accidents 199
5.9 Prohibition of interest 203
6. Conclusion: connection between the general institutional analysis and the case study on the MENA region 205
References 212
Data sources 227
Appendix A 229
Appendix B 232

Figures

Figure 2.1: emergence and alteration of institutions ... 21
Figure 2.2: institutional stickiness ... 24
Figure 3.1: deep determinants of growth ... 88
Figure 3.2: endogeneity and reverse causality ... 89
Figure 3.3: religious affiliation and informal institutions ... 100
Figure 3.4: religious affiliation and formal institutions ... 100
Figure 3.5: GDP per capita and trust ... 104
Figure 3.6: GDP per capita and control ... 104
Figure 3.7: GDP per capita and respect ... 105
Figure 3.8: GDP per capita and obedience ... 105
Figure 3.9: GDP per capita and inform4 ... 105
Figure 3.10: GDP per capita and xconst ... 106
Figure 4.1: GDP per capita for MENA and high income country groups ... 126
Figure 4.2: GDP per capita for MENA and world regions ... 127
Figure 4.3: GDP per capita for the MENA subgroups ... 127
Figure 4.4: MENA average GDP per capita growth rates ... 128
Figure 4.5: investment freedom in the MENA region ... 135
Figure 4.6: investment freedom in advanced economies ... 135
Figure 4.7: MENA average FDI inflows ... 136
Figure 4.8: government share of RGDPL ... 137
Figure 4.9: population growth ... 138
Figure 4.10: literacy rates (adults) ... 140
Figure 4.11: secondary school enrolment ... 140
Figure 4.12: MENA business freedom ... 142
Figure 4.13: advanced economies business freedom ... 142
Figure 4.14: MENA financial freedom ... 145
Figure 4.15: advanced economies financial freedom ... 146
Figure 4.16: MENA trade freedom ... 147
Figure 4.17: advanced economies trade freedom ... 148
Figure 4.18: MENA freedom from corruption ... 149
Figure 4.19: advanced economies freedom from corruption ... 149
Figure 4.20: MENA property rights ... 152
Figure 4.21: advanced economies property rights ... 152
Figure 4.22: MENA: voice and accountability ... 158
Figure 4.23: advanced economies: voice and accountability ... 159
Figure 4.24: MENA: regulatory quality ... 159
Figure 4.25: advanced economies: regulatory quality ... 159
Figure 4.26: MENA: government effectiveness. ... 160
Figure 4.27: advanced economies: government effectiveness ... 160
Figure 4.28: MENA: political stability ... 160
Figure 4.29: advanced economies: political stability ... 161
Figure 4.30: MENA: rule of law ... 161

Figure 4.31: advanced economies: rule of law 161
Figure 4.32: MENA: control of corruption 162
Figure 4.33: advanced economies: control of corruption 162
Figure 4.34: trust in MENA and advanced economies 172
Figure 4.35: control in MENA and advanced economies 172
Figure 4.36: respect in MENA and advanced economies 172
Figure 4.37: obedience in MENA and advanced economies. 173
Figure 4.38: live with parents, MENA and advanced economies. 173
Figure 4.39: women as single parents, MENA and advanced economies 173
Figure 4.40: women have to have children, MENA and advanced economies 174
Figure 4.41: divorce not justifiable, MENA and advanced economies 174
Figure 4.42: university important, MENA and advanced economies 174
Figure 4.43: men better politicians, MENA and advanced economies 175
Figure 4.44: politicians' beliefs in God, MENA and advanced economies 175

Tables

Table 3.1: regression results 115
Table 3.2: regression results 115
Table 3.3: regression results 116
Table 3.3: continuation regression results 117
Table 3.3: continuation regression results 118
Table 3.4: regression results 118
Table 3.5.1: regression results 119
Table 3.5.2: regression results 120
Table 3.6: data definitions and sources 121
Table 4.1: gross fixed capital formation as a percentage of GDP 134
Table 4.2: MENA business regulations 144
Table 4.3: MENA average xconst and polity2, 1990–2007 155
Table 4.4: MENA xconst and polity2, 2007 156
Table 4.5: MENA political freedom. 156
Table 4.6: advanced economies political freedom 157

Abbreviations and variables

Abbreviations	
FDI	Foreign direct investment
FEX	Foreign-introduced exogenous institutions
GDP	Gross domestic product
GCC	Gulf Cooperation Council
IEN	Indigenously introduced endogenous institutions
IEX	Indigenously introduced exogenous institutions
MENA	Middle East & North Africa
OECD	Organisation for Economic Co-operation and Development
OLS	Ordinary least squares
RGDPL	Real GDP per capita (Laspeyres)
RPLA	Resource-poor labor-abundant MENA countries
RRLA	Resource-rich labor-abundant MENA countries
RRLI	Resource-rich labor-importing MENA countries
TFP	Total factor productivity
2SLS / 3SLS	Two and three stage least squares
UAE	United Arab Emirates
WVS	World Values Survey
WDI	World Development Indicators
WGI	Worldwide Government Indicators

Country symbols	
DZ	Algeria
AUS	Australia
CDN	Canada
ET	Egypt
F	France
D	Germany
IR	Iran
I	Italy
J	Japan
HKJ	Jordan
MA	Morocco
N	Norway
SA	Saudi Arabia
CH	Switzerland
USA	United States

Variables

Chapter 2:

Institutional change and transplantation:

Z	Level of institutional stickiness
I	Institution

Shared-beliefs cum equilibrium-summary-representation approach:

$R = \{1,2,...,r\}$	Set of agents
$\Lambda_i = \{\lambda_i\}$	Set of technologically feasible actions of agent i $(i \in R)$
$\Lambda = x_i \Lambda_i = \{\lambda\} = \{\lambda_1,...,\lambda_i,...,\lambda_r\}$	Set of all technologically feasible action profiles
λ_{-i}	Agent i's expectations regarding others' actions $(i \in R)$
π_{-i}	Agent i's Nash equilibrium expectations regarding others' actions $(i \in R)$
$\Omega = \{\omega\}$	Institutional environment
ϕ	Consequence function
s_i	Agent i's private action choice rule
S_i	Agent i's set of action choice rules $(i \in R)$
σ_{-i}	Agent i's expectations regarding others' action choice rules $(i \in R)$
F	Transition function
$t;\tau$	Time
δ	Time discount factor
u_i	Agent i's utility function
$\Psi = \{\psi\}$	Exogenous environmental parameters
I	Institution

The form of societal organization:

E	Entrepreneurs
A	Agents
α	Agent's one-period payoff from cheating
δ	Agent's time discount factor
η	Agent's reservation utility
κ	Entrepreneur's payoff from noncooperation
γ	Entrepreneur's gross gain from cooperation
$W;w$	Wage
ξ	Termination probability

h_h	Probability that an unemployed agent who was honest in the last period he was employed will be hired in the current period
h_c	Probability that an unemployed agent who cheated in the last period he was employed will be hired in the current period
V_h	Present value of lifetime expected utility of an employed agent who, whenever hired, is honest
V_h^u	Present value of lifetime expected utility of an unemployed honest agent
V_c^u	Present value of lifetime expected utility of an unemployed cheater (who will be honest in the future if hired)
V_h^A	Present value of the entrepreneur's lifetime expected utility from being an honest agent
V_c^A	Entrepreneur's expected utility from being an agent who had cheated
V_c^E	Entrepreneur's expected utility from being an entrepreneur who cheated while providing agency services

Chapter 3:

Two stage least squares:

y	Dependent variable
x_i	Exogenous variables
μ	Endogenous variable
ρ	Instrumental variable
ε	Error term
β	Regression coefficient
θ	Regression coefficient

1. Introduction

In 2007, Germany realized a GDP per capita of USD 25,106, the United States of USD 38,063, and Norway of USD 42,065. However, Egypt's GDP per capita in 2007 amounted to USD 1697 and Yemen's merely USD 561. By contrast, the United Arab Emirates' (UAE) GDP per capita accounted for USD 26,071.[1] The relative numbers differed little in 1990, with Norway realizing the second highest GDP per capita behind the US. But why do some economies perform so much worse than others? Why are the per capita incomes and, therefore, living standards so much lower in some countries and why does the situation persist? Hence, why have many underdeveloped and less developed countries been unable to significantly improve their economic performances over recent decades?

Regarding the Arab region, GDP per capita virtually stagnated for more than 20 years from 1980. During the same period, GDP per capita in the world's highly industrialized states further increased and the gap between the MENA region and highly developed countries widened.[2]

However, the differences between Arab countries and highly developed Western states exist not only economically. The countries also differ regarding their political, legal, and social systems and, of course, regarding their histories.

In recent decades, and especially since 9/11/2001, the MENA region has moved into the public spotlight, not only because of its economic development, but also because of its domestic and external conflicts, oil richness, Islamic fundamentalism, and terrorism as well as cultural and religious differences.

Since the MENA region and highly developed Western states differ in so many variables, could it be the case that they are all linked? Can these different economic performances be traced back to varying political, legal, social, cultural, and historical paths?

Convergence in the neoclassical model

According to the neoclassical growth model, differences in growth performances can be explained by the fact that the observed economies are situated at different places on the model's growth path. In the long run, however, all countries will

---

[1] GDP per capita in constant 2000 US dollars. Data accessed July 2, 2009, from the World Bank World Development Indicators Online (WDI) database.
[2] MENA (Middle East and North Africa): Algeria, Bahrain, Djibouti, Egypt, Iran, Iraq, Jordan, Kuwait, Lebanon, Libya, Morocco, Oman, Qatar, Saudi Arabia, Syria, Tunisia, the UAE, West Bank and Gaza, and Yemen, according to the World Bank's WDI definition.

realize the equilibrium growth rate – that is to say the growth rate of technological progress.[3]

This argument is based on the assumption of diminishing returns to scale. Accordingly, less developed countries exhibit a relatively low capital stock. Therefore, every additional unit of capital causes relatively high returns. The more capital is accumulated the more the returns per unit of capital decrease. Therefore, less developed countries realize higher returns to scale and thereby higher growth rates. The more capital a country accumulates, that is to say the more developed it is, the lower the growth rates are. This process continues until a country has reached the equilibrium. Therefore, in equilibrium, the per capita growth rate constantly corresponds to the rate of technological progress (or is equal to zero depending on model assumptions). Hence, the growth rates of all observed countries converge to the rate of technological progress.

There are concepts of convergence that can be differentiated. β-convergence indicates that the growth rate is negatively correlated with the level of per capita income. Hence, poor countries will realize higher growth rates and, therefore, grow faster than rich countries. σ-convergence says that the disparities between income levels will decrease. That is to say, in equilibrium all countries will realize the same level of per capita income.

Furthermore, we can differentiate between conditional and absolute convergence. Here, the distinguishing characteristic is the steady state. If it is assumed that all observed economies realize the same preferences and production functions then the countries will move on the same steady state growth path and will at least be situated in the same steady state. That is to say, poor countries grow faster than rich ones and, therefore, realize higher growth rates. However, income disparities decrease and all observed economies will realize at least the same growth rates (zero or the rate of technological progress) and the same level of per capita income, since they all converge to the same steady state.

Conditional convergence emanates from varying preferences and production functions. Hence, decreasing returns to scale are assumed to hold for all observed economies, but the countries differ regarding their saving rates and population growth rates. Therefore, the economies move on different growth paths and will end up in different steady states. That is to say, poor countries will grow faster than rich ones, since decreasing returns to scale are assumed. But income levels will differ in equilibrium, since every economy realizes its unique steady state (Barro & Sala-i-Martin, 2004; Hagemann, Erber & Seiter, 1998; Reichart, 2005).

---

[3] If the model includes technological progress. In the case without technological progress, the equilibrium per capita growth rate is zero.

However, empirical evidence shows that growth rates and income levels do not converge on a global level. That is to say, convergence can be observed within certain groups of countries, so-called convergence clubs. These groups consist of relatively similar countries regarding their levels of factor accumulation and technology. Differences in growth rates and living standards indeed decrease within these groups, for example the Organisation for Economic Co-operation and Development (OECD) countries.

However, especially between poor and rich countries, convergence cannot be observed. But convergence theory insists that underdeveloped countries should realize higher growth rates and, therefore, close the gap in income levels and growth rates. Nevertheless, these two groups, underdeveloped and highly developed countries, drift further apart except for some exclusions.[4]

Why countries realize different growth rates and why poor countries should theoretically realize higher growth rates than rich countries was examined by Abramovitz (1986). Accordingly, poor countries have the potential to catch up. That is to say, because of their low levels of factor accumulation, underdeveloped countries are, assuming decreasing returns, able to realize higher growth rates per unit of capital than rich countries can. So far, the theory follows the neoclassical model. Poor countries benefit from the fact that they can adopt rich countries' technologies. That is to say, underdeveloped countries do not have to innovate by themselves but they can inherit technologies and ideas from highly developed countries. Poor economies can catch up by adapting such technologies. If these countries use their potential, adopt technologies, and thereby realize high growth rates, they are able to catch up to developed economies and thereby implement similar growth rates and income levels. However, if a former underdeveloped country is able to not only adopt technologies but also innovate and increase the pace of technological progress, it might even be able to forge ahead and overhaul the highly developed countries. By contrast, if an underdeveloped country is not able to use its potential to adapt the technologies of highly developed economies, it might not be able to close the gap and instead fall further behind regarding growth rates and income levels.

Abramovitz's theory explains why some countries are not able to catch up. Accordingly, the potential to catch up depends on a country's ability to adopt technology. Hence, when a country is not able to adopt the leading countries' technologies, it cannot use its potential. Then, the gap between the poor countries and highly developed countries might even widen. In this case, divergence instead of convergence is observed.

---

4 See, for example, Barro & Sala-i-Martin (1992); Baumol (1986); Ben-David (2000); Caselli, Esquivel & Lefort (1996); de la Fuente (2002); Islam (2003); Mankiw, Romer & Weil (1992); Quah (1996); Sala-i-Martin (1996); Temple (1999).

Hence, certain factors must determine an economy's ability to adopt technologies. Abramovitz introduced the term 'social capability', which is the decisive determinant of a country to catch up or fall behind. Social capability incorporates growth-relevant factors that are not included in a usual production function. Thus, apart from capital and labor, a country's growth performance might also depend on the historical, cultural, religious, political, and legal particularities that influence economic variables and a country's ability to adopt technologies. For example, certain religious or moral convictions might inhibit technological progress, human capital accumulation, and restrict the labor force. Certain norms might exclude particular parts of the population from the labor market or restrict research and development and education from applying certain methods, assumptions, theories, and so on. Social capability also influences the form of society, for example whether it is patriarchic and conservative or individualistic and modern.[5] Furthermore political, bureaucratic, financial, and legal structures are incorporated. Therefore, social capability is a so-called catch-all variable that cannot be clearly defined. It includes all the factors considered growth relevant but which are not directly included in the neoclassical production function. This broad definition makes it difficult to incorporate social capability in scientific work, whether theoretical or empirical.

Institutions

The concept of social capability is close to the concept of institutions. Institutions are rules that regulate human interactions. These rules can be informal and solely exist in human minds, for example certain codes of behavior. However, the rules can also be formally written down, for example laws and regulations. In any case, they regulate social interaction. This is possible since institutions allow the individual to establish expectations regarding other individuals' behaviors. Hence, people of the same culture act according to the same codes of conduct and, therefore, all individuals of the observed population know how the others will react. Similarly, people being subordinated to the same jurisdiction will behave accordingly; therefore, they can predict others' behaviors.

Institutions can be examined on a micro- or macro-level. In the micro view, the single individual's actions are of interest and it is investigated why an agent acts in a certain way. Since institutions regulate human behavior, they must play a role regarding the determination of an agent's actions.

However, institutions are also decisive from a macro point of view. Since a society's morals, values, norms, and so on are considered to influence societal

[5] See, for example, Adelman & Taft Morris (1967); Hall & Jones (1999); Temple & Johnson (1998).

organization, these factors are suspected of influencing economic development. The same holds for formal rules such as the political or legal system. Countries realizing significant differences in economic development often differ regarding their societal, political, and legal structures, too. Therefore, these 'macro' institutions, which are also rules regulating human interactions, might impact economic development.

Hence, institutions are obtained on a micro-level where they determine individuals' behaviors, but they also exist on a macro-level where their influence on economic growth becomes apparent. Therefore, comprehensive institutional analysis has to incorporate the micro view and thereby the single individual as well as the macro view, which analyzes the impact of institutional systems on economic development.

History matters

History plays a decisive role in questioning the emergence and development of institutions themselves (Lipsey, Carlaw & Bekar, 2005; North, 1990; North 2005; North & Thomas, 1973). A country's development path can suddenly change direction due to a historical accident. However, historical changes can also pass subliminally and not become obvious until a certain period of time. Nevertheless, historical accidents cause institutions to adapt and they result in an irrevocable alteration of an economy's development path. Hence, institutions clearly are path-dependent and usually neither their emergence nor later changes can be ascribed to conscious decisions. Once the path-dependent institutions resulting from historical accidents become 'locked in' change is almost impossible.

The importance of history in institutional development makes institutional analysis difficult. History is not a tangible variable that can be incorporated in theoretical and empirical models. The necessity to include history as a determining factor creates the need to deviate from standard economic analysis based on certain mathematical and empirical models. As good as these models are to examine particular issues they cannot incorporate historical incidents that accidentally appeared in a certain place at a certain point in time. Therefore, institutional analysis necessitates a *comparative institutional analysis* (Aoki, 2001). That is to say, institutional analysis must always be accompanied by historical research on the particular region. Otherwise the decisive institutional incidents cannot be detected.[6]

---

[6] See, for example, Aoki (2001); Greif (1994); Hedlund (2001, 2005); Lipsey, Carlaw & Bekar (2005).

Culture matters

Closely linked to history but less acknowledged as a growth-relevant factor is culture. However, culture in economic analysis seems to be gaining a growing audience even though its role is critically discussed.[7] In particular, mainstream economics that emanate from the assumption of the pure homo economicus do not ascribe a crucial role to culture. This is the case since humans are supposed to be rational and react to material incentives that ultimately overlie all other stimuli. Hence, even non-Western, non-individualistic, and maybe less materially focused societies pursue the same goal and realize the same utility functions. That is to say, despite different histories, beliefs, worldviews, morals, and thereby cultures all people are supposed to rationally maximize their material incomes. This argumentation is right from a pure theoretical viewpoint. That is to say, according to the assumptions the particular models make, they are right. Therefore, the application of these models is justified for the examination of certain economic issues. In any case, models that exclude cultural components might not be useful to explain long-term growth differences. It cannot be denied that in certain cases differences in economic growth performances correspond to cultural borders (Landes, 1998; Lipsey, Carlaw & Bekar, 2005; Olson, 1982; Pomeranz, 2001).

However, cultural determinism is not helpful either. Differences in development levels cannot be solely traced back to different cultures. They are rather initiated by a mixture of factors that varies from region to region. Nevertheless, culture is one component that needs to be taken seriously. This is the case since culture is highly correlated with history, which definitely is a determining force of economic development. Furthermore, culture determines human behavior. Since human behavior is what determines the economy, culture should affect economic outcomes.

However, to detect whether culture is a growth-relevant factor or not a more precise definition is necessary. The fact that culture is often not further defined is one reason why some mainstream economists dismiss culture and why cultural economists cannot bring out their arguments. Culture indeed is a broad concept that can incorporate quite different subjects. In economics, culture is usually defined as beliefs and preferences that differ between societies and, therefore, allow a differentiation between groups (Fernández, 2008). In institutional economics, culture can be used as a synonym for informal institutions. Therefore, culture has to be defined as beliefs, morals, norms, habits, conventions, codes of conduct, and so forth. That is to say, culture consists of rules that regulate human interactions on an informal level. With this definition we assume

---

[7] See, for example, De Jong (2009); Guiso, Sapienza & Zingales (2006); Harrison & Huntington (2000).

that beliefs, morals, norms, and so on – that is to say culture – determine the rules implemented by human beings and which might affect economic development. Whether culture affects economic growth is analyzed within this work.

The MENA region

To find out whether institutions influence economic development a theoretical analysis on the micro- or macro-level is necessary. However, since institutions are path-dependent and, therefore, dependent on historical accidents every single cause has to be examined itself. That is to say, the theory demonstrates how and why institutions in general influence economic development. But the theory will not tell us why a certain country realizes low levels of economic development. Therefore, empirical and especially historical investigation is necessary.

The MENA region is one of the world regions that cannot close the gap of living standards between itself and highly developed countries. On the contrary, the divergence of income levels and growth rates between MENA and highly industrialized countries can be observed. Hence, developments in the MENA region cannot be explained by the neoclassical model or the mainstream endogenous growth models.

However, differences between the Arab region and the economically successful countries of the Western hemisphere also exist on non-economic levels. The MENA countries differ regarding their political and legal structures and thereby their bureaucracies and regulations. Furthermore, cultures, religions, and histories differ widely between MENA and the Western world. Hence, the rules that regulate human interactions – the institutions – differ. Since discrepancies exist on the institutional level and regarding growth performances, one could assume that both are correlated, namely that the institutional environment of the MENA region is less growth supportive than the institutional environment of Western states.

That institutions do differ is demonstrated in chapter four via some descriptive statistics on formal and informal institutional indicators. Accordingly, current cultural, political, legal, and economic structures differ widely between Arab countries and highly industrialized states.

However, to explain these differences a historical comparative analysis is necessary. Such an analysis must highlight the developments and historical accidents responsible for the formation of the current institutional system in the corresponding region. Since institutions are path-dependent and since at least some of them are slow moving, the case study must start at an early point in time. Regarding institutional development in the MENA region, the analysis begins in the seventh century with the process of state building. Already at this point in time institutional developments differed widely between the Arab and Western (European) regions and had large impacts on the upcoming events. For the MENA region we can at least state that the phase of state building that began during Muhammad's lifetime (570–632) already demonstrated an institutional lock-in. This holds for political institutions and the relationship between the sacred and the secular. Incidents at this early point in time shaped the institutional structure of the Arab world sustainably.

However, from the phase of state building onwards several historical accidents and institutional developments had long-lasting effects on the institutional structure and the development path in general. Of course not all determining events can be listed since there are too many of them, several of which are unknown and will probably never be examined. Therefore, the current analysis does not claim completeness but wants to depict some decisive institutional developments that differed from those in Western Europe.

After this historical analysis it should be clear why the Arab region and highly industrialized Western states realize different economic performances and why the gap in living standards has widened.

Structure of the work

This dissertation project is differentiated into two parts. The first is a general section on institutions that incorporates a theoretical and an empirical analysis and examines whether institutions influence economic growth. The theoretical chapter deals with the definition of institutions and with equilibrium considerations. Hence, the observed economies develop equilibrium strategies and institutions according to their particular histories and environments. Although the economic and societal outcomes might differ, each society might be situated in an optimal state and realize optimal strategies regarding the prevalent conditions and thereby the specific histories of the countries. The empirical analysis deals with institutional data and measurement. A regression analysis demonstrates that informal and formal institutions have a significant impact on GDP per capita. Furthermore, a society's religious background seems to influence institutional development.

The second part of the dissertation project deals with the MENA region and its institutional development. The current institutional differences between the MENA countries and some highly developed economies are depicted. Within this analysis it becomes clear that institutions differ widely between the Arab region and Western hemisphere. That institutions have a significant influence on economic development is demonstrated in the general empirical analysis. We can conclude that the different institutional environments of the MENA region and the West continue to lead to varying growth performances. However, why institutions in the Arab region developed in their way and not in another is shown in the historical analysis. Here, the development path is partly reconstructed; emphasis, however, is placed on the very early phase of institution building. That is to say, we mainly concentrate on medieval times. It is argued that these early centuries were decisive for the institutional lock-in. Hence, the direction of the development path was determined during that time.

It should be noted that this study does not deal with the general economic history of the MENA region. Furthermore, it is not concerned with the Ottoman Empire, colonization, and the politically and economically crucial events of the 20th century. Emphasis is placed on current institutional differences as well as on selected events of the medieval period. This is the case since the study wants to demonstrate that early, seemingly unimportant incidents can have long-lasting effects on institutional and economic development. Later occurrences of course were also of crucial importance. However, they are not the content of this work.

This dissertation project demonstrates the importance of institutions regarding the analysis of economic growth and economic development. The MENA countries were chosen since at least in the past two decades (but also earlier) the region played a major role in public perception. Many of the region's conflicts, whether internal or external, can be traced back to the stagnating low living standards. High population growth rates and a high percentage of people under 25 years of age put pressure on the region's labor markets. To ensure employment for the growing part of the working age population, MENA's economic performance must improve significantly (Dyer & Yousef, 2007; Sala-i-Martin & Artadi, 2003; Yousef, 2004). However, if it is true that economic development depends on the institutional environment, then economic change would require institutional change. But the path-dependent nature of institutions inhibits fast change.

Although this might seem to be a depressing result for the Arab countries, this dissertation project nevertheless demonstrates that the particular institutional development in the MENA region is the decisive component for its economic performance. Since institutions are complex and complementary entities their development paths cannot be prophesied. Therefore, the MENA region might develop a solution strategy and improve its economic situation in a way that is yet unknown. Hence, since institutional development is unpredictable, the future Arab economic development can hold positive or negative surprises. However, this study demonstrates that the efficiency and optimality of institutions cannot be measured in economic successes and high living standards. A society's history and its institutional environment might result in low living standards and low growth rates. Nevertheless, regarding the prevailing conditions, the particular society might realize an optimal outcome.

2. Institutions – a theoretical approach

2.1 Introduction

Institutions constitute the social, political, legal and economic system of a state. According to North (1990), "Institutions are the rules of the game in a society or, more formally, are the humanly devised constraints that shape human interaction. [...] they structure incentives in human exchange, whether political, social or economic" (p. 1). Hence, institutions are the rules that regulate social interaction. Therefore, they establish the framework within which social life takes place. Institutions can take different forms, ranging from an individual's attitudes and beliefs to the legal system of a state. Regulations might, for example, be imposed on the distribution of power, the legal foundation (which must judge misconduct), and land tenure or ownership rights. Furthermore, economic regulations, which clarify expected costs and returns, can be established. However, these constraints – called institutions – must be implemented by humans to regulate their interrelationships. With institutions, people are able to assess others' behaviors since an institution by definition is universal, and thereby all members of the observed population adhere to the rule. The risk that somebody violates the rule is reduced, because the violator is punished and must pay a cost for their misconduct. Therefore, institutions make human behavior predictable. That is to say, human interrelations follow a given pattern, which allows preceding calculations. This is true for both formal rules such as laws and informal codes of conduct. It follows that, because of institutions, humans are endued with information on others' behaviors and, therefore, transaction costs can be reduced. The institution – whether a formal rule or morals and norms – provides behavior guidelines, which help an individual choose their own actions and predict others' behaviors. However, we should not mix this up with a situation of complete information, which does not exist. Therefore, transaction costs still exist and humans act in a state of uncertainty. Institutions reduce transaction costs and uncertainty by providing rules of conduct. Whether institutions are efficient cannot be easily stated and depends on the particular case and the applied theory. In fact, certain parts of the population can suffer from high transaction costs and uncertainty despite the implementation of institutions. Hence, institutions do not imply that all members of the observed population live a materially secure and satisfying life. However, to know about one's own and others' constraints opens up a clearly defined scope for action, even if the institutional environment is not efficient. Individuals can calculate their gains and losses resulting from specific behaviors. Hence, with distinct rules it is possible to determine whether an investment is worthwhile or not. Thus, the decisive property of institutions is that they set constraints on human behavior and so determine human action;

therefore, they reduce uncertainty and transaction costs. Hence, they create incentives for particular actions, since gains and losses become predictable.

Institutional analysis, however, is a complex field with several feedback mechanisms; it has 'no beginning' per se. Institutional development can be described as a circuit that continues indefinitely and for which a starting point cannot be detected. The crucial element, which determines and sustains societal organization, is human behavior. Hence, institutions are directly connected with human behavior, and this brings game theory as an analytical tool into play. To find the least common denominator, we can record that institutions are all about maximizing an individual's utility by optimizing their own behavior conditional on others' behaviors in time. Human behavior, however, depends on incentives and motivation. That is to say, institutions provide an incentive to act in a certain way – they motivate people to do something. In a world without institutions a human's reaction to a particular incentive is unpredictable. No patterns exist to help forecast human behavior. Furthermore, misconduct cannot be sanctioned since the difference between 'good' and 'bad' behavior is not defined. This world is characterized by uncertainty and, therefore, high transaction costs (Coase, 1937; Coase, 1960; Greif, 2006; North, 1990). Therefore, people strive for a situation in which others' reactions are predictable and thereby uncertainty and transaction costs can be reduced. To achieve their target, humans are prepared to impose constraints on themselves whereby codes of conduct emerge that afford reliable expectations and reduce uncertainty. Thus, the constraints are endogenous. At the same time, individuals are born into a world where restrictions already exist and which are, therefore, exogenous to them. That is to say, the constraints shape peoples' codes of conduct, whereas the latter determine the constraints. The restrictions, however, are called institutions. They are created by human beings – consciously or unconsciously – to impose binding rules on social interactions. Since almost all members of a society subordinate themselves to the self-imposed rules individuals achieve the maximal level of freedom under which the particular societal life is possible. Or, according to Hodgson (2006): "Regulation is not always the antithesis of freedom; it can be its ally" (p. 2).

However, the preceding explanation of institutional emergence should not be misunderstood. We do not emanate from a starting point where no institutions exist. Even an anarchical state, like every other, is distinguished by institutions.[8] However, a certain institutional environment might not lead to an effi-

[8] The only situation in which institutions are nonexistent is in a Robinson Crusoe world with only one individual alive. In this world, institutions cannot exist since there is no society, no reason for the prediction of other agents' behaviors, and no need for social interaction. However, even Robinson Crusoe might have already been shaped by the institutional environment he used to live in. Therefore, even Crusoe might act according to a particular value system and might possess certain habits – that is, at least some institutions might exist (Greif, 2006,

cient outcome and individuals might implement and alter institutions to optimize their living standards. To improve our understanding, we should consult Hodgson's (2006) definition that describes institutions as "durable systems of established and embedded social rules that structure social interactions … institutions are social rule-systems" (p. 13). Hence, social interactions require institutions and institutions require social interactions. Without institutions, social interactions cannot be realized, since an individual does not know what the other's behavior is meant to express. However, an institution cannot exist without interacting individuals, because otherwise there is no need for an institution. This is the beginning of the structure–agency debate and of a discussion that questions what came first, the individual or the institution. However, this study will not enter that particular debate. Instead, it is assumed that both approaches – structure and agency – must be applied and combined in a reasonable manner to examine institutions. Therefore, the present approach should be regarded as a mixture of agency and structure. Individuals make their decisions according to more or less rational reasoning. The micro view of the agency approach, however, suggests that they build institutions to regulate their social interactions. Anyway, individuals are a creation of their environments. Thus, prevalent norms and the social value system do influence their behavior and the decisions they make. Hence, on a macro level, individuals are born into an existing institutional environment that provides incentives and, therefore, regulates their behaviors. Individuals maximize their utility according to rational consideration. However, what they understand by rationality and utility maximization depends on the prevalent social value system and thereby the institutional environment. That is to say: "Human reasoning capacities are thus linked to their evolving social and biological contexts. Rationality is not detached from the world; it is situated in and operates through specific cues, triggers and constraints. These structures and circumstances are part of our biological and social heritage. Among them are institutions that frame our cognitions, enable some behavioural options and constrain us from others" (Hodgson, 2007, p. 8).

Individuals are utility maximizers and rational actors. However, rationality and logic are not exogenous entities; they emerge and exist in a certain social environment that is determined by individuals. The rules that determine the social value system are influenced by the individuals. But the individuals act according to the rules. That is to say, both structure and agency require each other (Lawson, 1987). Therefore, neither agency nor structure alone can solve the issues of institutional theory: "Institutions depend for their existence on individu-

Ch. 2, pp. 29–53). However, this idea further leads to the question of whether some institutions are predetermined in human nature and, hence, are settled in our genes. Anyway, this topic leads far into the realms of biology as analyzed by neuro-economists. Although interesting and important, it is not further ensued in this study.

als, their interactions, and particular shared patterns of thought. Nevertheless, any single individual is born into a pre-existing institutional world which confronts him or her with its rules and norms" (Hodgson, 2006, p. 7).

Therefore, the present work does not deal with the very beginning of institutions, but with institutional development over time. By the nature of its object of investigation institutional analysis cannot detect whether the individual or the institution was the starting point. We cannot draw a separating line between the micro- and macro-level. Institutions shape individual behavior, which in turn generates institutions that again determine behavior, and so forth. Nevertheless, for the purpose of analysis it might be useful to emanate from a pure rules-of-the-game approach.[9] Hence, certain questions might necessitate one approach while others are better solved with another. To depict the endogenous nature of institutions, the assumption of exogenously given institutions that determine an individual's behavior must be abandoned. Instead, an equilibrium approach that describes the endogenous, self-enforcing character of an institution can be applied (Aoki, 2001, Ch. 7, pp. 185–206).

A plausible scheme of institutions is given by Williamson (2000), who arranges institutions into four levels. The first is the social embeddedness level, which corresponds to North's (1990) informal institutions. It includes "norms, customs, mores, traditions, etc." and also "religion plays a large role at this level" (Williamson, 2000, p. 596). The first-level institutions are characterized by their robustness and durability – institutional change at this level happens very slowly, that is to say, in a dimension of centuries or even millennia.

The second level is called 'institutional environment'. This describes what we specify as formal institutions – that is, formal rules such as property rights, judiciaries, laws, or constitutions. The formal rules change faster than the informal institutions, between around 10 to hundred years according to Williamson (2000). The first two levels of Williamson's approach correspond to what North (1990) describes as formal and informal institutions. Williamson, however, further differentiates institutional analysis by introducing two additional levels.

Level three is called 'governance' and includes issues of private order, contract enforcement, and getting "the governance structures right" (Williamson, 2000, p. 599). Change on this level needs one to 10 years to happen. Level four,

---

[9] Interpreted in this way, the rules-of-the-game approach describes an exogenous understanding of institutions. That is to say, the institution – the rule – is exogenously attached to an individual, who adheres to the rules. North (1990), who determined the term 'rules-of-the-game', did not understand institutions as being purely exogenous to agents (North, 2005). This should be revealed to avoid misunderstanding. When we talk of the rules-of-the-game approach, we advert to the micro level where we observe one single individual who in fact takes institutions as exogenously given. Anyway, on the macro-level, institutions are endogenous and are shaped by society. That is to say, the rules-of-the-game approach must not mean that the particular author takes institutions as generally exogenously given. Institutions are still endogenous, but are exogenous to a single individual.

however, regards the economy from a macro-level and deals with resource allocation and macroeconomic optimality analysis.

The current study deals with levels one and two. These explanations demonstrate that a clear definition of institutions is difficult to state. What is defined as an institution and what is excluded depends on the kind of analysis. Institutions are entities that cannot be precisely described with certain terms. Institutions are a concept that must be understood and internalized; it makes no sense to desperately try to define them with a certain range of words. Therefore, whether organizations are defined as institutions or not and whether culture is an institution or not depends on the object of study and the idea being followed. Any definition of an institution cannot be described as wrong; every approach must be followed and discussed to find out whether it makes sense and whether further research should be conducted.

Therefore, informal institutions might be described as culture, the social value system, credible beliefs, habits, worldview, and so on. As a minimum they describe the broad, underlying basis of a society. They shape a society's mental model or its belief system, on which formal institutions might emerge. That is to say, this study will not commit to a certain restrictive definition of institutions. It rather seems to make sense to contribute to the understanding of the concept of institutions in general – which will hopefully be achieved by the end of the study – than to get lost in definition fetishism.

North's (1990) approach seems to include the most comprehensive and accurate definition of institutions. Based on his approach, further more or less restrictive definitions can be specified to analyze certain institutional issues. Some economists use the term 'rules-of-the-game approach' to describe institutions as purely exogenous (Aoki, 2001; Greif, 2006). However, North's approach is not tempted to understand institutions as pure exogenously given entities. Nevertheless, the exogeneity assumption might be true from an individual, micro point of view. Greif (2006), for example, specifies the assumption that institutions "are exogenous to each individual whose behaviour they influence" (Greif, 2006, p. 30) as a determining characteristic of institutions. In any case, at least from a macro point of view, institutions are endogenous. This is demonstrated, for example, by Aoki's (2001) equilibrium view of institutions. Both approaches are 'right' depending on the point of view – micro or macro – and, as will be seen, complement each other.

2.2 Formal and informal institutions

The current study follows North's (1990) approach and differentiates between formal and informal institutions. This is the case since it should be emphasized that institutions do not only correspond to formal entities – that is, to certain laws and regulations that are officially written down. Some empirical analyses, although very important for examining institutions and their effects on economic development, convey the impression that institutions correspond solely to a form of government, a legal system, property rights, or business regulations, but do not correspond to the sociocultural value system.[10] Of course, the fact that empiricists concentrate on formal measures of institutions is an issue of data availability, since a country's social value system is difficult to measure. However, the availability of survey data has led to some interesting results in recent years.[11] In any case, the objective of the current study is to include informal institutions or the embeddedness level in its analysis (Williamson, 2000). It is important to define precisely our understanding of the terms 'formal' and 'informal' institutions, since different definitions and approaches exist and are often mixed up (Hodgson, 2006).

In general, rules that constitute the political, legal, economic, and social environment and are formally written down in a rulebook, be it for example a legal text or a constitution, are called formal institutions. Formal institutions imply an official formal enforcement mechanism in case the rules are violated. However, life is not constrained solely by formal institutions. Morals, norms, values, conventions, traditions, and codes of conduct also influence human behavior. These cultural and societal factors are called informal institutions. They are not officially written down and a violation might not lead to state-run, but rather societal punishment. Usually, informal institutions underlie formal institutions because they determine a society's basic attitudes and beliefs and, hence, its value system (Aoki, 2001; Boettke, Coyne & Leeson, 2008; Greif, 2006; North, 2005). North (1990) reverts to a plausible example of rules in sports to describe the difference between formal and informal institutions. Thus, formal institutions can be compared to rules that are written down in a rulebook, whereas informal institutions are "unwritten codes of conduct that underlie and supplement formal rules, such as not deliberately injuring a key player on the opposing team" (p. 4).

In the present study, informal institutions are defined as values, beliefs, morals, convictions, norms, habits, and codes of conduct and the term is used as

---

[10] See, for example, Acemoglu, Johnson & Robinson (2001); La Porta et al. (1999); La Porta et al. (2004); Rodrik (2000); Rodrik, Subramanian & Trebbi (2004); Persson & Tabellini (2008).

[11] See, for example, Fernández & Fogli (2007); Guiso, Sapienza & Zingales (2006); Knack & Keefer (1997); Knowles & Weatherston (2006); Tabellini (2005); Tabellini (2008a); Tabellini (2008b); Williamson (2009).

a substitute for culture. However, institutions can range from the general to the specific. Thus, culture can be defined as an institution that corresponds to the broadest categorization; further, values, beliefs, morals, norms, convictions, and so on can be categorized as culture or informal institutions. Hence, particular values or norms correspond to specific categories.

Culture is used as a substitute for informal institutions since at least in the current definition it depicts the rules that regulate human interactions. Culture restricts human behavior since individuals belonging to a certain culture share the same values and beliefs and, therefore, share norms, codes of conduct, habits, and traditions. Hence, they will behave according to certain defaults, and misconduct will be punished. Furthermore, culture offers incentives. Culture provides a metaphysical incentive in the sense that people want to act in a particular way because they are persuaded that they are 'right'. Hence, they act according to religious or other metaphysical beliefs, such as altruism or abstinence. They do so because they are persuaded by a particular belief system or because they fear societal or divine punishment. Furthermore, culture offers the incentive of becoming a member of a cultural group by practicing particular traditions and codes of behavior.

If, however, new beliefs and convictions become accepted by the individual, at least parts of a society's belief system and its worldview can be consciously altered by its members. Take, for example, attitudes regarding gender equality, political equality, vigilantism, the death penalty, or the rule of law. These institutions have been altered in some societies because the attitudes concerning the individual and social coexistence changed. These changes can be traced back to conscious decisions that were taken because of rational and logical reasoning. However, institutions can also emerge or be altered unconsciously. Hence, rules to regulate social interaction are established unconsciously, and after their implementation individuals adhere to the rules without consciously questioning them.

Individuals might feel constrained by informal institutions rather than by formal institutions, because informal institutions are connected to their personal convictions. That is to say, formal and informal institutions are not clearly separable. According to Hodgson: "… the idea that there is a dividing line between institutions that are entirely "formal" on one hand and entirely "informal" institutions on the other is false, because "formal" institutions […] always depend on nonlegal rules and inexplicit norms in order to operate. If laws or declarations are neither customary nor embodied in individual dispositions, then – "formal" or not – they have insignificant effects" (2006, p. 18).

Hence, a society's value system or its culture determines its worldview and its general understanding of the state and of society. Thus, a conservative or non-modern value system might unconsciously support a hierarchical societal structure, an authoritarian government, and a restricted judiciary. On the contrary, a liberal and modern social value system might be supportive of a horizontal societal structure, political participation, civil liberties, and an independent judiciary. However, since the institutional system is influenced by many exogenous and endogenous factors, exceptions to the hypotheses might be found.

The differentiation between formal and informal institutions seems reasonable since it clarifies that not only formal rules are institutions. Nevertheless, one should not forget that a clear separation between formal and informal institutions is not possible since both are connected in several ways and both merge into each other. Anyway, depending on the object of study, the distinction might be useful.

Once established formal institutions also impact informal institutions. A democratic state that practices the rule of law and in which civil liberties and political rights are implemented might induce self-reliant and self-dependent individuals who are able to question their political and societal environment. They might be able to critically reflect on themselves and on the surrounding structures. An autocratic or patrimonic state that oppresses its citizens and does not imply civil liberties such as freedom of the speech does not necessarily bring up critical and self-reliant individuals. Education also plays a major role. Individuals with access to a modern educational system will probably develop different personalities compared with individuals with no or less access to education.

Of course, formal institutions, such as in the form of government, property rights, the legal system, business regulations, and so on, influence a country's development and thereby its growth performance. Opinions are mixed about informal institutions. The current study's hypothesis is that informal institutions influence economic development because cultures differ between societies. Hence, values, beliefs, worldviews, morals, codes of conduct, and so on differ between cultural groups. Therefore, preferences, incentives, and utility functions differ. These differences lead to varying strategies on the individual level, but also regarding collective behavior. Hence, the impacts on economic development vary. If, for example, a society has a positive attitude concerning materialism, it will probably accumulate more capital and invest more than a society in which materialism is considered negative.

If societies differ concerning their cultural characteristics, aggregated behavior will vary and affect economic outcomes differently. The following sections will examine institutional properties, institutional emergence and change, and the transmission channels between formal and informal institutions and economic growth.

2.3 Growth-supporting institutions

Since we are interested in the impact of institutions on economic growth and economic development, we should define the meanings of growth-supporting and growth-inhibiting institutions before we examine the issue of institutional efficiency and change. An institution that has a positive effect on the growth rate is called growth supporting, whereas an institution that has no effect, or that is detrimental to economic growth, is called growth inhibiting. A general classification in growth-inhibiting and growth-supporting institutions is impossible because the economic impact of an institution depends on several influencing factors such as other institutions, history, geography, ecology, the level of economic development, and so forth. Depending on the prevalent environment, an institution that supports growth in one country might have a different impact on the growth rate in another country. However, assuming equal initial conditions, certain institutional features are generally described as growth supporting. These institutions are considered to be property rights, an independent judiciary, the rule of law, and political participation, although the detected effect of democracy is mixed.[12] Property rights are growth supporting in two ways. First, they expand the possible use of an asset. That is, besides its direct utilization as a living space, office, production facility, showroom, farmland, and so forth, the asset can be used as collateral and thereby can create new capital (De Soto, 2000). Second, clearly defined ownership rights guarantee individual utility maximization since the owner can use the asset in a way that best fits her or his interests. Therefore, secure property rights are accompanied by higher growth rates (Acemoglu & Johnson, 2005; Williamson & Kerekes, 2009). However, property rights are useless if they cannot be enforced by an independent judiciary; hence, as long as the state or private interest groups are able to appropriate private property or influence the allocation of assets. La Porta et al. (2004) examine the effect of judicial independence and constitutional review and discover that an independent judiciary matters most in the attainment of economic freedom. Political participation guarantees that it is not possible for a minority, which is not legitimatized, to determine the institutional form. That is, political participation prevents interest groups from exerting de facto political power solely based on their resources (Acemoglu, Johnson & Robinson, 2005; Rodrik, 2000; Rodrik, 2007). On the informal level, a societal structure of generalized morality (Platteau, 2000; Tabellini, 2005; Tabellini, 2008a; Tabellini, 2008b), high levels of trust (Akerlof & Kranton, 2000; Knack & Keefer, 1997), convictions concerning destiny and predetermination, and the level of respect for other people (Knowles & Weatherston, 2006; Tabellini, 2005) are proven to support economic growth.

[12] See, for example, Barro (1999); Persson & Tabellini (2006); Persson & Tabellini (2008); Persson & Tabellini (2009).

As already indicated, the economic impact of institutions depends on other institutions, historical accidents, further factors, and reverse causality. The informal institutional environment, for example, might not match the relevant formal institutions – that is, a culture of property rights, rule of law, and political participation might not exist. In this case, the assumed growth-supporting institutions might not support growth. However, if countries could change their institutional environments in a way that fits the above-named growth-supporting institutions then efficient production would be possible and would result in optimizing the growth rate. Of course, this is an unrealistic and less helpful assumption. It reveals that if we emanate from a growth model similar to, for example, the neoclassical model, then the mentioned institutions will support growth. However, this is precisely the problem. Real conditions do not correspond to the model world. But models can be used in a way that makes sense. Hence, we can detect which institutions – emanating from our perfect model world – would support growth. Then, we can continue and examine how far the prevalent situation differs from the model and draw conclusions regarding institutions and growth. That is to say, we can compare the model world and the real world; but the objective should not be to change and perfect the real world according to the model world, but to detect differences.

However, in institutional economics the 'strongest' (meaning the economically most efficient) institution might not prevail and survive. The corresponding hypothesis cannot be brought into line with the persistence of many economically, politically, and socially inefficient informal and formal institutions. Furthermore, the theory of multiple equilibria has taught us that inefficient states can emerge and persist, although they are detrimental to economic growth and development. This is not astonishing since utility maximization does not necessarily correspond to material utility maximization. An individual's utility can also be influenced by certain beliefs and convictions. Furthermore, stability and security can be rated higher than economic profit, depending on risk adversity, societal dullness, values, attitudes, and beliefs. Hence, the persistence of institutions might lead to a state of general inefficiency – that is, even if informal and formal institutions are inefficient from an economic point of view they might persist because of the complexity and difficulty of institutional change. Thus, even if we consult informal institutions and immaterial incentives, the persistence of inefficient institutions cannot be easily explained. But since institutions are inertial but changeable, marginal alteration is always possible. Nevertheless, as we will see in the following sections, possibilities to accelerate the process of change are limited because of the complexity of the institutional system.

2.4 Transaction costs

Transaction costs are the costs that arise from transactions such as information costs, policing costs, and enforcement costs. To accomplish a transaction, information concerning the relevant commodity, its value, the seller, the contractual arrangement, and relevant laws must be gathered. Aside from the commodity's price, costs for contract enforcement, information about the goods, and information about the business partner are incurred. Additionally, a risk premium must be considered.

According to North (1990), the theory of institutions is a combination of a theory of human behavior and a theory of transaction costs. Since institutions have binding rules, they are created in a way to reduce transaction costs (Coase, 1937; Coase, 1960). Hence, via institutions humans try to reduce, as far as possible, expenditure on information, monitoring, and enforcement. A clear system of rules that punishes offences decreases enforcement costs. Hence, acts of sale are well regulated and correspond to specified patterns. The consolidation of procedures, through business regulation and laws (for example, contract law, patent rights, and the protection of intellectual property) constrains human action and fosters predictability. Therefore, even if we are not endued with personal information about our potential seller, we take less risk in doing business with him since we know he must adhere to the rules otherwise he will be punished. This means the introduction of relevant institutions has decreased risk and thereby transaction costs. Institutions have superseded the need for information and monitoring and have facilitated enforcement, since binding rules exist that can be used by individuals to predict others' behaviors. The possibility to predict human actions increases security. We can rely on people acting under these rules since a violation is connected with costs. Since the constraints are binding, the environment in which humans act is stable. Thus, institutions decrease transaction costs and increase security and stability. Hence, under these conditions, individuals maximize their utility.

Institutions not only increase material utility but also increase immaterial utility by providing a stable mental and metaphysical environment that permits the prediction of others' reactions and thereby decreases transaction costs. How individuals rate material and immaterial utility, (what they assess as being more important) depends on individual attitudes and beliefs.

However, institutions are not necessarily economically efficient and a particular institutional environment might not maximize the utility of an individual or a society. Consider what happens if somebody achieves maximal personal utility by general destabilization. In this case, the individual might try to rearrange institutions that best fit their interests, for example, if it is an unstable environment. This could be true for certain minorities that consciously destabilize a particular region to enforce their own interests, for example Iraq or Afghanistan in the past couple of years. However, from a societal point of view, this approach is not desirable since it usually leads to the oppression of large sections of the population and economic disadvantages. In any case, the utility of the minority, which possesses de facto political power, is maximized.

Utility is maximized under certain assumptions. The assumptions correspond to the prevalent institutional environment and depend on individual preferences. That is, institutions allow individuals to maximize their utility presupposing the institutional environment. For example, in a dictatorship that oppresses its citizens individuals can maximize their utility by adhering to the rules and constraints set by institutions. However, if an individual's utility can be increased by revolting against the authority and the established institutional system, it will act accordingly. Nevertheless, such an approach is accompanied by high costs, which might, in part, explain the persistence of authoritarian regimes.

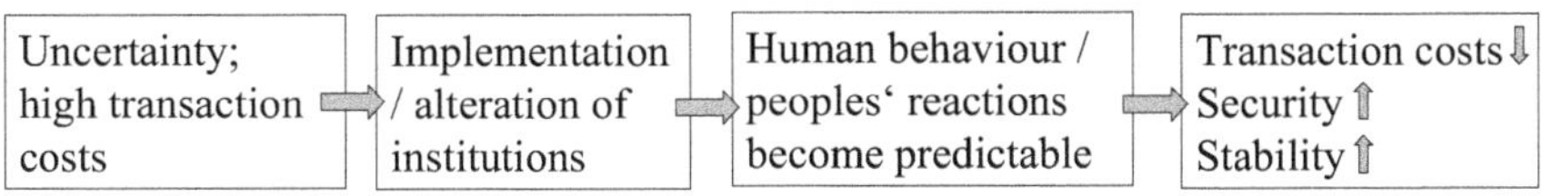

Figure 2.1: emergence and alteration of institutions. Source: own calculation.

Figure 2.1 demonstrates the emergence and alteration of institutions. The state of prevalent institutions is affected by uncertainty and high transaction costs. This might be for different reasons, for example historical accidents, increasing dissatisfaction regarding the current situation (cognitive disequilibrium), and so on. In this situation, humans impose further constraints on themselves, or alter existing constraints, to regulate their relationships – that is, they implement or alter institutions. Institutions make human behavior predictable; hence, institutions reduce transaction costs and increase security and stability. Within this environment, people will maximize their individual utility, which includes immaterial utility. Utility, in general, is an irrational concept since it depends on individual attitudes, convictions, and beliefs – that is, the social value system and the prevalent culture.

2.5 Institutional change and transplantation

Ascribing underdevelopment to institutional quality poses challenges for the theory of economic growth in several ways. First, a general growth model, which determines the reasons for growth and provides overall solutions that can be applied to every economy, cannot be found. Second, this makes it difficult to give instructions for improvements in growth performance, since the success of reform activities depends on the prevalent conditions. If Pareto-optimal growth is the target, it is possible that existing institutions could hinder its implementation. Hence, to realize Pareto-optimal growth institutions must be altered in a way that supports growth. Thus, the problem could be solved by adopting institutions from economically successful countries and implementing them in economically backward countries. However, as the previous section has already suggested, institutional development and change are subject to several influencing factors and institutional properties, which can make the adoption of such a policy difficult. In addition, institutions differ in relation to the nature of change and, in particular, to the speed of change. This section, therefore, deals with the issue of institutional change and transportability.

To expand this idea, we will refer to the approaches of Boettke, Coyne and Leeson (2008) and Roland (2005). These two studies incorporate the basic facts of the subsequent argument and will now be summarized.

Roland (2005) establishes the concept of slow- and fast-moving institutions. Institutions can change slowly and continuously, or rapidly and irregularly. Culture depicts a typical slow-moving institution. Thus, culture is rooted in religion or other beliefs that have hardly changed over time. Since it is an institution that constitutes the identity of the society, only marginal change is possible. Hence, we are talking about a slowly but continuously changing institution.

By contrast, for example, political institutions can be changed rapidly and irregularly. A military coup or a rebellion can alter the power structure of a state overnight or at least within a few weeks or months. Legal institutions can be seen as in-between, since the revision of statutes does not occur very quickly, but does not take centuries either.

However, a relationship between fast- and slow-moving institutions exists, since institutions are complementary and build systemic consistency (Roland, 2005). In examining institutions we deal with a system of institutions that influence and complement each other. Therefore, slow-moving institutions such as culture can be understood as the slow, but continuously altering, underlying foundation that influences the fast-moving institutions and vice versa. Fast-moving institutions can change during no observable modification to a slow-moving institution. Yet, after a long period of marginal change in slow-moving institutions, the aggregated shift might suddenly lead to a rapid and irregular adjustment in fast-moving institutions. Hence, inconsistencies between slow- and fast-moving institutions lead to changes (Roland, 2005). The fact that institutions interact and build complementary systems has far-reaching policy implications. Disturbing the complex institutional apparatus might result in equally complex inconsistencies and might have unpredictable consequences. Hence, replacing an apparently growth-inhibiting institution by a seemingly growth-supporting institution can be risky.

Another approach that sheds light on the issue of institutional change and transportability comes from Boettke, Coyne and Leeson (2008). The authors assign a crucial role to 'institutional stickiness', that is, "the ability or inability of new institutional arrangements to take hold where they are transplanted" (p. 332). Within the model, institutions are categorized as 'indigenously introduced endogenous institutions' (IEN), 'indigenously introduced exogenous institutions' (IEX), and 'foreign-introduced exogenous institutions' (FEX). Here, *foreign-introduced* means institutions designed by outsiders such as foreigners, whereas *indigenously introduced* denotes institutions established by insiders or locals. *Exogenous* is meant to describe institutions implemented by a subordinate entity, which could be the local government or a foreign organization or force. *Endogenous*, on the contrary, depicts institutions that are not formally designed but developed spontaneously from within the community of indigenous individuals.

Boettke, Coyne and Leeson (2008) use the philosophical term *métis* to describe the societal and cultural basis that underlies all human and societal life. Since *métis* depicts the origin of the natives' mentalities, beliefs, and practices, it is durable and nearly unchangeable. Hence, the stronger an institution is connected to *métis*, the stickier it will be. Since IEN institutions are rooted in *métis*, they constitute the stickiest of all institutions. Thus, the further an institution is situated from *métis*, the less sticky it will be.

IEX institutions are not endogenous but formally created by a superior entity. However, this entity must be indigenous, which implies it must concern a local institution, for example, the local government. Since an indigenous authority is familiar with local customs, attitudes, and practices, IEX institutions will, in general, be consistent with IEN institutions and *métis*. Hence, IEX institutions are less sticky than IEN institutions, but more inertial than institutions introduced by an outsider. Consequently, FEX institutions are the least sticky since they are created and implemented by foreigners and are sparsely, or not at all, correlated with *métis*.

Figure 2.2 demonstrates the closeness of the particular institutions to *métis* and to each other and, therefore, their degree of stickiness. The institutions within the outermost circle are the easiest to modify, whereas a change becomes catchier the further inwards we go.

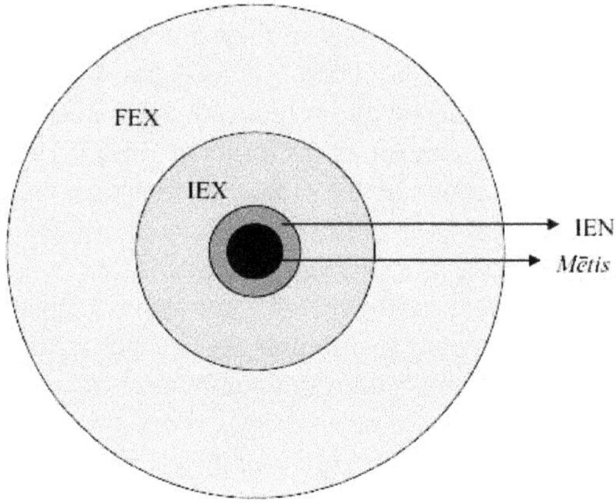

Figure 2.2: institutional stickiness. Source: Boettke, Coyne & Leeson, 2008, p. 344.

However, according to Boettke, Coyne and Leeson (2008), the stickiness of an institution depends on its stickiness in the former period, hence:

$$Z_t^I = Z_t^I\left(Z_{t-1}^I\right) \tag{2.1}$$

$$Z_{t-1}^I = Z_{t-1}^I\left(Z_{t-2}^I\right) \tag{2.2}$$

$$Z_{t-n}^I = Z_{t-n}^I\left(Z_{t-(n+1)}^I\right) \tag{2.3}$$

where Z denotes the level of stickiness and I the particular institution. Accordingly, the stickiness of an institution today at least depends on the stickiness at its date of emergence N periods ago. That is:

$$Z_{t-N}^I = Z_{t-N}^I\left(I^{IEN}, I^{IEX}, I^{FEX}\right) \tag{2.4}$$

where:

$$Z^{I^{IEN}} \rhd Z^{I^{IEX}} \rhd Z^{I^{FEX}}. \tag{2.5}$$

Hence, the stickiness of an institution today depends on its past stickiness, which depends on its level of connection with *métis*.

This model shows that institutional transplantation can be disputed. Adopting institutions from an economically successful country and implementing them in an underdeveloped economy is consistent with adding or changing FEX institutions. These institutions do not match the societal basis and do not complement IEN and IEX institutions. The more the endogenous and exogenous institutions differ, the less sticky FEX institutions will be. However, one should not conclude that IEN and IEX institutions must be economically efficient and support growth. If it is not possible to implement particular institutions because they do not fit *métis*, the prevalent institutions are not necessarily 'better'. On the contrary, the *métis* and the IEN and IEX institutions can be growth inhibiting. However, transplanting institutions that are supposed to be growth supporting might not necessarily improve the situation; instead, it could worsen it.

The model of institutional stickiness can easily be connected to Roland's (2005) theory of fast- and slow-moving institutions. IEN institutions are slow moving since they are rooted in hardly changing beliefs and practices. IEX institutions can be considered fast or slow moving depending on which particular institution is involved – which is also true for FEX institutions. However, both concepts of institutional change emphasize the rootedness of informal institutions in a societal and cultural foundation on which a society's identity depends. Thus, less connection between the foundation and the institution makes modification or transplantation easier. However, less connection also implies that the institution will eventually not fit the complex institutional system in a particular country; this could mean it might not be accepted, might be seen as useless, or might even be abolished. Thus, an institution that leads to economic growth in one country might be unsuccessful in another country. Consequently, encouraging economic growth in a country in which growth-inhibiting informal and formal institutions are prevalent is a complex and difficult task, especially for outsiders not connected to the country's *métis*.

Dolfsma and Verburg (2008) also develop an approach to institutional change. Like Roland (2005), they emphasize tensions as the trigger for institutional change. Accordingly, sociocultural values (which we determine as informal institutions) shape the institutional setting. However, the authors differentiate between three examples of institutional change. First, value tensions are seen as crucial, since new sets of sociocultural values might conflict with old values. Thus, a new constellation between values and institutions might emerge. The second possibility for institutional change is tensions between institutions. Third, tensions between values and institutions can trigger institutional change, since sociocultural values alter over time and can no longer match the institutional setting. At this point, institutions have to adjust.

However, the three outlined theories of institutional change all originate in the context of a connection between a sociocultural foundation and a formal superstructure. The sociocultural values, or the general value system, determine the formal institutional structure. The closer the informal and formal structures are, the more inert they become. However, tensions between or within the structures cause institutional change.

Furthermore, institutional change depends on the ability to cooperate. If the majority of the population wants to change the institutional environment but is not able to cooperate or form an organized representation of interests, it is easy for a small group of oppressors to restrict those particular individuals. Individuals might not be willing to subject themselves to the high costs of institutional change. However, in this case this means that the current institutions, introduced, for example, by a dictator, do their jobs.

As previously mentioned, interactions between institutions are crucial. The absence of institutional change not only depends on costs and the fear of oppression, but also on the interplay of a myriad institutions. Hence, an inefficient political and legal system might be preserved because of its connectedness with history and culture.

Because individuals are unsure how others will react to a new situation, people are uncertain whether an institutional change will improve or worsen their living conditions. To avoid a deterioration in their living standards, they will try (consciously or not) to preserve the status quo. In the case of informal institutions, the preservation of the status quo might be a matter of the subconscious.

However, since informal institutions determine self-identification, they build the foundation of a society and of an institutional system. Further, formal institutions are based on the fundamental structure of values and beliefs. Institutions that determine an individual's identity are the stickiest, since people do not easily give up their convictions, belief systems, or origins – that is their identity. Informal institutions construct a system of mental guidance and affiliation and, therefore individuals identify with a certain culture. They define a society's identity, shape its worldview, and establish a feeling of affiliation. Hence, informal institutions are hard to change; external and internal changes are slow moving.

The complexity of the institutional system has consequences for the issue of institutional transfer. If the institutional arrangement is crucial for economic development, it seems logical that less well developed countries will adopt the institutions of rich countries – which we define as growth-supporting institutions. It is argued that underdeveloped countries should replace their growth-inhibiting institutions by growth-supporting institutions, since this would solve their issue of underdevelopment. However, it is not easy to conduct a transfer of institutions. The reasons for this have already been examined. Informal institutions equal culture; cultures differ between regions since cultural components such as values, norms, beliefs, conventions, worldviews, and attitudes can all differ. In general, since these informal institutions build the fundament of institutional structure, institutions will differ between societies. Therefore, fundamental institutions, as well as institutional superstructures, can vary greatly and (to make it even more complicated) a country's development path can also be hit by historical accidents.

Institutions that are exogenously transplanted into an economy correspond to FEX institutions. If an external organization, such as the World Bank or the International Monetary Fund, forces a country to liberalize its financial system or forces privatization, these are examples of FEX institutions. However, these FEX institutions are transplanted into a complex institutional system consisting of institutions that are, more or less, connected to the informal foundation and complement each other. Substituting one institution for another, or adding a new one, can disturb the complex structure and lead to severe consequences. Thus, the new institutions (or the institutional changes) might not be accepted because they do not match the system. Since FEX institutions are not connected to IEN and IEX institutions – that is, to relevant informal and formal institutions – they might be dismissed by the institutional structure and then quickly retracted. They might also be bypassed and subsequently malfunction. In the worst case scenario, they might disturb institutional equilibrium and impact on other institutions, in turn, making them unsound. If this occurs, the FEX institutions would have an inhibiting effect on economic growth. Hence, a transplanted institution is not usually rooted in the informal institutional structure. It does not match the institutional system, and the consequences of its adoption are incalculable since a calculation would require a complete knowledge of the total institutional structure, which is impossible.

However, institutional transplantation can work. If the FEX institution matches the underlying system, the expected positive effects on the growth rate can be realized. As a consequence, the chance of success is higher if the transplanted institution better fits the informal structure. Take, for example, the exogenous institutional innovations in Japan and West Germany after World War II, which showed that institutional transplantation can have positive impacts. However, if the transplanted FEX institution does not match the informal institutional structure, the outcome of the transplantation is not predictable and the risk of a worsening economic situation is high. Hence, if countries' formal institutional structures differ, the transplantation of institutions should be reconsidered.

However, historical accidents can also alter the institutional system in the short- or long-term.[13] Historical accidents are events that randomly change the

[13] It has also been suggested that historical accidents are responsible for the emergence of institutions, in so far as they are the catalysts for the implementation of certain institutions.

institutional environment, for example wars, civil wars, natural disasters, political upheavals, migrations, or economic crises. Since rapid institutional changes correspond to FEX or IEX institutions, the theory of institutional stickiness predicts that alterations are not durable. However, in relation to how much damage is done – that is, to what extent the original institutional system has been demolished – and in relation to power allocation, historical accidents can lead to lasting institutional changes. If a historical accident causes an indigenous or exogenous minority group to have sufficient resources (and thereby power) to create institutions that best fit their interests and enforce the compliance of those institutions, then these, potentially inappropriate institutions, might persist. Since institutions influence each other, the prevalent environment might eventually adjust or the new institutions might never be totally accepted. In this case, they might one day be abolished, even if it is a long period of time between implementation and abolishment.

Hence, history can be a catalyst of institutional implementation and is responsible for the shape institutions assume. This shape can differ from that which humans had originally created. The outcome depends on how long the situation persists, the prevalent institutional system, further historical accidents, and other unpredictable factors. Again this demonstrates the complexity and unpredictability of institutional systems and institutional changes.

History, in the sense of experience, is also crucial. In the case of informal institutions, historical events can influence value systems, societal attitudes, morals, and beliefs. At the same time, history influences each individual and their personal experiences, values, beliefs, morals, and so on. Since people's experiences can be traced back to general historical events, many will experience the same event; for example, individuals who experience the cruelties and the destruction of war. Every individual makes their own experiences; however, on an aggregate level, their experiences are similar and, therefore, society is also shaped.

2.6 Institutions and technology

> "Technology relates to a broader set of beliefs about the operation of the physical world and about the nature of interactions between humans and their physical environment. [...] it is the interaction between institutional change and technology that drives economic growth" (Roland, 2005, p. 13).

Hence, historical accidents might not only change the institutional environment, they might also be the starting point of the emergence of a new institution. This is the case when a historical accident alters the environment in a way that makes the implementation of new constraints necessary.

Technology is the body of knowledge available to society that creates economic value. Technological progress is the alteration of the relationship between inputs and output and, therefore, can be defined as a change in knowledge. Hence, if the same amount of output can be produced with fewer inputs, or if more output can be produced with an equal amount of inputs, we talk about technological progress. Technological progress is a change in the knowledge about products, about the production process, and about the organization of production. This knowledge differs between societies. However, this could be the case because one society could, potentially, be further behind other societies on its development path. In this situation, time is the decisive factor, because the society that is behind will further evolve over time and will equal the level of technological knowledge of the more developed countries. In any case, this implies that all societies exhibit equal initial conditions, which is not a realistic assumption. Therefore, differences in technology can be traced back to different initial conditions, such as geography or institutions (Rodrik, 2003; Rodrik, Subramanian & Trebbi, 2004). We are interested in the technological differences that can be traced back to institutions. We argue that some societies possess a body of knowledge that creates economic value, whereas other societies do not have such technologies or at least not to the same extent. According to the current hypothesis, the available technological knowledge depends on the prevalent informal and formal institutions. Reverse causality also exists – that is, institutions influence technology and technology influences institutions.

According to Lipsey, Carlaw and Bekar (2005), technological progress is the main driver for long-term growth. The ability to use tools, to invent, and to innovate are the crucial properties that led to the unique evolution of the human race. Thus, rearranging knowledge about existing technologies and developing completely new ideas, make production more efficient and lead to technological progress.

Economic development did not spread evenly around the globe and nor did technology. At certain times in history, some societies were, technologically, very sophisticated, whereas others were totally backward. However, the rank order of the technological leaders has changed several times, and progressive societies have suffered setbacks while underdeveloped societies took over the technological and scientific leadership. The most remarkable progress took place in Britain and spread to Western Europe at the beginning of the 19th century.

However, if technological progress is crucial, then societies with knowledge that creates economic value have an advantage, since they are able to rearrange technologies and generate new ideas. That is, innovating societies are better off compared with non-innovating societies when the goal is per capita income maximization.

Whether a society can be described as innovating or non-innovating depends on several factors. Lipsey, Carlaw and Bekar (2005) specify five classes of reasons for why a society can be non-innovating. Here, we will discuss how much of a role institutions play.

- The ability to innovate depends on the prevalent opportunities and challenges the society faces. Hence, some societies are well adapted to their environment and for them there is no need to innovate; the prevalent technological standards might also be low compared with those in other societies.
- It is possible that people do not realize the opportunities for technological progress and further development. This is because they interpret their environment in a way that makes technological progress unnecessary. Lipsey, Carlaw and Bekar (2005) state that "someone whose worldview is mechanical, as was common with Europeans in early modern times, will tend to look for mechanical solutions. Someone whose worldview is mystical will tend to look for magical solutions" (p. 70).
- Societies might be non-innovating because they do not receive the full return of their efforts, for example, because of insecure property rights.
- Innovating efforts can be restricted by the government in power or by powerful interest groups. Also, certain innovations can be forbidden for religious reasons.
- Humans' energy to innovate can be influenced by diseases or other circumstances that leave no space and strength for innovating activity.

Institutional matters relate to points one to four. Individuals need incentives to innovate. The innovation must improve their current situation. Hence, the expected returns must be high enough to take the costs of innovating. If individuals do not receive the full return from innovating, the remaining return might be under the critical level that does not make innovating worthwhile. In relation to the role of property rights, people will not use their assets in an economically efficient way if they cannot be sure whether their ownership will endure and whether they will receive the profits from using the assets. Property rights can be restrained by an inadequate legal system, by political power, or by powerful interest groups. Hence, property rights, which are an institution in themselves, depend on further political and legal institutions. Thus, a society can be described as non-innovating because it has insecure property rights and an inadequate legal system.

As already mentioned, even if property rights exist powerful interest groups might be in a position to ignore them. Furthermore, since particular interest groups might possess de facto political power or might be able to influence de jure political power, they can change the formal institutional environment in a way that best fits their interests and thereby they can abolish property rights (Acemoglu, Johnson & Robinson, 2005).

Furthermore, formal and informal institutions, which preclude individuals from freely accumulating knowledge, constrain technology and technological progress. In such cases, beliefs, values, and convictions can restrict knowledge accumulation; or there might be formal restrictions, such as particular laws or political restraints. An authoritarian regime, which oppresses freedom of opinion and controls publicly expressed ideas as well as teachings in schools and universities, does not support the free accumulation of knowledge and thereby does not support technological progress.

Civil rights, especially freedom of speech, rule of law, and material and intellectual property rights, seem crucial for knowledge accumulation and technology. However, the absence of property rights, civil rights, and an independent judiciary can lead a society to be non-innovating since it hinders the individuals from receiving their full returns from innovating.

Lipsey, Carlaw and Bekar (2005) mention several situations in which informal institutions preclude people form innovating. Here, individuals might not realize the opportunities that are offered to them by innovation. In history, most economically viable innovations are grounded in scientific and mechanical research. To innovate, humans have to examine the physical world and accept the laws of nature. Therefore, if people support a more mystical worldview, which often has its roots in religious beliefs, they might not identify the ideas that are necessary for economically relevant innovations. A person who believes that, every second, God creates a feature of the world anew and who believes that everything (at least in the physical world) can be totally changed in a moment is not persuaded by the laws of nature. Hence, this individual cannot develop a naturalistic and mechanical worldview. Therefore, their basic beliefs shape knowledge and thereby technology.

Furthermore, informal institutions might place constraints on human behavior and bar individuals from innovating. Religious doctrines or other metaphysical convictions can restrain scientific research and technological progress. Even if people receive the full returns for innovating, they might be persuaded that their proposed method of innovating was wrong and might not innovate at all. People might also put so much time and energy into religious and other metaphysical activities, that there are not enough resources left for the innovation itself.[14]

Here, it is argued that the institutional environment influences a society's ability and desire to innovate. Hence, technological progress depends on the particular institutional structure. Since the institutional system per se is complex, the connections and transmission channels between institutions and technology are also complicated and difficult to see through. Owing to institutional complementarities, institutions that hinder technological progress might not always

[14] Barro and McCleary (2003), for example, find that the number of church attendances is negatively correlated with the growth rate, whereas religious beliefs, in general, have a positive impact on growth.

be growth inhibiting. The concentration of power, for example, might hinder innovative activity since individuals do not receive the full returns from innovating. However, a powerful interest group (such as a government) might also be able to channel resources into the relevant sectors, for example research and development, and thereby support innovation and technical progress in a way that exceeds private innovating behavior.

The relationship between institutions and technology is not causal. That is to say, a change in technology might influence living standards and, therefore, might lead to a change in priorities and preferences. As a result, the feelings of material and immaterial stability might be modified and at least some informal institutions might change. Hence, a change in the value system, and even in worldviews and beliefs because of technological progress, is possible. Nevertheless, technology and technological progress emerge from the interplay of institutions, historical accidents, and further technological progress.

Hence, the hypothesis at hand is that informal institutions, which are not supportive of a naturalistic, scientific, or mechanical worldview, do not encourage economically viable innovating activity and thereby do not encourage technological progress. That is, knowledge depends on general beliefs and attitudes concerning worldviews and ideology. As regards formal institutions, secure property rights will create the maximal incentives for innovation by guaranteeing the owner of an asset the full returns from innovating. An independent judiciary and civil rights will also support innovation and technology, since they guarantee freedom of action, at least within the boundaries of the rule of law. Hence, every individual can use their assets in a way that maximizes utility. When property rights, civil rights, and an independent judiciary exist, the question of whether individual utility maximization supports innovation and technological progress depends on the informal institutional setting, because here innovating activity is solely restricted by worldviews and beliefs.

Therefore, the particular development that took place in Western Europe can be led by the kind of technological knowledge and the special institutional environment that have been prevalent. That is to say, the Industrial Revolution could only occur in Europe, since the required conditions were available. Furthermore, it started in England since this was the leading country concerning Newtonian mechanics. The point in time of the Industrial Revolution was affected by the interdependencies between sciences, technology, and institutions. Hence, it could have happened sooner or later depending on external influences. But it could not have happened anywhere else (Lipsey, Carlaw & Bekar, 2005).

The process of industrialization since 1820 is related to the development of modern sciences, Newtonian mechanics, and the mechanical worldview that pervaded all of Western European society. The diffusion of the mechanical worldview can be traced back to the emergence of modern sciences whose basis was the acceptance of naturalism. The decisive point is that the ideas of naturalism, the belief in the laws of nature, modern sciences, and a mechanical worldview were able to penetrate all of society and build the basis of the society's identity. Hence, Western European technology is related to the prevalent beliefs, worldviews, and convictions concerning the physical world and its components. The informal and formal institutional environment permitted and supported the development of the Industrial Revolution. Historical accidents and the emergence of relevant formal institutions such as independent universities, the structure of the educational system, the role the church played in education, the emergence of corporate bodies, and the legal system supported a unique development path, which was accompanied and correlated by a body of technological knowledge that led to high economic growth. The fact that naturalism could at least not be abolished by the Catholic church depicts one of the stochastic historical accidents; another one is depicted by the fact that in Europe political pluralism was prevalent, which also supported its development (Grant, 1996; Huff, 2003; Jacob, 1997; Lipsey, Carlaw & Bekar, 2005).

However, technology and institutions are highly correlated. A society's stock of knowledge, its beliefs and worldviews, and its attitudes concerning the fundaments of the physical world differ between cultures. Hence, technological developments vary. Therefore, a specific cultural background constrains the development of knowledge and thereby of technology. In addition, it determines formal institutions, which further influence the development of knowledge and technology.

2.7 Equilibrium view of institutions

2.7.1 General remarks

This part of the dissertation project demonstrates a more formal approach to institutions. That is to say, game-theoretic analysis is used to describe the formations of self-enforcing strategies and, therefore, institutional persistence. It has already been stated that, depending on the object of study, different approaches of institutional analysis are reasonable. The rules-of-the-game or design view, which depict institutions as exogenously given to human agents, neglect the endogenous character of institutions. Anyway it makes sense to consult this view for the examination of several issues. With the assumption of exogenously given constraints, we can examine the impact of these constraints on behavior and, for example, on economic development. That is to say, we can assume the legal system, or in the case of informal institutions the level of trust, is exogenously given and study its impact on a situation in which there is no feedback mechanism. Regarding a single individual or a certain period of time, this proceeding can be considered to describe the real world truthfully.

The equilibrium view, however, tries to explain the self-enforcing character of institutions. This approach is useful for an understanding of institutional persistence and institutional diversity. It incorporates feedback mechanisms and describes institutional self-preservation in an equilibrium state. The equilibrium view demonstrates the circular flow between humans' actions and institutions; that is, institutions determine human behavior, but they are also determined by human actions.[15] Institutional persistence and the self-enforcing character of institutions are institutional properties that cause problems for less developed economies. If institutions could easily be changed, we could just establish the institutions of economically successful countries in underdeveloped economies and the problem of underdevelopment would be solved, apart from geographical factors. Therefore, it is the robustness of an established institution that causes the problems.

In the subsequent model the reason for institutional robustness is an equilibrium state. The only possibility for an alteration of an equilibrium state is an exogenous shock. Without the appearance of an exogenous shock, the equilibrium state will exist indefinitely. Therefore, a pretend 'inefficient' equilibrium, in which only low living standards and low growth rates are implemented, is hard to abolish. However, an equilibrium state suggests that optimal strategies are implemented and thereby the state cannot be inefficient. That is to say, societies might be situated in an equilibrium state in which only low living standards are realized. Nevertheless, contingent on the prevalent conditions, the state might present an equilibrium. In economics, however, we are looking for Pareto-optimal results. Hence, a state in which no individual can be better off without putting another individual in a worse position. In any case, an institutional equilibrium might not be Pareto-optimal. But, according to the equilibrium view, the strategies are optimally chosen regarding the prevalent conditions. Hence, the individuals choose their strategies in a way that maximizes their utility. Therefore, strategies are optimal, but not necessarily Pareto-optimal (Greif, 2006, pp. 407–420). When multiple equilibria are possible, multiple optimal states exist. Thus, different equilibrium strategies are possible. Then, however, equilibrium behavior or rather equilibrium codes of conduct differ. Different strategies originate in different institutions. Hence, varying value or belief systems are

[15] However, historical path dependence and historical accidents play a decisive role in institutional development (Aoki, 2001; David, 1994; Greif, 1993; Greif, 1994; Greif, 2006; North, 1990; North, 2005). According to Aoki (2001), institutional development cannot be solely described by analytical tools and game theory. Historical events must be consulted to understand a society's institutional environment. That is why Aoki describes his approach as comparative institutional analysis – that is an analytical, comparative, and historical analysis (Aoki, 2001, p. 3).

equal to different institutions, which determine different optimal strategies (the strategy determined by the institution corresponds to the optimal strategy that is derived through utility maximization). Since institutions become visible through behavior, different institutions become visible through different forms of societal organization. Hence, according to the equilibrium view of institutions, an equilibrium corresponds, for example, to a certain form of societal organization. Therefore, forms of societal organization vary and correspondingly result in different economic performances. Comparing societies regarding their economic performances or even their institutions and concluding that the society with less economic growth or a low living standard is 'worse' is wrong. An institutional standard that must be fulfilled to be considered a 'good' institution does not exist. Every society optimizes its strategies and, therefore, realizes its individual optimal institutions and strategies. Institutions that lead to (Pareto-)optimality in one country are not (Pareto-)optimal in another country. Hence, a normative comparison of institutions and growth performances is – according to the equilibrium view – not possible.

Greif's (1994) model, which is depicted in the next section, demonstrates that two varying societies that reside in their particular equilibrium realize different economic outcomes. Nevertheless, both implement optimal strategies. Hence, the state will endure indefinitely – or until an exogenous shock occurs – although one society might realize significantly lower growth rates and living standards than the other one. The present study differentiates between generalized and limited morality. Chapter three describes the two concepts in more detail.[16] Here, we define limited morality as a traditional and conservative form of societal organization where hierarchical and paternalistic structures are prevalent. Societies realizing limited morality are marked by the importance of group affiliation, for example the family, the tribe, the clan, the religious group, and so on. Furthermore, individualism is less pronounced since the collective is emphasized. Generalized morality describes a modern, individualistic society where civil liberties are realized. Group membership is not the decisive factor; instead individuals cooperate independent of affiliation.

2.7.2 Shared-beliefs cum equilibrium-summary-representation approach

This part of the present study demonstrates Aoki's (2001) shared-beliefs cum equilibrium-summary-representation approach of institutions. According to Aoki's definition: "An institution is a self-sustaining system of shared beliefs about how the game is played" (Aoki, 2001, p. 185). This definition includes

[16] In his paper (1994) and his book (2006), Greif refers to individualist vs. collectivist societies instead of generalized vs. limited morality.

three important statements. First, we are entering the sphere of game theory, which is unavoidable if we want to study strategic behavior, that is situations in which an outcome depends on an agent's own actions and on other agents' actions. Second, an institution is defined as self-sustaining. That is to say, when the institution is established (that is when it is implemented in peoples' minds and behaviors), it resides in an equilibrium state and, therefore, is self-preserving. Third, the institution is a system of shared beliefs. Hence, institutions are built from expectations regarding one's own and others' behaviors. That is to say, certain beliefs about behavioral patterns are established and every agent believes that the other agents behave according to these beliefs. Therefore, the agent himself will also act according to the beliefs. The result is a Nash equilibrium, as will be seen and thereby there exists no incentive for an unilateral deviation.

According to Aoki (2001, Ch. 7, pp. 185–206), five properties characterize institutions. First, institutions are endogenous. That is to say, the beliefs about how the game is played are not exogenous, but emerge from an equilibrium state of the society. Second, the beliefs enable agents to predict others' behaviors and thereby optimally choose their own actions. Therefore, the institution contains all the information necessary for the agent to choose his own behavior. This is called the *summary representation* of an institution. Third, institutions are characterized by their robustness or durability; that is institutions are inertial and change slowly. Therefore, we can assume institutions are constant at least for a certain period of time. Change comes along through a shock or other exogenous influences. However, change can also occur because a critical mass of agents considers the rules – no matter whether formal or informal – as unsatisfying and tries to change them. Such a situation corresponds to a general cognitive disequilibrium (Aoki, 2001, p. 240). Nevertheless, change implies the abandonment of an equilibrium path. Hence, the shared-beliefs cum equilibrium-summary-representation approach examines institutional existence, and persistence, in equilibrium. Fourth, institutions are universal to all agents. Since institutions regulate human interactions, they have to be universal. An institution becomes an institution because agents adhere to it. They do so because an equilibrium institution establishes a Nash equilibrium and thereby the agents have no incentive to unilaterally deviate. Finally, since institutions are not given by a natural order but develop spontaneously, multiple institutional systems can emerge within technologically similar environments. That is to say, multiple equilibria are possible.

Our definition of institutions now becomes more analytical. However, this does not change anything regarding the general content. Institutions are necessary to regulate strategic interactions between agents. That is to say, an agent maximizes his utility by optimally choosing his action. An agent's utility, however, depends not only on his own action but also on others' actions. Hence, to maximize his utility the agent must anticipate other agents' actions and choose his own behavior accordingly. That is to say, a utility function must incorporate an agent's actions as well as expectations regarding other agents' actions. Decisions that depend on one's own and on others' actions are called 'strategic'.

The technologically feasible actions determine a society's environment. The environment influences an agent's action, but a single agent's action choice has no impact on the environment. Thus, the environment consists of exogenous rules (institutions, geography) that influence an individual's action choices.

Before the model is presented some general remarks are necessary. As mentioned, institutions reduce uncertainty regarding others' behaviors and, therefore, decrease transaction costs. Hence, an institution includes information regarding others' actions and lets an agent choose his optimal action given the expectations concerning the others' behaviors. A certain moral, for example, makes individuals behave in a particular way; hence, an agent knows how to behave (how others expect him to behave) and he knows how the others will act. Thus, codes of conduct based on a certain moral or worldview emerge. The same holds for formal institutions, for example a certain law, although the motivation might differ.[17] However, this is a typical problem solved by game-theoretic analysis: to predict behavior in a strategic situation – that is, in a situation in which the outcome does not solely depend on one's own action but also on other individuals' behaviors. According to Greif, game-theoretic analysis deals with the issue that: "For player A to choose behavior, he has to know what B will do, but for B to choose behavior, he has to know what A will do" (Greif, 2006, p. 408). This, however, is exactly the problem of social interaction and the reason why humans impose institutions. Institutions let player A know how B expects him to behave as well as how B will behave, and vice versa. Then it is optimal for A to behave like B expects him to do. Hence, with an institution being established, a Nash equilibrium is implemented since no player has an incentive to unilaterally deviate; and we can observe the self-enforcing character of institutions: "if each individual expects others to follow the behaviour expected of them, he finds it optimal to follow the behaviour expected of him" (Greif, 2006, p. 408).

Classical game theory, however, has its drawbacks. As with every theory, at least some of the assumptions are unrealistic. In any case, as already argued the reasonableness of a theory depends on the object of study. That is to say, the unrealistic assumptions of complete information, rationality, and homogeneous agents, for example, might be acceptable when the objective is to demonstrate the self-enforcing character of institutions. Here, however, we want to demon-

[17] The adherence to an informal institution might originate in a metaphysical belief, whereas the adherence to a formal institution might be rooted in the fear of official punishment. However, since formal and informal institutions cannot be clearly separated, usually both motivations are mingled.

strate that institutions are self-enforcing and explain institutional persistence. To do so, we will show that the five characteristics of institutions defined above hold in the model. Other questions, of course, are better solved using other models, and thereby other assumptions, for example bounded rationality in evolutionary game-theoretic approaches.

2.7.2.1 Model I

Below Aoki's shared-beliefs cum equilibrium-summary-representation model is demonstrated (Aoki, 2001, Ch. 7, pp. 185–206). However, the model described here partly deviates from Aoki's model and the interpretation might differ at some points. Therefore, the core model is adopted but modifications are made.

To analyze institutions, we now deal with the most elementary actors, the single agents themselves. Institutions as mental models or belief systems are irrelevant as long as they are not implemented by human behavior. Hence, human behavior makes institutions visible.

The model demonstrates the self-enforcing character of institutions. That is to say, an institution depicts the equilibrium state of a strategy. The pure existence of an institution implies a Nash equilibrium, since the agents have no incentive to unilaterally deviate. This, however, implies that the institution is self-sustaining and will persist until an exogenous shock or a cognitive disequilibrium leads to a deviation from the equilibrium path.

The domain of the game includes a finite number of agents – that is, the set of agents $R=\{1,2,...,r\}$ as well as the sets of physically feasible actions $\Lambda = x_i\Lambda_i = \{\lambda\} = \{\lambda_1,...,\lambda_i,...,\lambda_r\}$ $(i \in R)$. The action profile $\lambda(t)$ consists of the actions chosen by all agents in period t. The action profile actually implemented is called the internal state of the domain. The technological and institutional environment of the domain – the exogenous rules – is depicted by the consequence function. For the moment, we assume the environment to be stationary. Time is infinite and agents choose their actions in every period.

Notation:

$R=\{1,2,...,r\}$	set of agents
$\Lambda_i = \{\lambda_i\}$	set of technologically feasible actions of agent i / agent i's action profile $(i \in R)$

$\Lambda = x_i \Lambda_i = \{\lambda\} = \{\lambda_1, ..., \lambda_i, ..., \lambda_r\}$	set of all technologically feasible action profiles
λ_{-i}	agent i's expectations regarding others' actions
$\Omega = \{\omega\}$	set of physically possible consequences / institutional environment
$\phi(\Lambda) = \Omega$	consequence function
$s_i(\Omega) = \Lambda_i$	private action choice rule
s_{-i}	all agents' action choice rules omitting agent i's action choice rule
π_{-i}	agent i's Nash equilibrium expectations regarding other agents' action choices
σ_{-i}	agent i's expectations regarding others agents' action choice rules
u_i	agent i's utility function
δ	discount factor

At first, the relationship between an agent's action and the environment is depicted. Ω presents the already existing institutional environment – that is, the institutions exogenous to the single agent. Λ_i is the set of a single agent's possible actions. Λ, by contrast, represents the general set of possible actions – thereby all agents' possible actions. Agent i's action Λ_i depends on the existing institutional environment, which is exogenous to the single agent. This is demonstrated by:

$$s_i(\Omega) = \Lambda_i . \tag{2.6}$$

s_i presents an agent's private action choice rule or his strategy. Hence, the environment – the prevalent formal and informal institutions – determines an agent's behavior. How the environment influences an agent's action is described by s_i. Instead, the environment Ω is determined by the set of all technologically feasible action profiles Λ:

$$\phi(\Lambda) = \Omega. \qquad (2.7)$$

A function ϕ assigns to every element of Λ an element of Ω. ϕ is the consequence function, that is, the functional form that describes how Λ and Ω are assigned to each other. Thus, the environment Ω is determined by the technologically possible actions of all agents, Λ. Anyway, an individual agent who maximizes his utility by optimally choosing his technologically feasible actions Λ_i takes Ω as exogenously given. Agents observe the environment Ω in period t. Thus, the decision regarding an agent's action in period t+1 is based on the environment in period t. Hence, we have:

$$\lambda_i(t+1) = s_i(\omega(t)) \qquad (2.8)$$

s_i assigns to every $\omega(t)$ an action $\lambda_i(t+1)$.That is to say, an individual's action depends on the institutional environment in the preceding period. The environment itself is constituted by the set of all technologically feasible actions of all agents, Λ.

Therefore, we have:

$$s_i(\omega(t)) = s(\phi(\lambda(t))), \qquad (2.9)$$

$$\lambda_i(t+1) = s_i(\omega(t)) = s(\phi(\lambda(t))), \text{ and} \qquad (2.10)$$

$$\lambda(t+1) = s(\phi(\lambda(t)) = F(\lambda(t)) \text{ for all t.} \qquad (2.11)$$

$F(\lambda(t))$ is the transition function, which describes the transition of the internal state of the domain from one period to the next.

The steady state equilibrium of the internal state is determined by:

$$\lambda(t) = \lambda(t+1) = \lambda(t+2) = \ldots = \lambda^* \quad \text{with } \lambda^* = F(\lambda^*). \qquad (2.12)$$

The next step, however, is to explain the action choice rule s_i in more detail and to demonstrate how the equilibrium state is achieved.

Let us introduce u_i as agent i's utility or payoff function and δ as the agent's discount factor. First, we assume $\delta = 0$, thereby the agent's optimization problem is limited to the current period. Let Λ_{-i} describe the action profile without agent i's action – that is, the actions chosen by all agents in period t omitting agent i's action.

Now we add agent i's expectations regarding the other agents' behaviors. Another agent's behavior might cause agent i to reconsider his strategy. Therefore, agent i's utility function includes his own actions as well as his expectations regarding other agents' actions. However, $\lambda_{-i} \in \Lambda_{-i}$ depicts agent i's expectations concerning the other agents' action choices $(i \in R)$. We assume that the expectations regarding others' actions correspond to the actions that are actually chosen, and that an agent's action choice is always the best response. Hence, there exists a Nash equilibrium: agents act as they expect each other to act and their behavioral response is optimal; there is no incentive for a unilateral deviation.

Thus, there exists a Nash action profile $\lambda^{Nash} \in \Lambda$ such that:

$$\pi_{-i} = \lambda_{-i}^{Nash}, \quad \text{and} \tag{2.13}$$

$$\lambda_i^{Nash} \in \arg\max_{\lambda_i \in \Lambda_i} u_i(\phi(\lambda_i, \pi_{-i})) \qquad \text{for all i.} \tag{2.14}$$

π_{-i} depicts agent i's Nash equilibrium expectations regarding other agents' action choices. Agent i's utility depends on his own action λ_i and on his (Nash equilibrium) expectations regarding other agents' action choice rules, π_{-i}. Hence, agent i chooses $\lambda_i \in \Lambda$ so that u_i is maximized. Then, under the assumption that expected actions and actual actions coincide, and that λ_i is best response, the resulting λ_i^{Nash} is a static Nash equilibrium. The agents act in the way agent i expects them to act, and agent i himself knows how the other agents expect him to behave and since he has no incentive to deviate, he delivers. With the transition function transferring the internal state from one period to the next we have: $\lambda(t) = \lambda(t+1) = \lambda(t+2) = ... = \lambda^{Nash}$.

Now the conditions for the subgame are imposed. A subgame includes the history up to a specific point in time, the internal state. In the current model, $\lambda(t)$ depicts the internal state including the history up to period t. All following events are based on $\lambda(t)$.

Therefore, let us assume that an agent's decision regarding his action choice rule $s_i(.)$ is made once and for all in period t, depending on the internal state

$\lambda(t)$. Hence, s_i in the period $\tau \geq t$ is contingent on the internal state $\lambda(t)$.That is to say: $s_i(\tau : \lambda(t))$.

At some point in time, the equilibrium state λ^{Nash} has to emerge; hence, the particular action has to appear for the first time. From then on, it is a Nash equilibrium. Thus, the observed game starts at a certain point in time, at which λ^{Nash} is determined. We are not directly interested in the history up to that point in time, but the history is indirectly included through $\lambda(t)$. The period in which the internal state λ^{Nash} is generated for the first time is defined as period t. Furthermore, suppose $\delta \triangleright 0$. Now the agent must incorporate his own and other agents' future action choices. For simplicity, let us further assume $\Omega = \Lambda$ and accordingly $\omega(t) = \lambda(t)$; that is the institutional environment is one-on-one determined by the set of all technologically feasible action profiles in the particular period.

The game evolving since period t, and thereby the game contingent on the internal state $\lambda(t)$, is called a subgame. That is to say, for $\tau \geq t$ an agent's set of technologically feasible action choices, Λ_i, is determined by the set of all technologically feasible action choices, Λ. The functional form which maps Λ_i and Λ, $s_i(.)$ is constant for every period $\tau \geq t$.

Suppose $\sigma_{-i}(.)$ denotes agent i's expectations regarding other agents' action choice rules, $s_{-i}(.)$. Assume that the expectations regarding other agents' action choice rules correspond to the real action choice rules and that, therefore, agent i's action choice rules are the best response. Hence, agent i's expectations regarding other agents' action choice rules are equal to the agents' action choice rules omitting agent i's action choice rule:

$$\sigma_{-i}(\tau : \lambda(t)) = s_{-i}(\tau : \lambda(t)). \tag{2.15}$$

s_{-i} are the agents' strategies omitting agent i's strategy. The terms in brackets indicate that s_{-i}, and therefore σ_{-i}, is a function of $\lambda(t)$, the set of all technologically feasible action profiles. However, we observe s_{-i}, and thereby σ_{-i}, as a function of τ contingent on the internal state $\lambda(t)$.

Agent i's utility, however, depends on his own action choice rule $s_i(\tau : \lambda(t))$ and on his expectations regarding other agents' action choice rules, $\sigma_{-i}(\tau : \lambda(t))$. Now agent i maximizes his utility u_i by optimally choosing his action choice rule s_i:

$$s_i^{opt}(.) \in \arg\max_{s_i} \sum_{\tau \triangleright t} \delta^{\tau - t} u_i(s_i(\tau : \lambda(t)), \sigma_{-i}(\tau : \lambda(t)) \tag{2.16}$$

for all $\lambda(t) \in \Omega, t \geq 0$, and i.

s_i^{opt} is agent i's optimal action choice rule or strategy. It is a subgame perfect equilibrium. Agent i's utility depends on his own action choice rule and on his expectations regarding the other agents' actions. Both variables, s_i and σ_{-i} are a function of the environment – that is, to say, of the set of all technological feasible actions $\lambda(t)$. The expectations, however, are consistent with the agents' actual actions. Hence, every agent acts in the way the other agents expect him to act. Agent i chooses his action choice rule so that his utility is maximized. The agents have no incentive to unilaterally deviate. Therefore, the action choice rule s_i becomes self-enforcing. This is what Greif (2006) means when he writes: "Behaviour is self-enforcing if, when players expect it to be followed, it is indeed followed because each player finds it optimal to so expecting the others to follow it" (p. 410).

So far, we have established strategies, or action choice rules, for the agents' actions that are self-enforcing in equilibrium. That is, the function that converts the exogenous environment or the set of all feasible technological actions into an individual's action is constant in equilibrium and does not depend on time. Hence, the transition function of the internal state is constant as is the internal state itself. Without an exogenous shock, the state will continue indefinitely. Hence, we demonstrated how human behavior in a society can become persistent. However, the strategies or action choice rules, s, are not institutions yet. A strategy misses an institution's summary representation function. An institution is a bundle of information that includes the information relevant for the agent to decide on his strategy or action choice rule, s_i.

For now we know that the action choice rule or the strategy s_i is the function that maps the set of all technologically feasible actions, $\lambda(t)$. s_i can be understood as the strategy behind the behavior; that is to say, s_i is the reason for (or the consideration behind) a certain behavior. However, s_i is included in the utility function. An agent's utility is maximized by optimally choosing s_i, the agent's strategy or action choice rule. Now, assume that we have already maximized utility and got an equilibrium strategy profile:

$$s^* = (s_1^*, \ldots, s_i^*, \ldots, s_n^*) \in S = x_i S_i \,. \qquad (2.17)$$

S_i is the set of strategies or action choice rules of agent $i(i \in R)$. Now suppose that there exists a function $I_i^*(.)$ associated with the equilibrium that incorporates all information necessary to achieve s*. Hence, $I_i^*(.)$ summarizes the relevant information for the equilibrium strategy; other information is not necessary. As soon as $I_i^*(.)$ is the functional form of a strategy, s_i is the equilibrium strategy or action choice rule: $I_i^*(s) = I_i^*(s^*)$ for $s \in x_i S_i$.

Therefore:

$$s_i^*(\phi(s)) = s_i^*(\phi(s^*)). \tag{2.18}$$

That is to say, if agent i's strategy is in equilibrium, then the set of all strategies (all agents' strategies) are in equilibrium. Since $I_i^*(s^*)$ includes all relevant information, it is defined as agent i's *summary representation*.

An institution, however, is defined to be robust within a certain environment. That is to say, institutions do not adjust to small modifications in the exogenous rules; instead most of them are inertial and only extreme external shocks cause institutional change. Here, we do not deal with institutional change but with the institutional self-enforcement that causes institutional persistence. Therefore, we assume the exogenous environment to change within a certain range. A change beyond the range would cause institutional adjustment.

$\Psi = \{\psi\}$ depicts the exogenous environmental parameters. $\hat{\Psi}$ is the subset of the environmental parameters within which the environment can vary without causing institutional change. Hence, within the subset $\hat{\Psi}$, $s^*(\psi)$ exists. That is to say, the set of all action choice rules now depends on the environmental parameters. As long as the environment varies within a certain range, $\hat{\Psi} = \{\psi\}$, s* remains the equilibrium strategy, since an environmental variation within the range causes no strategic changes. Hence, the agent might not directly maximize his utility contingent on his own action choice rule, $s_i(\tau : \lambda(t))$, and on the expectation regarding other agents' actions, $\sigma_{-i}(\tau : \lambda(t))$. Instead, $I_i^*(s^*)$ incorporates all information necessary for s*. Therefore, I_i^* is implied by:

$$I_i^*(s^*(\psi)) \qquad \text{for any } \psi \in \hat{\Psi}. \tag{2.19}$$

The last term indicates that, as long as the environment varies within the range $\psi \in \hat{\Psi}$, I_i^* is the summary representation of the internal state that agent i observes, and on which his strategy and actions are based.

Now assume that the environmental parameters are given by the subset $\hat{\Psi} = \{\psi\}$, but that different sets of equilibrium action choice rules, $\{s^{**}(\psi)\}, \{s^{***}(\psi)\}, \ldots$, exist contingent on $\hat{\Psi}$. Hence, there also exist different equilibrium summary representations, $I^{**}, I^{***}, \ldots$, emanating from the subset of environmental parameters $\hat{\Psi}$. That is to say, despite the same underlying exogenous parameters, multiple equilibrium paths are possible.

Therewith the summary representation I^* can now be defined as an institution. Aoki's (2001) five characteristics of institutions, depicted with his shared-beliefs cum equilibrium-summary-representation view of institutions, are observed in the model: I^*, the institution, is endogenous; it is a summary representation of the decisive information; it is robust; it is universally relevant to all individuals (shared cognition); and multiple institutional equilibrium paths are conceivable, based on equal technological and ecological environments.

The institution, however, includes all relevant information the agent needs to optimally choose his strategy. With the institution in place, the agent does not consciously choose a strategy; the only possible strategy adapted from the institution is the optimal strategy. The strategy, however, is decisive for the agent's action. Hence, an individual's behavior is based on the prevalent institution.

That is to say, without the institution in place, the agent has to consciously maximize his utility as depicted in this section to achieve his equilibrium strategy. With an institution in place, the derivation is not necessary. The institution includes all relevant information and lets the individual know – without further consideration – how others will behave and how they expect the individual to behave. This is a Nash equilibrium since an incentive for an unilateral deviation does not exist. The state will continue until it is disturbed by an exogenous shock.

This applies as long as the environment varies within a certain range. An environmental change exceeding the particular range is similar to an exogenous shock and thereby causes institutional adjustment. Hence, the equilibrium state is disturbed and a new equilibrium must emerge. As long as the equilibrium does not exist, an institution cannot be observed. In this case, the specific universal rule regulating social interaction does not exist within the examined domain. An institution becomes obvious when it is already implemented in human behavior. Hence, it becomes obvious when an equilibrium is realized. Therefore, an institution is unobservable until an equilibrium state is present. Hence, the institution is associated with the equilibrium. However, other institutions, depicted by the exogenous environment Ω, do exist. Applying the equilibrium view of institutions I^* refers to the one institution under consideration, but of course other institutions are prevalent.

The model is unsatisfying in the sense that it does not describe the emergence of an institution. The institution is suddenly there. However, institutional emergence can have several origins. It depends on the definition of an institution and its borderlines. Institutions can obviously emerge from other institutions or historical accidents. In any case, often institutional emergence cannot be traced back to a certain starting point. Invisible random events might, influenced by other exogenous events or shocks, generate a new institution without anybody recognizing it. Institutional emergence can be a conscious process, that is consciously initiated by individuals to regulate their interactions. However, institutions can also emerge unconsciously (and probably most institutions do); nevertheless, their intentions are to regulate social interaction.

So far, we cannot explain the emergence of an institution. At least when it comes to the origin of informal institutions, other disciplines such as neurology, genomics, evolutionary theory or in general biology and anthropology must be consulted. However, if we want to explain certain codes of conduct within a society, we can resort on a particular social value system or worldview. These are often based on a certain religion, although this might not be the case. Behavioral patterns originate in a society's tradition and culture but the roots of the culture are difficult to assess.

Therefore, the model and the equilibrium view of institutions in general have their drawbacks. However, the theory should be used to demonstrate the persistence of institutions and the issue of equilibrium strategies and inertial behavior; no more and no less.

The case study in chapter five demonstrates the emergence of a new worldview in the Arab region during the early Middle Ages because of societal, historical, religious, and accidental reasons. Starting with subtle changes, institutional modifications were put into motion that, together with external random events, altered the existing institutional environment and created a new starting point for technological development, modern sciences, and economic growth.

According to the equilibrium view, it could be argued that external shocks and a cognitive disequilibrium originating in a new worldview disrupted the institutional equilibrium and ended up, after hundreds of years, in a new stable equilibrium that seems to be less growth supportive, at least from a Western economist's point of view. Now, institutional persistence makes it difficult to change institutions in a growth-favoring way.

However, the institutional equilibrium that might become disrupted does not have to relate to the general institutional system of a state or a society. Institutional systems emerge within institutional systems. This is what makes the topic so complex. An institutional equilibrium might exist on a low level; hence, a certain institution might regulate the interactions of a certain group of individuals in a particular case. That is to say, talking about institutions does not necessarily mean talking about the 'big' institutions, such as the constitution, the jurisdiction, property rights, or the general social value system. A certain institution can be relevant for only a few individuals. Therefore, it is important to define the observed population. Institutions might exist within a circle of friends, the family, colleagues, a firm, a nation, and so on. Other institutions might be relevant not only for a country but for a whole cultural area, which might cross national borderlines. That is to say, the term 'institutional persistence' does not intend to suggest that all institutions within a state are in equilibrium and cannot be changed. Instead, an institutional system consists of a myriad institutions, formal and informal, relevant to a certain group or to all individuals in the system. All institutions interact with each other, are influenced by exogenous factors, and, of course, change. One institution in the system might be disrupted and modified. This can be without result for the other institutions, it can have consequences for a few institutions, it can have a sudden impact on the whole institutional system, or it can have a slow but strong influence on the other institutions. In the model, for example, we demonstrated institutional persistence for a certain domain, and thereby for the observed set of agents and their physically possible actions. The model can be applied to a large state-level institution or an informal institution affecting only a few individuals, but it cannot be applied to the whole institutional system.

For example in the Arab case, we cannot say that the institutional system per se experienced an exogenous shock and, therefore, deviated from the equilibrium path. Some institutions changed, others did not, and some were modified subtly, others consciously. However, some of the changes had long-lasting effects on societal and economic development. An institutional system is a dynamic entity with some constraints never changing and others being modified constantly. Thus, the equilibrium view of institutions should not be misunderstood. The model deals with only one institution for a given population. It emanates from partly unrealistic assumptions. Therefore, it cannot be applied one-on-one on the institutional environment of a state. The objective is merely to demonstrate the issue of equilibrium strategies in the case of institutional analysis. Hence, when individual and collectivist behavior is in equilibrium, codes of conduct cannot be changed. Thus, we cannot just change institutions because they are economically inefficient. Even if they result in low economic growth rates, the individuals' strategies are optimal regarding the prevalent conditions.

2.8 The form of societal organization

Institutions, however, are the reason for a certain form of societal organization. Societal organization describes the collective behavior of the members of a society. Hence, with societal organization we can examine the impacts of different institutions on collective behavior. When different institutions lead to different individual and, since institutions are universal, to different collective behavior, different forms of societal organization are the consequences. Thus, choosing societies that vary in their form of organization means we can demonstrate the impact of different institutions on, for example, the equilibrium wage.

However, how does the issue of institutional persistence adhere to societal organization? Well, if optimal strategies are realized, then the value system and, therefore, norms and codes of conduct will not change until an exogenous shock causes a deviation from the equilibrium path. In any case, this means the form of societal organization is persistent. Hence, limited or generalized morality will survive, no matter which outcomes they produce. Outcomes, however, can vary widely depending on societal organization.

The next model demonstrates the impacts of different forms of societal organization. Again it is important to note that the objective of the analysis is not to identify the 'better' form of societal organization. Both societies cannot be normatively compared. In both societies, optimal strategies are implemented contingent on the corresponding prerequisites. Individuals maximize their utility by choosing the optimal strategy contingent on the others' behaviors and at least indirectly contingent on the institutional environment. Hence, it is demonstrated that different forms of societal organization cause different results. No statement is made regarding which result and which organizational form is 'better', since every form and every result is optimal per se.

2.8.1 Model II

This section partly depicts the model by Greif (1994). Greif, however, examines the development paths of a collectivist and of an individualist society, where the former corresponds to the concept of limited morality and the latter is similar to a society practicing generalized morality.

The original paper from 1994 combines the game-theoretic analysis with a historical case study of Genose and Maghribi merchants of the 11th and 12th centuries.[18] Here, however, only the theoretical part will be presented.

The model depicts the agency relationships between entrepreneurs and agents. The one-side prisoner's dilemma game demonstrates that different forms of societal organization lead to different patterns of agency relations that are separately in equilibrium. Agents can decide whether to cheat and earn a one-period gain from cheating, or whether to play honest and earn the regular wage. Entrepreneurs, by contrast, can hire an agent or decide to work on their own and not hire an agent. Whether to hire an agent or not depends on the possibilities of avoiding cheating. Thus, the entrepreneur, who pays the agent's wage if he hires the agent, can provide an incentive to play honest by correspondingly choosing the wage. The wage must be higher than the gain through cheating. Then again the entrepreneur must decide whether it is worthwhile paying the wage. Thus, the incentive structure works via a wage, which must be high enough to provide an incentive for the agent not to cheat. The wage must also be low enough to provide an incentive for the entrepreneur to hire an agent, since he can also do the work himself.

The equilibrium wage that ensures that an agent is hired, and that the agent plays honest, is calculated using the players' corresponding utility functions. When the wage is fixed, however, the differences between societies practicing

[18] See also Greif (1993).

limited rather generalized morality become obvious. It is demonstrated that, depending on the form of societal organization, the equilibrium wage and societal structures differ.

Notation:

E	entrepreneurs
A	agents
$E \lhd A$	agents are more numerous than entrepreneurs
$\alpha \rhd 0$	agent's one-period payoff from cheating
δ	agent's time discount factor
$\eta \geq 0$	agent's reservation utility
$\kappa \rhd 0$	entrepreneur's payoff if he does not hire an agent / payoff from noncooperation
γ	entrepreneur's gross gain when he hires an agent / gross gain from cooperation
$W \geq 0$	wage
ξ	termination probability

Players live indefinitely. An entrepreneur hires one agent and an agent can work for only one entrepreneur per period. Entrepreneurs and agents meet randomly; however, the entrepreneur can exclude certain groups of agents from the possible pool according to the information available to the entrepreneur. When the agent is employed he can decide whether it is worthwhile playing honest or to cheat. The reservation utility η is the utility the agent receives from being unemployed. Furthermore, the agent runs the risk that, even when he plays honest, the agency relationship is terminated. This could be the case because the entrepreneur becomes ill or retires. ξ depicts the probability that the entrepreneur terminates the relationship even though the agent plays honest. All players are aware of the history of the game.

Agent playing honest:

When the entrepreneur hires an agent and the agent plays honest, the entrepreneur receives $\gamma - W$; that is the gross gain from cooperation minus the wage. The agent receives the wage W.

γ	entrepreneur's gross gain from cooperation
$\gamma - W$	entrepreneur's net payoff from cooperation
W	agent's payoff from cooperation

Cooperation is assumed to be efficient, that is $\gamma \triangleright \kappa + \eta$. The left-hand side of the inequality depicts the gross gain from cooperation, thereby the entrepreneur's and the agent's payoffs. γ includes the entrepreneur's net gain plus the agent's wage. The right-hand side describes the gain from noncooperation, thereby the entrepreneur's payoff κ plus the agent's reservation utility η.

Agent playing cheat:

0	entrepreneur's payoff
$\alpha \triangleright \eta$	agent's payoff

If the agent cheats the entrepreneur receives zero payoff. Hence, the entrepreneur prefers noncooperation over being cheated or having to pay $W = \alpha$ since noncooperation provides him with $\kappa \triangleright 0$.

Derivation of the equilibrium wage:

Up next the players' utility functions are described, which are then used to derive the equilibrium wage.

h_h	probability that an unemployed agent who was honest in the last period he was employed will be hired in the current period
h_c	probability that an unemployed agent who cheated in the last period he was employed will be hired in the current period

V_h	present value of the lifetime expected utility of an employed agent who, whenever hired, is honest
V_h^u	present value of the lifetime expected utility of an unemployed honest agent
V_c^u	present value of the lifetime expected utility of an unemployed cheater (who will be honest in the future if hired)

One period of cheating must be less attractive than the utility an agent receives from playing honest in every period. Hence:

$$V_h \geq \alpha + V_c^u \qquad (2.20)$$

must hold for the agent to play honest.

Utility functions:

$$V_h = W^* + \delta(1-\xi)V_h + \xi V_h^u \qquad (2.21)$$

$$V_i^u = \delta h_i V_h + \delta(1-h_i)(\eta + V_i^u) \qquad i = h, c \qquad (2.22)$$

To gain the equilibrium wage W^* we have to dissolve equations (2.21) and (2.22) for V_h and V_c^u, which we then have to insert in the above inequality (2.20). The full derivation is demonstrated in appendix A.

Dissolve (2.21) for V_h^u:

$$V_h^u = \frac{V_h \Sigma - W^*}{\xi} \qquad \text{with: } \Sigma = 1 - \delta(1-\xi) \qquad (2.23)$$

From (2.22); setting i=h:

$$V_h^u = \delta h_h V_h + \delta(1-h_h)(\eta + V_h^u) \qquad (2.24)$$

Dissolve (2.22) with i=h for V_h^u:

$$V_h^u = \delta H_h V_h + \delta P_h \eta \tag{2.25}$$

$$\text{with} \quad H_i = \frac{h_i}{[1-\delta(1-h_i)]}$$

$$P_i = \frac{1-h_i}{1-\delta(1-h_i)} \qquad i = h, c$$

Similarly; setting i=c in (2.22):

$$V_c^u = \delta H_c V_h + \delta P_c \eta \tag{2.26}$$

Equalizing (2.23) and (2.25):

$$V_h = \frac{\delta P_h \eta \xi + W^*}{\Sigma - \delta H_h \xi} \tag{2.27}$$

Remember:

$$\Rightarrow V_h \geq \alpha + V_c^u \tag{2.20}$$

Insert (2.26) in (2.20):

$$V_h \geq \frac{\alpha + \delta P_c \eta}{1 - \delta H_c} \tag{2.28}$$

Insert (2.27) in (2.28):

$$\frac{\delta P_h \eta \xi + W^*}{\Sigma - \delta H_h \xi} \geq \frac{\alpha + \delta P_c \eta}{1 - \delta H_c} \tag{2.29}$$

Dissolve (2.29) for W*:

$$W^* \geq \frac{\alpha(\Sigma - \delta H_h \xi)}{1-\delta H_c} + \delta\eta_u \left(\frac{P_c(\Sigma - \delta H_h \xi)}{1-\delta H_c} - P_h \xi \right) \qquad (2.30)$$

$$W^* = w(\delta, h_h, h_c, \xi, \eta, \alpha) \rhd \eta . \qquad (2.31)$$

w decreases in the agent's time discount rate δ and in the probability of hiring an honest agent h_h. w increases in h_c, the probability of hiring a cheater; in ξ, the termination probability; in η, the reservation utility; and in α, the payoff from one period of cheating.

Hence, the optimal wage is $W^* = w(\delta, h_h, h_c, \xi, \eta, \alpha) \rhd \eta$ with $\delta \in (0,1)$ and $h_c \lhd 1$.

Until now no difference has been made between limited and generalized morality. The optimal wage depends on the agent's discount factor, on the probability of hiring an honest agent or a cheater, on the termination probability, the reservation utility, and the agent's payoff from one period of cheating. Altogether the wage has to be greater than the reservation utility since it must provide an incentive to an unemployed agent.

The two observed forms of societal organization differ regarding the probabilities of hiring an honest agent h_h or a cheater h_c. A society that practices limited morality is characterized by informal networks of social interaction. Within these networks or groups, information is transposed at no charge. That is to say, an entrepreneur is told which of the agents have cheated in the past. Hence, the entrepreneur has information on which of the agents have cheated and, therefore, is able to employ only from the group of previously honest agents. With limited morality, $h_h = 1$ and $h_c = 0$. An entrepreneur will not employ an agent who cheated in the past since he knows the agents' histories. He will hire an agent from the pool of honest agents.

In a society practicing generalized morality, no such informal information networks exist. Hence, an entrepreneur does not know whether the considered agent is a cheater or not. Therefore, $h_h = h_c \rhd 0$. The probability of hiring a cheater is equal to the probability of hiring an honest agent. The entrepreneur does not know the agents' histories. Entrepreneur and agent are randomly matched and agents are chosen from among the pool of all agents. Hence, the entrepreneur must pay a wage high enough to prevent agents who previously cheated from cheating in the current period.

In the case of limited morality, the entrepreneur knows that the hired agent will play honest. Hence, an incentive to keep the agent honest is not necessary. The wage must merely be higher than the agent's reservation utility, since only then it is worthwhile for the agent to get a job.

Hence, under limited morality the optimum wage is lower than under generalized morality. Societies practicing generalized morality possess no informal information network to provide the entrepreneurs with the agents' histories. Thus, the probability of employing a cheater equals the probability of employing an honest agent. Therefore, agents must be provided with an incentive to play honest.

As long as $\gamma - W^* \geq \kappa$ holds, both strategies constitute a subgame perfect equilibrium. That is to say, the net gain from cooperation has to be greater than or equal to the equilibrium wage. If this condition holds, it is worthwhile for both the entrepreneur and the agent to cooperate. Hence, both have no incentive to unilaterally deviate. The wage is low enough to make cooperation efficient for the entrepreneur and the wage is high enough to provide an incentive for the agent to play honest. Under limited morality, an incentive to play honest is not necessary. Thus, the wage has merely to be higher than the agent's reservation utility. In this case, work is more efficient to the agent than unemployment. The probability of employing a cheater is zero. Under generalized morality, history is irrelevant. The wage provides an incentive for the agents not to cheat, but cooperation is still worthwhile for the entrepreneurs. Since agents play honest under the equilibrium wage, cheating never occurs in equilibrium, neither under limited nor under generalized morality. Both the entrepreneur and the agent know how the other player will act, thereby expectations correspond to real actions; the players behave as they are expected to since this strategy is the best response. Thus, entrepreneur E knows how agent A will behave and agent A knows how entrepreneur E will behave. Behavior that violates the expectations will not occur since entrepreneur and agent would put themselves in a worse position.

This first result demonstrates that different equilibrium states can exist. Each state implicates another outcome W^*. However, both states are optimal even though wages differ. Hence, strategies can be in equilibrium even though economic outcomes differ. However, even the society with the lower equilibrium wage realizes its optimal wage. The generalized strategy is to hire from the pool of all agents, whereas the limited strategy is to hire only from the pool of honest agents.[19]

[19] Strategies off-the-path-of-play are not depicted here, however, corresponding evidence can be found in Greif, 1994, p. 920 and p. 945.

2.8.1.1 Horizontal and vertical societal structures

The informal information network plays a major role in the model since it exists only in the case of limited morality. A further important assumption refers to the collective punishment strategies. Limited morality needs informal collective punishment strategies, since otherwise the information network would be futile. A third-party enforcer does not exist; however, official formal rules would be necessary for such an enforcement mechanism to exist. Since the rules regulating social interactions consist of norms, traditions, habits, and so on they are informal and no legitimate third-party enforcement exists. Thus, regulation and enforcement have to be provided informally.

Regulation is guaranteed by informal institutions, whereas the enforcement of the institutions is ensured by unofficial collective punishment strategies. Hence, society itself and not a third party such as the state punishes the violators. Of course, informal enforcement results in subjective punishment strategies. These are governed by subjective sentiments and might seem rude and unjustified to observers that are used to the rule of law and an independent judiciary. Nevertheless, these informal enforcement mechanisms are optimal strategies for the particular society.

In the case of our model, informal enforcement has nothing to do with crude punishment but with the fact that society punishes cheaters because entrepreneurs do not employ agents who cheated in the past. Hence, unemployment is the punishment strategy applied for dishonest agents.

Now it is assumed that entrepreneurs can work as agents for other entrepreneurs. In the original model by Greif (1994), entrepreneurs are restricted to merchants, since the historical case study deals with two groups of merchants. Regarding the historical example of Maghribi and Genose traders, it was in fact the case that merchants installed agency relations with other merchants. This made sense since merchants were situated at different locations and thereby a merchant in one place could act as an agent for a merchant situated in another location. Or, a merchant who was travelling between places could act as an agent for locally bound merchants. Merchants who were members of a society practicing limited morality (the Maghribi) actually preferred to hire other merchants from the particular society as agents. For reasons considered below, merchants were more trustworthy than pure agents.

However, in the present model we now add the possibility that entrepreneurs can be hired as agents by other entrepreneurs. In addition, pure agents exist (who can only work as agents and not as entrepreneurs). Hence, an entrepreneur can choose between employing an agent or employing an entrepreneur who provides agency services. An entrepreneur who provides agency services can either cheat or play honest.

If the entrepreneur is *honest* while providing agency services we obtain:

V_h^A	entrepreneur's expected utility from being an agent
$\frac{\gamma - W^*}{1-\delta}$	entrepreneur's expected utility from being an entrepreneur
$V_h^A + \frac{\gamma - W^*}{1-\delta}$	entrepreneur's lifetime expected utility if he is always honest

If the entrepreneur *cheats* while providing agency services we obtain:

α	gain from cheating while providing agency services in the current period
V_c^A	entrepreneur's expected utility from being an agent
$\gamma - W^*$	payoff from being an entrepreneur in the current period
V_c^E	entrepreneur's expected utility from being an entrepreneur
$\alpha + \gamma - W^* + V_c^E + V_c^A$	present value of the lifetime expected utility of an entrepreneur who cheated while providing agency services

An entrepreneur should not gain from one period of cheating while providing agency services, That is:

$$V_h^A + \frac{\gamma - W^*}{1-\delta} \geq \alpha + \gamma - W^* + V_c^E + V_c^A. \tag{2.32}$$

If this inequality holds, the entrepreneur will play honest while providing agency services.

For a pure agent to play honest

$$V_h^A \geq \alpha + V_c^A \tag{2.33}$$

must hold.

The difference between generalized and limited morality becomes visible via the punishment strategy. By assumption, under limited morality an entrepreneur who cheated while providing agency services gets punished by withholding information from him. Thus, the entrepreneur does not learn which of the agents cheated in the past. Hence, he has to pay a higher wage, since he has to choose his agent from the pool of all agents, which includes honest agents and cheaters. Therefore, the entrepreneur has to provide an incentive for the agent to play honest. If the entrepreneur himself plays honest while providing agency services, he will not get punished and thereby gets to know the agents' histories and can choose from the pool of honest agents. Then, he does not have to provide an incentive to play honest and can pay a wage that is higher or equal to the agent's reservation utility.

The argumentation, however, might seem far-fetched. But Greif (1994) demonstrates that exactly the punishment strategy described above was applied by the Maghribi traders in the 11th century.

Under limited morality, an entrepreneur who cheated while providing agency services has to pay a higher wage to his agent, since he does not know his history. Therefore, the lifetime expected utility of the entrepreneur decreases. That is to say, V_c^E on the right-hand side of equation (2.32) decreases and thereby it becomes less attractive for an entrepreneur to cheat while providing agency services, since cheating decreases his future utility because of higher labor costs. Thus, cheating while providing agency services influences the entrepreneur's utility of being an entrepreneur.

$$\frac{(\gamma - W^*)}{(1-\delta)} \triangleright \gamma - W^* + V_c^E \tag{2.34}$$

Equation (2.34) includes the gains from being an entrepreneur. The left-hand side depicts an entrepreneur's gains from entrepreneurship when he plays honest while providing agency services; the right-hand side represents the gains from entrepreneurship when the entrepreneur cheats while providing agency services. Again, V_c^E decreases and thereby it becomes more attractive to play honest.

However, because under limited morality cheating as an agent impacts on an entrepreneur's utility from entrepreneurship, the entrepreneur has more to lose from cheating than under generalized morality. Therefore, the probability that the entrepreneur cheats while providing agency services is lower under limited morality. Hence, under limited morality entrepreneurs prefer to employ other entrepreneurs as agents, since for them cheating is less attractive because it has a negative influence on their utility from entrepreneurship.

A society practicing generalized morality misses the informal information network and the collective punishment strategy – that is to say, history is irrelevant. Therefore, an entrepreneur who cheats while providing agency services does not get punished and might not pay a higher wage. However, as has been proved before, the equilibrium wage under generalized morality is higher since the probability of employing a cheater equals the probability of employing an honest agent.

In any case, under generalized morality, we observe:

$$\frac{(\gamma - W^*)}{(1-\delta)} = \gamma - W^* + V_c^E . \qquad (2.35)$$

That is to say, the lifetime expected utility from entrepreneurship of an entrepreneur who plays honest when providing agency services equals the lifetime expected utility from entrepreneurship of an entrepreneur who cheats when providing agency services. Hence, under generalized morality entrepreneurs do not prefer to hire other entrepreneurs for agency services. Since an entrepreneur who provides agency services realizes an income from entrepreneurship, his reservation utility might be higher than that of a pure agent. Therefore, under generalized morality, entrepreneurs might prefer to employ pure agents instead of entrepreneurs providing agency services, since the latter might demand a higher wage for playing honest because of their higher reservation utility.

It can be concluded that under limited morality, entrepreneurs prefer to hire other entrepreneurs providing agency services instead of pure agents. The collective punishment strategy deprives an entrepreneur who cheated as an agent of the information regarding the honesty of other agents and entrepreneurs. Hence, the cheating entrepreneur has to pay a higher wage since he does not know whether the hired agent is honest or not. Therefore, entrepreneurs providing agency services have more to lose when working as an agent. Thus, they need a lower incentive to play honest and thereby a lower wage.

Under generalized morality, entrepreneurs prefer to hire pure agents. Since a collective punishment strategy does not exist, and since the agents' histories are irrelevant, the entrepreneurs anyway pay a higher equilibrium wage. However, because of the high reservation utility of entrepreneurs providing agency services, entrepreneurs prefer to employ pure agents.

Thus, limited morality advances a horizontal social structure, whereas generalized morality results in a vertical social structure. This is what we would expect according to our previous definition of generalized and limited morality. Hence, limited morality is characterized by group affiliation. Within these groups, informal networks and punishment strategies exist. Wages are lower compared with individualistic societies. Limited morality results in a horizontal social structure. Hence, income differences are less notable. Social mobility is constrained since there is not much space for up- or downward movement. This matches the significance of the collective. Less social mobility hampers incentives to invest. Hence, incentives and preferences differ compared with a vertical social structure. This might result in less productivity, economic growth, and consequently lower living standards.

Generalized morality describes an individualistic society. Group affiliation is not important. Transactions are conducted independent of certain memberships and are regulated via formal rules. These are enforced by a third-party enforcement mechanism. Since informal networks do not exist, wages are higher and a vertical social structure is realized. Hence, social mobility is possible and income differences are bigger compared with limited morality. Therefore, incentives and preferences differ. Incentives to invest are higher and productivity and living standards might be higher compared with a collectivist society.

Greif (1994) indeed proves that the Maghribi traders of the 11th century realized a horizontal structure. A clear dividing line between a class of merchants and a class of agents could not be drawn. On the contrary, the society of the Genoese merchants of the 12th century was structured vertically. Merchants rarely functioned as agents and instead a relatively rich class of merchants and a relatively poor class of agents emerged (Greif, 1994, p. 928).

The current chapter shows that different institutions – and thereby the rules that regulate human interactions – lead to different behavioral patterns and that these cannot be easily changed once implemented. This can be demonstrated with the equilibrium view of institutions and a model that presents the issue of institutional persistence via equilibrium strategies. These strategies can only be changed by an exogenous shock; otherwise they persist indefinitely. However, multiple equilibria are assumed to be possible and different equilibrium strategies can occur. Since institutions determine an individual's behavior, they also determine the societal patterns of behavior since they are universal to all members of the observed population. Hence, different institutions imply different individual and collective behaviors. Although behavior differs, it might correspond to an optimal strategy regarding the particular population. Varying behavior can result in different economic outcomes, as Greif's (1994) model shows. However, although one society might realize lower economic growth rates and living standards compared with another one, it might still realize equilibrium strategies. Hence, the outcome might be optimal regarding the particular society and the prevalent basic conditions. Hence, a bad economic performance does not imply that the societal structure per se is inefficient and has to be changed. If change is still to be promoted this might be a difficult task. Since institutions are the main drivers for behavior, institutions must then be modified. However, according to the equilibrium view, institutions are associated with an equilibrium and thereby the implemented strategies are equilibrium strategies. Therefore, a modification of collective and individual behavior is only possible by a preceding institutional modification, which can only occur via an exogenous shock.

Hence, two points should be stressed: first, if a society's institutions do not promote high economic growth this does not mean that the society itself is in disequilibrium and, therefore, inefficient. Second, institutional change is not easily conducted.

Until now the institutional analysis in this thesis has been conducted theoretically. The next chapter, however, depicts an empirical analysis of institutions. It will be demonstrated how formal and informal institutions can be measured. Furthermore, issues of the empirical examination of institutions are presented. Then, a regression analysis is run that examines whether informal and formal institutions influence per capita income. Hence, it will be examined whether the theoretical consideration can be empirically verified.

3. Institutions – an empirical approach

3.1 Informal institutions

Informal institutions are defined as morals, values, conventions, norms, traditions, codes of conduct, habits, attitudes, and beliefs. They incorporate culture in general and, therefore, the societal value system. Hence, the term 'informal institutions' is used as a substitute for culture or cultural factors. The corresponding transmission channel is the individual himself as informal institutions affect economic development on an aggregated level through their influence on people's behaviors.

However, even Adam Smith (1759) discussed the impact of cultural traits on economic development in his *The Theory of Moral Sentiments*. Later, Banfield (1958) and Putnam (1993), inter alia, composed popular writings connecting culture and specific developments.

After cultural and institutional impacts on economic growth had been forgotten for a while, North (1990) surged ahead with his popular publication *Institutions, Institutional Change and Economic Performance*. His approach was to help growth theory out of the stagnation concerning the explication of persistent growth differences between countries. However, the often mathematically sophisticated models of endogenous growth theory, which tried to improve the inconsistencies of neoclassical theory, turned out to be too abstract to explain the real world. As good as these models were, they were not able to explain why the proximate determinants of growth varied that much between countries and why differences in productivity between countries could not be solved by applying the sophisticated economic knowledge that the models offered.

North and Thomas (1973) and North (1990) brought institutions as the decisive missing link back into play. Furthermore, North's theory of institutions incorporated cultural factors since he faced the fact that informal institutions are constraints implemented by individuals to regulate social interaction. However, North (1990) constitutes the chronological and content-related starting point of the recent study.

The effect of culture on economic development was then emphasized by Landes (1998), who traces the Western European economic success back to its supportive culture. whereas in other regions of the world, such as the Middle East or China, the existing cultural conditions were not favorable for an Western-style Industrial Revolution.

However, starting with these works cultural economics experienced a gentle revival from the beginning of the 1990s, as observable in de Jong and Eelke (2009), Platteau (2000), North (2005), Inglehart and Welzel (2005), and Harrison and Huntington (2000). Furthermore, several journal articles dealing with culture, informal institutions, and economic development appeared.[20] Since informal institutions are a subjective matter, cannot always be explained rationally, and cannot be measured in generally accepted units, the formal incorporation in economic models is a difficult task. Because direct observations are not possible, proxy variables must be used instead. That is to say, data that permit inference on a society's organization, beliefs, and values are used instead of the cultural variables themselves, which are not directly observable. However, we will revert to the issue of the measurement of informal institutions later.

For now we will concentrate on the theoretical argumentation of informal institutions and their impacts on economic growth. An early example regarding informal institutions and their influences on economic development is Max Weber's popular thesis concerning the Protestant work ethic (Weber, 2002). Weber argues that the emergence of capitalism was closely related to the belief and thereby the resulting behavior of the Protestant population. Following his argument, work was not just a means to an end but the purpose of life and God's will. People believed that God's chosen ones were blessed with a materially good and safe life. Hence, everybody tried to achieve a high living standard in order to believe that they were a chosen one. In other societies, where material standards play no role regarding God's goodwill, people lack the accordant incentives to work hard and invest. Therefore, according to Weber, countries with a high proportion of Protestant citizens were economically more successful than those without. Consequently, the beliefs, attitudes, and codes of conduct resulting from such a religious affiliation affect the development of economies. Weber's thesis comes close to this work, because religious origins result in the norms and values that people implement in their everyday lives. For now we will skip the religious dimension but will refer to this point later.

The hypothesis states that particular attitudes, norms, values, and codes of conduct support factor accumulation and technological progress whereas others do not. The challenge is to measure informal institutions and point out concrete features with which the impact on economic growth can be analyzed. Hence, we must consider which human properties can be depicted and demonstrate a clear relationship to culture. That is, the accordant characteristics must depend on values, norms, convictions and so forth, and must differ according to those criteria.

[20] See, for example, Barro & McCleary (2003); Dolfsma & Verburg (2008); Fernández (2008); Fernández & Fogli (2007); Gorodnichenko & Roland (2010); Greif (1994); Guiso, Sapienza & Zingales (2003); Guiso, Sapienza & Zingales (2006); Knowles & Weatherston (2006); Porta & Scazzieri (1997); Tabellini (2005); Williamson (2009).

3.1.1 Trust

An often used indicator for culture and societal organization is the level of trust. The role of trust in an economy has been studied for some time, especially in game-theoretic approaches. "In prisoner's dilemma type of situation, interactions between trusting individuals are more likely to lead to efficient outcomes, whereas lack of trust make it more difficult to overcome the inefficient equilibrium" (Tabellini, 2005, p. 9). An individual's level of trust depends on their cultural and societal background, as well as on experiences, which again are shaped by society, culture, and history (Putnam, 1993). If children are taught to trust other people, they will apply what they have learned without critical request, eventually for all their lives, and will pass their attitudes onto their own children. The same is true if we are taught not to trust others or not to trust a certain group or certain people. Knack and Keefer (1997), for example, find that the level of trust is higher in countries with less ethnical and class discrepancy. Hence, it might be true that in hierarchical societies, among which the affiliation to the family or tribe is very distinct, the level of trust within the group is high, but beyond it people might not trust others. In how far individuals of a society trust each other and trust the members of other societies depends on upbringing, (religious) beliefs, historical accidents and experiences, and traditions. Since trust is an informal institution, it is slow moving and can be characterized as an IEN institution. That is to say, the attitudes and beliefs that shape the level of trust change slowly and an external alteration is difficult. Nevertheless, change is possible, since experiences and historical accidents never stop shaping an institution. Furthermore, individuals might alter their attitudes and beliefs after logical reasoning or because they become persuaded by something else, although this way of change might be rare and take a long time.

However, because of the characteristics of slow-moving institutions, trust represents a stable determinant that does not change in an obvious way for a long time. Hence, once established the influence of trust on economic outcome is durable and must be taken for granted. Nevertheless, we will not define trust as an exogenous parameter since it can be influenced by per capita income. Because of its slow convertibility the assumption of trust being an exogenous variable might be justifiable in empirical work in some cases.

However, trust has several impacts on economic performance. Trust regulates social interactions and lowers transaction costs. In high-trust societies, information is replaced by trust. Hence, the corresponding monitoring expenses are lower. Furthermore, people in high-trust societies might not record every detail of an act of sale and spend less time and money on lawyers and the monitoring process. The business environment and, in general, economic transactions can be less regulated than in low-trust societies. People in high-trust societies might also place more confidence in the government and other official agencies, which might result in higher credibility. However, incentives to innovate and invest are higher in high-trust societies. Since transaction costs are low, more capital and time is available for innovation and investment. This also means that the expected returns are higher since fewer costs and a lower risk premium can be discounted. Hence, the innovator and the investor retain their full returns. Furthermore, investors in a high-trust society will realize the optimal investment strategy over the long run rather than the short run.

Trust enhances anonymous market exchange and decreases the need for formal institutions and, therefore, external enforcement. That is to say, trust also increases the gains from labor division and trade (Knack & Keefer, 1997, p. 1252). La Porta et al. (1997) find that trust increases judicial efficiency, bureaucratic quality, tax compliance, and decreases corruption (p. 335).

However, these examples already indicate the ambiguous character of institutional relations since an adequate regulatory structure and legal system might also increase the level of trust. At least higher per capita incomes might lead to a general change in perspectives and priorities and thereby modify a society's level of trust in the long-term. Thus, a clear causality between trust and the respective formal institutions rather than per capita income does not exist. In any case, it is obvious that a high level of trust decreases transaction costs, whereas increasing the quantity of transactions. Therefore, trust is associated with higher economic growth (Knack & Keefer, 1997; La Porta et al., 1997; Putnam, 1993).

3.1.2 Limited and generalized morality

The concept of generalized and limited morality corresponds to the organization of society per se. The societal organization can be seen as the general framework that depends on the prevalent morals, norms, beliefs, and values. Institutions are implemented through behavior, and thereby societal organization allows inferences regarding the institutional environment. Hence, knowing the societal order, we might be able to deduce the value system and vice versa. However, limited morality (collectivist societies) characterizes hierarchical societies, in which high levels of trust and cooperation are prevalent inside groups such as the family, the clan, the tribe, and religious or ethnic groups. That is to say, within the respective group transaction costs are low and business is done. However, beyond the group mistrust is dominant. Cooperation between members of different groups depends on high monitoring and information costs and thereby transactions between the groups are rare. Hence, a hierarchical society with distinct familial or tribal structures suffers from restricted economic relations because of high transaction costs. Contracts between affiliates of the same group are closed according to informal rules. Hence, traditions, morals, and codes of conduct play a decisive role in business relationships. The same holds for enforcement mechanisms, which are conducted informally regarding morals and traditions. Official formal institutions are either nonexistent or individuals ignore the formal rules. Hence, an official enforcement mechanism implemented by a third party does not exist. Instead, informal rules and enforcement mechanisms (collective punishment) regulate social interaction. The macroeconomic outcome and thereby per capita income, could be increased by optimizing business relations, trade, and production in general. However, this is not possible because of certain morals and norms, which stand in the way of the corresponding economic activity. Hence, in societies where limited morality is prevalent, innovation, investment, factor accumulation, trade, and thereby economic development per se is restricted through the limited possibilities of cooperation. Nevertheless, the members of the society optimize their strategies and achieve an equilibrium state. Hence, the societal organization of limited morality and its economic outcome cannot be described as inefficient per se (Platteau, 2000; Greif, 1994; Greif, 2006; Zweynert & Goldschmidt, 2006).

By contrast, societies in which social interactions are conducted independent of familial or tribal affiliation practice what is called generalized morality. Transaction costs are reduced via formal rules that regulate, for example, the formation of contracts and enforcement mechanisms. Hence, societies that realize a form of generalized morality need to develop a formal institutional framework to regulate their interactions and decrease transaction costs. That is to say, a third-party enforcement mechanism and authorized punishment strategies are necessary. Thus, economic transactions are conducted independent of group affiliation and unfamiliar informal rules. Therefore, high efficiency gains can be realized. Furthermore, in a society where generalized morality is prevalent, the free-rider issue on public goods might be less dominant. Since people trust each other and legitimized punishment strategies are conducted by a third party, public goods might not be misused. Hence, transaction costs are low and the scope of cooperation increases. Innovation and investment are stimulated and so the concept of generalized morality supports economic development.[21] Generalized morality is a form of societal organization that emerges from a strategy optimization and depicts a different equilibrium state than does limited morality. Therefore, because we are talking about two completely different entities, a comparison that rates the societies according to their economic performances is pointless. Both societies realize their individual optimal outcomes.

However, the transition from limited to generalized morality is fluent. We can imagine that norms of good conduct and trust decrease with distance. Hence, a society that practices generalized morality concerning its own members might mistrust geographically or culturally distant societies. That is to say, even if

[21] See also Greif (1993); Greif (1994); Platteau (2000); Tabellini (2005); and Tabellini (2008a,b).

generalized morality is prevalent within the society, limited morality might be practiced if we extend the geographical scope.

However, Tabellini (2008b) argues that limited and generalized morality not only shape economic development, but also are a matter of the development progress itself. Accordingly, "at early stages of development, transactions are mainly local, and both values and cooperation remain more limited in scope. As development progresses, and impersonal transactions gain relevance, this is accompanied by a generalization of the scope of values and cooperation" (p. 932).

Hence, Tabellini hints at the issue of reverse causality, since societal organization influences economic development, whereas economic development impacts values and beliefs and, therefore, societal organization. In another article, he demonstrates that democratic political institutions support the realization of generalized morality, whereas countries that practice generalized morality possess better government indicators and legal institutions (Tabellini, 2008a). However, we should not rely on the fact that economic development shapes values and beliefs in a way that supports generalized morality and, therefore, further progress. The interdependencies between economic development and generalized versus limited morality can also lead an economy to be stuck in a state of backwardness. Societies that practice limited morality can have less respect for the law and be more tolerant of lax law enforcement, since informal institutions govern their interrelationships. By contrast, the quality of law enforcement strengthens sound values, beliefs, and morals (Tabellini, 2008b). Accordingly, "in Western Europe impersonal exchange took place in anonymous markets supported by specialized institutions obeying formal procedures. In East Asia markets were organized through a web of kin-based social structures linked by personal relations (Greif, 2005). [...] these different arrangements are likely to encourage the diffusion of different values: in the West a generalized respect for the individual and their rights, in the East a culture of loyalty to the local community or to a network of relatives and friends. [...] these different values facilitated the evolution of different political and economic arrangements, with feedback effects in both directions" (Tabellini, 2008b, p. 930f.). Hence, this might explain why "... distant historical circumstances have such long lasting effects, and why some societies might remain trapped in cultural, institutional and economic backwardness" (Tabellini, 2008b, p. 938).

The form of societal organization allows us to draw conclusions regarding the institutional environment. Hence, a society practicing limited morality will be characterized by a conservative value system and corresponding attitudes. A society realizing generalized morality is assumed to be indicated by modern values and morals. However, the equilibrium view demonstrates that whether conservative or modern every society acts optimally given the prevalent conditions.

3.1.3 Beliefs that encourage the accumulation of physical and human capital

However, to examine the impact of informal institutions on economic development theoretically and empirically, it is not enough to speculate on beliefs, values, norms, and attitudes in general. To make meaningful statements research must become more concrete. Therefore, particular informal institutional features will be singled out, which are also used in the empirical analysis, and their influence on economic development will be described. Since beliefs and attitudes influencing economic activity are manifold, we concentrate on the particular variables that can be measured empirically and have been used in econometric analysis before. This allows us to demonstrate the empirical results later on and to use the particular variables for the following analysis. However, many other beliefs, attitudes, and so forth exist, which influence an individual's economic behavior and aggregated economic outcome. Hence, the following enumeration is not complete and is thought to demonstrate a few examples.

3.1.3.1 Destiny

An informal institutional feature that depends on the cultural environment and influences economic activity is an individual's conviction concerning their control over their own life. However, destiny as a relevant determinant of economic development might first appear to be somewhat abstract. Nevertheless, the belief concerning one's destiny is an informal institution that perfectly demonstrates the interrelationship with economic growth. If people are persuaded of being able to influence destiny they will try to improve their situation and be proactive. If, by contrast, people believe in predestination, they are not in the position to better their situation through their own initiative. Hence, investment in physical and human capital will in general be lower than in a society in which everybody works hard and invests to improve her or his life. That is to say, the individual has no incentive to innovate and invest. The attitude concerning control over one's own life originates from religious beliefs since in some religions God determines everything in life rather than the individual itself. However, even the belief concerning one's destiny is subject to reverse causality and influenced by the institutional environment. A higher per capita income might change one's worldview and purpose in life and people might rather feel that they are in control of their fate. Furthermore, an authoritarian political system that domineers over its citizens combined with bad economic performance, and thereby low per capita income, probably does not entail self-confidence but resignation. In any case, believing in predestination rather inhibits growth on an aggregated level.[22] Several approaches use World Values Survey (WVS) data to measure the impact of culture or informal institutions on economic development using *control* as a single variable or as part of an indicator (Knack & Keefer, 1997; Knowles & Weatherston, 2006; Tabellini, 2005; Tabellini, 2008a).

3.1.3.2 Life after death

However, as already indicated, institutions do their jobs through incentives. Hence, if people believe in life after death or reincarnation, these beliefs influence people's behaviors since they offer an incentive to live life in a certain way. Thus, abiding by the religious rules might guarantee a good life after death or a reincarnation on a higher level. However, not only life after death but also the belief in heaven and hell offers incentives to abide by certain rules. Living life according to a certain morality might guarantee a place in heaven, whereas breaking the rules might lead to hell. The rules that must be followed to arrive in heaven might inhibit economic growth. If, for example, a population is required to live an abstinent, traditional life without any luxury, this does not boost factor accumulation. Hence, if materialism and luxury are regarded as a sin, this does not foster growth. The same is true concerning the accumulation of human capital. Certain beliefs and attitudes concerning the natural world might prevent individuals from becoming educated. Furthermore, a belief in God or being religious per se makes believers live their lives following religious doctrines. This can be the case because individuals are persuaded by what they believe and thereby what they do or because they fear hell or another kind of divine punishment. Anyway, every restriction provides an incentive to act in a certain manner. Of course, the beliefs might not promote behavior that supports growth. On the contrary, if, for example, materialism and modernism are banned by religious doctrines, if women are not allowed to work, if naturalism is regarded as blasphemy, then the believers have no incentive to accumulate physical capital and to use their human capital in a productive way. According to Weber (2002), the contrary is true concerning the Protestant work ethic. Calvinism propagated that all humans belonged either to the group of chosen ones or to the group of not-chosen ones. Who is a chosen one and who is not is predestined and cannot be influenced by the human being. However, since work effort and economic success are signs of being a chosen one and dawdling and accumulating luxuries are a sin, people worked hard to prove to others and to themselves that they belonged to the chosen ones. Hence, the fear of not being a chosen one drove people to work hard and be economically successful. That is to say, the religious

[22] Data on the attitude concerning control over one's own life (*control*) is taken from the WVS. The relevant question text can be found in the data description at the end of the chapter.

doctrine stimulated growth since it indirectly forced people to accumulate capital and invest. However, the argument is not without controversy. It has also been stated that the economic success of the Protestant work ethic depended on the fact that people became better educated since they had to be literate to read the bible (Becker & Wößmann, 2009).

Nevertheless, we can imagine that widespread beliefs that directly or indirectly influence factor accumulation, investment, innovation, technological knowledge, and so forth can inhibit or support growth on an aggregated level. Religious doctrines or other convictions regarding destiny, life after death, reincarnation, or God's goodwill offer incentives for people to act in a certain way. We can also imagine non-religious incentives that are rooted in tradition and other cultural traits other than religion. However, the incentives can be either growth supporting or growth inhibiting.

This section already hinted at the role of religion regarding economic development and institutions. Several of the mentioned informal institutions are influenced by religious doctrines. This leads us to the question of what determines informal institutions. We will leave it at that for now but will return to the question later.

3.2 Formal institutions

Since institutions can be classified from general to specific categories – that is, for example, from the categorization of political, legal, and social institutions to regime type, electoral rule, business regulations, and so forth – formal institutions are manifold and cannot be enumerated completely. However, some formal institutions turn out to be growth supporting in general. Hence, guaranteeing these formal institutions basically stimulates growth unless they do not match the prevalent informal institutions. If this is the case, economic progress will be difficult to prevail. However, the most basic formal institutions thought to support growth if matched by the informal environment are depicted in this section.

3.2.1 Property rights

Regarding formal institutions, the protection of property rights is usually described as the decisive institutional feature concerning growth (De Soto, 2000; Kerekes & Williamson, 2008; North, 1990; Platteau, 2000; Rodrik, 2000; Williamson & Kerekes, 2009). Property rights afford the individual the right to decide on their labor supply, physical and human capital, and the goods and services they possess (North, 1990, p. 33). That is to say, the individual has the exclusive rights to decide on their assets. Hence, the owner benefits from the complete returns on the usage of the property. The exclusiveness and irreproachable allocation of ownership offer the crucial incentive to invest. Furthermore, property rights highlight the economic potential of an asset, since the owner will use his property in a way that maximizes his utility. Therefore, it is assured that the asset is used optimally. However, since we do not emanate from a pure homo economicus, individual utility maximization might not be equated with profit maximization. It is assumed that individuals are selfish and want to maximize their own utility. Anyway, individual utility is not equal to material utility. People might want to maximize their immaterial utility – that is, they might be altruistic because it makes them feel better or they might abstain from something because they are persuaded of doing the right thing. Hence, abstaining from something, abiding divine rules, or being altruistic makes people feel good and, therefore, maximizes their individual, eventually immaterial, utility. Nevertheless, the owner is most suitable to value his asset.

However, since property rights reveal an asset's economic potential, property can be used as collateral and can generate new capital and receive credit. De Soto (2000) explains that one of the foremost problems of underdevelopment is that in many underdeveloped countries property is not clearly assigned to a particular owner and cannot be used as collateral and to generate new capital. However, property rights, coupled with an appropriate law to protect them are, according to De Soto (2000), the lifeline of economic success in Western economies.

Despite the direct channel on income, the dominance of secure property rights also makes a statement concerning the political and legal environment of a state. Property rights are usually not afforded in dictatorships or authoritarian states, where expropriation by the political power or even by private interest groups is possible since no appropriate law and no independent judiciary exist. Hence, unsecure property rights are accompanied by less political and economic freedom, fewer civil rights, and a manipulable judiciary. To maximize economic outcome the opposite situation is necessary.

Therefore, economic success depends on secure property rights. But who decides on the protection of ownership, and, thus, the structure of the legal and economic system? Acemoglu, Johnson and Robinson (2005) developed a theoretical approach that ascribes the emergence of the political, legal, and economic institutional environment to resource endowment and, therefore, to property rights. In their model, political power is crucial regarding the formal institutional environment of a state — that is, the elites in power will arrange formal institutions in a way that best fits their interests. The essential theoretical feature is the differentiation between de jure and de facto political power. The former depicts the legitimate or official political power, whereas de facto political power is not legitimized, but able to enforce its interests. Hence, legitimate governance can, but might not necessarily, possess de facto political power. Instead, de facto political power depends on resource endowment. Thus, an interest group with an adequate endowment of capital and other resources might be able to determine formal institutional properties. The exercise of de facto political power can vary. One possibility is a military coup in which individuals equipped with arms and money, and eventually supported by further interest groups, use their resources to overthrow the current government. Then, the de facto political power will implement formal institutions that fit its interests, that is, the retention of political power. Therefore, civil property rights and political participation will not be afforded, since this would endow individuals with resources that could be used to overthrow the rebels.

A less martial example is lobbying. Even in democratic states, particular industries or other interest groups use the power resulting from their resource endowment to determine the institutional form in a way that best fits their interests, that is, the further accumulation of resources.

Hedlund (2001, p. 217–227; 2005) describes the historical dimension of the implementation of property rights in Russia. His article and book demonstrate that property rights necessitate a culture and tradition of private property. Hence, in a country's history historical accidents and path-dependent developments must have led to the convention of property rights implemented by the citizens and the executive. If a tradition of property rights is missing and if a society never experiences being entitled to private property, the positive effects of private ownership cannot be implemented. Hence, property rights might not be understood as a natural right, they might also occur through convention (Hedlund, 2001, p. 217). Since conventions differ between states and regions, not every country could develop a tradition and culture of private property.

3.2.2 Legal system – the rule of law

Property rights are useless if they are not secured by an appropriate law. Hence, to utilize the full potential of property rights the legal system must guarantee the owner complete freedom of choice and exclusiveness with respect to the relevant asset. Hence, neither state-run nor private expropriation can be tolerated.

However, complete secure property rights can only exist under the rule of law and thereby with an independent judiciary. Any other legal system offers a possibility for private or state-run interest groups to intervene. Even if a non-democratic government provides secure property rights, the form of government permits minorities to enforce their interests via a coup d'etat or bribery, for example. Hence, de facto political power is able to determine the legal environment to the detriment of property rights. Therefore, the rule of law and an independent judiciary are essential for secure property rights. The rule of law and an independent judiciary are guaranteed in democratic states.[23] Hence, the allocation of secure property rights is usually accompanied by a democratic system and postulates an independent judiciary. This is the case since the legal system must be able to enforce property rights against governmental and private offences. Democracy ensures that formal institutions cannot be changed on behalf of a certain interest group that possesses the appropriate resources. Property rights in conjunction with civil liberties guarantee the efficient use of every asset in a society, and thereby the optimization of per capita income. Nevertheless, property rights can also exist and be protected in other political systems, but since their application will probably be constrained in a non-democratic state, total economic efficiency will be adversely affected (Besley & Kudamatsu, 2008; Rodrik, 2007). Furthermore, to develop their full potential ownership rights must be accompanied by a free-market system that allows any individual to use their assets in a way that maximizes their utility. Then, the economy can realize its maximal growth potential on an aggregated level.

La Porta et al. (2004) examined a sample of 71 countries and found that judicial independence is a strong predictor of economic freedom. However, as in the case of property rights, the rule of law corresponds to an institutional entity that depends on random historical developments, too. Hence, the rule of law necessitates a tradition of private property and of generally accepted rights that hold for every member of society. Therefore, the rule of law also necessitates a certain understanding of the state. The state must be constrained and subordinated to the rule of law; however, it must also enforce the rule. Hedlund (2001, 2005) describes the difference between a state that subordinates itself to the law and a one that overrides the law with the terms 'rule of law' rather 'rule by law'. Rule by law, as in the Russian case, does not support a tradition of property rights, civil liberties, and equality before the law. On the contrary, a tradition of rule by law inhibits confidence in the state. Instead, it conveys the impression of a state that officially adheres to the law but can override it whenever in the mood. Hence, the relationship between the members of the society and the state per se differs compared with a society with a tradition of the rule of law. This has impacts on all further developments. When a country accidentally strokes the way of rule by law, the emergence of a constitutional state and secure property rights is impossible. Even if foreign or indigenous forces try to implement the rule of law at a later point in time, a tradition and culture of property rights and the rule of law will be missing. Hence, FEX or IEX institutions will not match IEN institutions and will, therefore, remain ineffective.

[23] La Porta et al. (2004) examined the effect of judicial independence and constitutional review empirically and affirmed the hypothesis that indicial independence guarantees economic and political freedom by the protection of property rights inter alia.

3.2.3 Form of government – democracy

Democracy is a broad concept with which we usually associate power being directly or indirectly exercised by citizens through a system of representation. Furthermore, universal suffrage, civil rights, the rule of law, and the separation of powers are components of democracy. Since definitions are broad and different concepts of democracy exist, we borrow the Polity IV definition, which states that democracy is conceived as three elements (Jaggers & Marshall, 2005):

> 1) "The presence of institutions and procedures through which citizens can express effective preferences about alternative policies and leaders" (p. 13).
>
> 2) "The existence of institutionalized constraints on the exercise of power by the executive" (p. 13).
>
> 3) "The guarantee of civil liberties to all citizens in their daily lives and in acts of political participation" (p. 13).
>
> "Other aspects of plural democracy, such as the rule of law, systems of checks and balances, freedom of the press and so on are means to, or specific manifestations of, these principles" (p. 13).

Since different political regimes determine different economic and legal institutions their impact on economic growth varies. The question is whether democracy yields institutions that support growth rather than autocracy.

Democracy inhibits resource-rich minorities from implementing institutions that best fit their interests. Hence, the possibility that a minority overthrows the government by using its resources, for example money or weapons, is lower than in an autocracy where no separation of power and thereby no independent judiciary gives shelter to the head of state. In a non-democracy, the elites in power will enforce the institutions that best fit their own interests. In the majority of cases, these interests will increase their profits and power, but will be detrimental to aggregated economic growth. Hence, improvements in the general living standard are not optimized. Institutions in a democracy might not be growth maximizing, and political participation and universal suffrage will inhibit the establishment of institutions that benefit a small elite. Hence, democratic institutions might not maximize growth, but, compared with other institutional environments, democracy guarantees the most efficient economic outcome.

What mostly affects the efficiency of democracies is the freedom it guarantees its citizens. Civil liberties are constrained by institutions such as constitution and the rule of law, which optimize social coexistence in decreasing transaction costs and guarantee individual utility maximization. Property rights, freedom of opinion and speech, and the right to physical integrity offer incentives to accumulate physical and human capital and to invest. Democratic institutions allow the largest possible individual freedom. The constraints, thereby the institutions, that characterize democracy are there to afford maximal individual freedom since less restrictions would mean that the individuals themselves would reduce their freedom through uncertainty. Hence, transaction costs would be high and capital accumulation and investment would be lower.

However, the growth effect of democratic institutions again depends on the complex system of institutions and other relevant determinants. Just to say that democracy is the most efficient institutional system is too simple in reality. A country's political system is determined by the prevalent deep determinants - that is, geography, institutions, and history. Therefore, the implementation of democracy might not be efficient if a country has a non-democratic history, is embedded in a non-democratic institutional environment concerning its neighboring countries, or if its formal and informal institutions do not support democracy. Hence, democratic institutions might not have positive growth effects if they are implemented in a non-democratic environment. This is the case because the implementation will fail. That is to say, the relationships and dependencies with the prevalent institutions will not come about. Hence, the democratic institutions will exist in isolation and will have no effect at all. In this case, they will be abolished as soon as possible. However, the implemented democratic institutions can even have detrimental effects if they demolish parts of the existing institutional system. By contrast, it might also happen that the prevalent institutional system adjusts to democracy and supports it. However, this process will take time and come at some cost.

Empirical evidence on democracy and its influence on growth is mixed. Rodrik (2007) finds that a participatory political system guarantees less volatile growth rates, better adjustment regarding external shocks, and less distributive inequality.

Persson and Tabellini (2009) examined the economic effects of political regimes. Via a panel estimation they analyzed data from up to 155 countries for up to 180 years. Accordingly, democracy supports economic growth via physical capital accumulation, which in turn fosters democracy. However, high per capita income does not encourage a transformation from autocracy to democracy. Democratic capital, which is defined as a society's civic values that support democracy, plays a decisive role. Therefore, a virtuous circle can emerge, because democratic experience supports capital accumulation (also democratic capital) and thereby fosters democracy.

Persson and Tabellini (2006) demonstrate that economic liberalization must precede political liberalization. That is to say, economic liberalization followed by democracy has a positive and significant effect on economic growth, whereas democracy followed by economic liberalization has a negative and significant impact on the growth rate.[24]

3.3 Measuring institutions – a literature review

It is not enough just to form a theory about the influence of institutions on economic growth nowadays. In the past 20 years, the revival of growth theory has been based on a mixture of theoretical and empirical reasoning. The term 'informal institutions' has been known since North's work in 1990. Despite that, empirical measures of institutions were predicted from factors describing formal institutions, because determinants such as values, norms, morals, attitudes, habits, and codes of conduct cannot be easily measured. However, since the incorporation of societal and cultural factors into economic theory has gained more acceptance research projects dealing with the issue have emerged. The WVS, for example, is an oft-used data source for indicating and measuring informal institutions (Inglehart & Welzel, 2005; Inglehart et al., 2004). It is based on surveys and is separated into different parts dealing with topics such as "perceptions of life", "politics and society", and "religion and morals", inter alia. This section provides a short overview regarding influential empirical work on informal and formal institutions.

An influential work concerning culture and its impact on GDP per capita, which is based on the WVS data, is Tabellini (2005). The author examines data on European regions and identifies history as the decisive determinant of economic growth. He argues that culture depicts the connection between history and current economic development. That is to say, historical accidents shape a society's values, attitudes, and morality. Values, attitudes, and morality determine peoples' behaviors and, therefore, economic development on an aggregated level. Since culture is slow moving and only marginal change occurs from one generation to the next, values, attitudes, and morality are persistent determinants, which indirectly connect history with current economic performance. Hence, Tabellini has had to identify a variable that reflects culture, is shaped by history, and influences current economic growth. Therefore, he created a cultural indicator using the WVS data set. The indicator is meant to measure individual values and beliefs and thereby comprises data on the level of trust and respect for other people as well as on the confidence and self-determination of the individuals taken from the WVS. Accordingly, trust, respect for other people, and individual self-determination encourage economic development, whereas obedience, seen as a measure of the hierarchical structure of a society,

[24] Further references on democracy and the economy include Acemoglu & Robinson (2005) and Acemoglu et al. (2008).

is detrimental to economic growth. Tabellini uses the percentage of the population being Protestant (La Porta et al., 1999) and, in another regression, literacy rates in 1880 and political institutions between the 17th and 19th centuries as instrumental variables for culture. All variables are explained in detail in the appendix of his paper. His argument is that the instrumental variables do not influence current economic outcome directly, but only through their effects on culture. Hence, European regions that were poorly educated at the end of the 19th century differ from better educated regions regarding their cultural characteristics even today. The same is true for early political institutions, which affected cultural patterns and thereby current income. However, Tabellini detects that early political institutions have had a significant influence on economic performance today. Culture, as explained by historical variables, is a decisive determinant of regional economic development and performance in Tabellini's work. Particular cultural traits – that is, trust and respect on the one hand and individual confidence and self-determination on the other hand – are found to be favorable to economic development. Furthermore, no primacy of formal institutions over culture or informal institutions can be observed. On the contrary, both interact with each other and thereby shape the economic environment. Tabellini's accurate article became a guideline for further research since he explains his theoretical, empirical, and methodical proceedings in detail and is correct in his analysis. Furthermore, the cultural indicator created by Tabellini has been used in several studies on the impact of culture or informal institutions on economic performance since then.

Tabellini (2008a) also uses survey data from the WVS, which measure the level of trust and the level of respect for other people as proxy variables for the character of morality – that is, generalized vs. limited morality. Via a probit model he estimates the effect of the ancestors' countries of origin on the current level of trust. Furthermore, Tabellini uses certain language properties (rules on the use of pronouns) as instrumental variables for values. He finds that there exists a correlation between grammatical rules and his proxies of morality. Then, Tabellini regresses the first-stage results on the measures of the quality of government and trade. However, he detects that generalized morality is correlated with better government indicators and vice versa. In addition, a connection between the prevalent character of morality and the specialization in certain sectors can be found.

Knowles and Weatherston (2006) rely on the WVS data set to measure the effect of informal institutions on economic growth. The authors refer to the deep determinants of growth literature and incorporate proxies for institutions, geography, and openness as independent variables in their regression analysis on per capita income.[25] They differentiate between formal and informal institutions,

[25] See also Rodrik (2000); and Rodrik, Subramanian & Trebbi (2004).

which are defined as conventions, norms, and codes of behavior. Informal institutions are measured using an indicator similar to Tabellini's cultural index (Tabellini, 2005). The authors add together Tabellini's variables regarding the levels of trust and respect (*TRUST*, *RESPECT*) and control over one's own life (*CONTROL*) and call their indicator *INFORM.* Formal institutions are measured by the 'average protection of risk against expropriation' taken from the International Country Risk Guide and 'constraints on the executive' from the Polity IV data set. Since formal and informal institutions are endogenous, Knowles and Weatherston run two and three stage least squares (2SLS and 3SLS) regressions using the proportion of the population speaking English, the proportion of the population speaking a major European language (Hall & Jones, 1999), state history (Bockstette, Chanda & Putternam, 2002), population density in 1500 (Glaeser et al., 2004; McEvedy & Jones, 1978), and the proportion of the population being Protestant (La Porta et al., 1999) as instrumental variables. Of course, they also use instruments for geography and openness; nevertheless, this is not our current topic. However, the authors find significant effects of formal and informal institutions and geography on per capita income. Accordingly, informal institutions are no less decisive for economic performance than formal institutions are.

Williamson (2009) examines the relationship between different formal and informal institutional arrangements. Her aim is to detect whether institutions are transferrable and, therefore, whether the institutional structure of economically successful countries can be imposed on underdeveloped economies. She uses a modified indicator of Tabellini's cultural index on a country level to measure informal institutions (Williamson & Kerekes, 2009; Williamson, 2009).

Guiso, Sapienza and Zingales (2006) use the WVS data to measure the effect of culture on expectations and preferences and their impacts on economic outcomes. They estimate, for example, how far trust influences the probability of becoming an entrepreneur (data source: WVS and General Social Survey) and how cultural traits affect saving decisions and political preferences such as redistribution. They use religion (proportion of people of the different religious denominations in each country) and ethnicity (ancestors' countries of origin) as instrumental variables for culture, since both measures are nearly time-invariant and thereby the causality issue can be faded out. Cultural traits are measured using questions on redistribution and the importance of thriftiness from the WVS. However, cultural traits are highly correlated with countries' saving rates and governmental redistributive policies, whereas the endogenous cultural variables are highly correlated with data on religious denomination and ancestors' origins.

In an earlier work, Guiso, Sapienza and Zingales (2003) analyzed the influence of religion on particular cultural traits measured via the WVS data. By using the answers to questions that ask for the frequency of attending religious services and whether the particular person was raised religiously, they studied the degree and the type of a person's religiosity. The religious variables are then regressed on the societal attitudes that are shown to be supportive of growth, such as attitudes towards trust, thriftiness, cooperation, the market economy, and so forth.

Knack and Keefer (1997) estimate the effect of interpersonal trust and norms of civic cooperation on economic performance. Trust (TRUST) is measured via the corresponding answers to the question from the WVS (see appendix). Norms of civic cooperation (CIVIC) are measured via a questions asking if certain statements can be justified, with the possible answers ranging from 1 (never justifiable) to 10 (always justifiable). The statements are: "Claiming government benefits to which you are not entitled"; "Avoiding a fare on public transport"; "Cheating on taxes if you have a chance"; "Failing to report damage you've done accidentally to a parked vehicle"; and "Keeping money that you have found". They find that TRUST and CIVIC are correlated with economic outcome, secure property rights, and contract rights.

Fernández and Fogli (2007) study the effect of culture on economic performance, using work and fertility rates of second-generation American women. Accordingly, culture influences peoples' beliefs and preferences and thereby peoples' attitudes concerning, for example, the role of women in society. Therefore, conservative societies exhibit low female labor supply and high fertility rates, since the predominant opinion is that women should stay at home and raise children. On the contrary, modern societies feature high female labor supply and lower fertility rates. However, when individuals emigrate they take their culture with them, but live in a new institutional environment. If culture is partly responsible for the large variation in incomes per capita, it should be persistent. Hence, ancestors' beliefs and preferences should equal the beliefs and preferences of their descendants. If culture adjusts immediately to the new environment, it is not a deep determinant of growth and cannot help explain per capita income differences. Therefore, Fernández and Fogli use data on labor and fertility of second-generation American women, who were born and raised in the United States. Hence, these women grew up within the same institutional environment, but their cultural heritage differs according to their parents' countries of origin. The authors use 1970 values of female labor force participation and total fertility rates as proxy variables for culture. They use female labor force participation and total fertility rates from the woman's country of ancestry in 1950 as instrumental variables for culture. They then run several regressions using different techniques and variables and find that past female labor participation of the ancestors' countries of origin and past fertility rates of the ancestors' countries of origin have a significant effect on female labor participation and fertility today. The results are robust to the inclusion of women's education data, husbands' education data, husbands' incomes, data on institutions and markets, and so on. Thus, culture decisively influences the proximate determinants of growth and thereby a country's economic performance.

Since empirical analyses on formal institutions are manifold, the following summary is incomplete. However, the most influential approaches concerning the dissertation thesis are depicted. Several approaches explain the economic success of Western industrialized countries with certain institutional prerequisites that were prevalent in these countries.

Hall and Jones (1999), for example, estimate the impact of *social infrastructure* on per capita income levels. They define *social infrastructure* as the institutions and government policies that determine the economic environment within which individuals act (Hall and Jones, 1999, p. 84). To measure *social infrastructure*, the authors create an indicator called "government antidiversion policies" (p. 97) from Political Risk Services data. Hence, they use data on law and order, bureaucratic quality, corruption, risk of expropriation, and government repudiation of contracts (p. 97f.). They further include a measure for a country's openness to international trade. Since causality between *social infrastructure* and output per worker (the dependent variable) can run both ways, Hall and Jones (1999) conduct an instrumental variable estimation. The fraction of the population speaking English or a major European language and distance from the equator are used as instrumental variables for *social infrastructure*. The choice of instruments is justified by the fact that these variables are said to measure the extent of Western European influence and are positively correlated with *social infrastructure*. Hence, countries that were influenced by Western Europe developed a growth promoting *social infrastructure*, whereas others did not. According to the authors, early Western European influence can be measured through the extent to which English, French, German, Portuguese, and Spanish are spoken as first languages today (Hall and Jones, 1999, p. 100). Concerning distance from the equator, Hall and Jones argue that "Western Europeans were more likely to migrate to and settle regions of the world that were sparsely populated at the start of the 15th century ... such as the United States, Canada, Australia, New Zealand, and Argentina ... [and] it appears that Western Europeans were more likely to settle in areas that were broadly similar in climate to Western Europe" (Hall and Jones, 1999, p. 101). They discover that *social infrastructure*, and thereby political and economical institutions, have a significant effect on economic development. Accordingly, differences in capital accumulation, education, and productivity can be partly explained by differences in *social infrastructure*.

Another approach that emphasizes Western European influence comes from Acemoglu, Johnson and Robinson (2001). The authors trace current economic performance back to particular colonization strategies. That is to say, current economic performance depends on current formal institutions. The quality of current formal institutions, in turn, depends on the quality of early institutions.

Hence, a country that possessed growth-inhibiting formal institutions in the past is still characterized by growth-hindering formal institutions today. However, the quality of early institutions depended on the colonization strategy. Where Western Europeans settled, they replicated European institutions, emphasized property rights, and restricted governmental power. In areas where Europeans could not settle they set up extractive institutions that helped exploit resources but did not protect property or constrain the particular government. Whether Europeans were able to settle was dependent on their probability to survive. Acemoglu, Johnson and Robinson (2001) use records of the 18th and 19th centuries concerning the mortality rates of soldiers, bishops, and sailors in former European colonies to create a measure of 'settler mortality', which is then used as an instrument for current institutions. They do so because settler mortality in the 17th and 19th centuries should have no effect on current economic performance other than through institutions. Data on the risk of expropriation (Political Risk Services) and on constraints on the executive (Polity IV) are used as proxies for current institutions. However, the authors obtain high correlations between mortality rates and European settlements, between European settlements and early institutions,[26] and between early and current institutions.

Moreover, Acemoglu, Johnson and Robinson (2002) demonstrates a 'reversal of fortune'.[27] It shows that former European colonies, which were relatively rich before colonization, are relatively poor today and vice versa. Data on urbanization and population density in 1500 is used as a proxy for economic prosperity before colonization. However, the authors find a negative relationship between economic prosperity in 1500 and economic prosperity today. Again, they trace the development back to colonization strategies and institutional quality. Accordingly, the colonizers preferred to settle in places that were sparsely populated and did not settle in regions that were densely populated. In regions where Europeans settled, they established secure property rights and restricted governmental powers, whereas extractive institutions were introduced, or could remain, in populated places. Again, average protection against expropriation risk (Political Risk Services) and constraints on the executive (Polity III) are used as proxies for current formal institutions. In both papers, Acemoglu, Johnson and Robinson (2001, 2002) control for many additional variables on geography, policy, history, and ethnicity, and conduct several tests of robustness.

Acemoglu and Johnson (2005) examine the importance of property rights institutions and contracting institutions. Although contracting institutions correspond to transactions between private individuals or parties, property rights in-

---

[26] Early institutions are measured with data on constraints on the executive in 1900, an index of democracy in 1900, and constraints on the executive in the first year of independence (Polity III).
[27] See also Przeworski (2004).

stitutions regulate the relationships between private citizens and the political power. The authors detect that countries with secure property rights (measured with 'constraints on the executive' taken from the Polity IV data set) have significantly higher per capita incomes. However, contracting institutions seem to affect financial intermediation, but have no impact on per capita income once property rights are controlled for.

Further important empirical work on formal institutions comes from La Porta et al. (1999), who examine the influence of political and cultural institutions on government performance (thereby on another institution). Governance performance is measured with several indices measuring government intervention (property rights index, business regulation index, top marginal tax rate) and government efficiency (corruption, bureaucratic delays, tax compliance, average government wages). The independent variables are: ethnolinguistic fractionalization, which is used as a proxy for political institutions; legal origin, also used as a proxy for political institution; and the religious affiliation of the population, used as a proxy for cultural institutions.[28] The authors discover a positive relationship between government performance and per capita income. However, their results "present clear evidence of systematic influence of historical circumstances, as captured by ethnolinguistic heterogeneity, legal origins, and religion, on government performance" (La Porta et al., 1999, p. 265).

La Porta et al. (2004) focus on legal institutions. They regress measures of political and economic freedom (for example, a property rights index, a democracy index, a political rights index) on proxies for judicial independence and constitutional review. They find that especially judicial independence is correlated with economic and political freedom.

Rodrik, Subramanian and Trebbi (2004) deal with the so-called deep determinants of growth such as institutions, geography, and integration and with the question of which of these determinants is most important for the level of per capita income. They measure the quality of (formal) institutions with an indicator from Kaufmann, Kraay and Zoido-Lobatón (2002). The indicator is composed of data "that capture the protection afforded to property rights as well as the strength of the rule of law" (Rodrik, Subramanian & Trebbi, 2004, p. 138). Integration is measured with the ratio of trade to GDP, and several measures of geography are used, for example, distance from the equator and an index of malaria risk. Furthermore, the authors use several instrumental variables depending on the particular country sample. For example, they use the Frankel and Romer (1999) instrumental variable for integration and the settler mortality variable from Acemoglu, Johnson and Robinson (2001) as an instrument for institutions. Further instruments are the proportion of the population speaking English or a

[28] La Porta et al. (1999) focus on Catholic and Muslim religions "which have been recently singled out by Landes (1998) as hostile to institutional development" (p. 224).

Western European language. The dependent variable is GDP per capita. However, the results suggest that institutions matter the most for the level of per capita income. In any case, the authors stress the policy implications that could be deduced from the regression results and emphasize that they do not provide a general pattern to increase income in individual countries.

Glaeser et al. (2004) critically regard current empirical approaches on institutions and growth. They emphasize the causality issue in institutional economics and bring human capital into play as a decisive determinant of growth. They demonstrate that democracies exhibit higher educational levels than autocracies, whereas causality cannot be determined. Hence, it is not clear whether democracy supports education or whether education supports democracy. However, both factors probably influence each other and neither can be exposed as the starting point. Glaeser et al. (2004) argue that constraints on political power might be overrated as a growth-relevant determinant. Accordingly, this is the case since human capital accumulation is decisive. Economic growth, it is argued, can also be obtained in autocratic regimes where the political power is unconstrained. Furthermore, the measures for institutions are criticized, since many of them measure choices rather than constraints. Hence, no clear causality from institutions to growth can be determined. However, Glaeser et al. (2004) describe Polity IV's 'constraints on the executive' as being the best available proxy for formal institutions. The authors emphasize instrumental variable estimation as a valid method to solve the causality issue. They challenge the usage of 'settler mortality' by Acemoglu, Johnson and Robinson (2001) as instrument for institutions, stating that the fact that European settlers brought their human capital along is more decisive than the institutions they established. In addition, the exogeneity of the instrument is questioned. The authors run several regressions including educational variables and demonstrate a significant relationship between education and income.

Glaeser et al. (2004) are right in their critical reflection of empirical institutional analysis. However, every economist engaged in the field should be aware of these issues otherwise reliable research is impossible. Nevertheless, research should be performed using the available data. It is in the hands of the particular researcher to conduct serious work and be aware of the respective methodical issues and data problems.

Glaeser et al. (2004) also use a disputatious variable, namely the initial years of schooling, to measure human capital. First, reverse causality and correlation with the error term might also be an issue regarding years of schooling. Second, years of schooling might not be a valid measure for human capital. It excludes many important properties, such as the subjects taught, the quality of education, the human capital acquired outside schools or universities, and so on. Hence, it might be incomplete and not comparable across countries. Nevertheless, it is often used as a proxy for human capital since it probably is the best available measure.

However, Glaeser et al. (2004) are right that human capital should be studied in relation to institutions. Informal institutions such as beliefs, attitudes, worldviews, and so on are definitely correlated with educational standards and the subjects taught. For example, morality and beliefs might hinder the teaching of certain subjects such as evolutionary theory. Furthermore, traditional societies might despise the role of education and hinder parts of the population from becoming educated. For example, in many underdeveloped countries girls are not allowed to go to school or they go to school only to learn the essential basics such as how to read and write. Comparable attitudes still exist in some developed societies or in parts of nearly every society.

Furthermore, the level of education influences an individual's general understanding of the state and society. Hence, highly educated societies tend to be democratic as shown by Glaeser et al. (2004).

3.4 Endogeneity

The empirical analysis of institutions is particularly hampered by the fact that "institutional quality is as endogenous to income levels as anything can possibly be" (Rodrik, 2007, p. 185). Institutions influence each other and are influenced by further factors. That is to say, institutions impact per capita income and vice versa.

However, the transmission channels between informal institutions and economic development have already been described using several examples. Particular norms and values lead to behavioral patterns that do not necessarily support growth. Take, for example, the exclusion of women, and thereby a large part of the potential workforce, from education and economic life in several societies. By contrast, it is conceivable that income levels also influence cultural features. In general, institutions are characterized by their stickiness. In any case, institutions can be changed, although this might take time, especially if informal institutions are involved. As usually only marginal progress is made from one generation to the next, a change in norms, values, and conventions can take decades or centuries (Boettke, Coyne & Leeson, 2008; Roland, 2005).

Institutions emerge to reduce transaction costs, uncertainty, and instability. Informal institutions guarantee a kind of non-material or social stability, whereas formal institutions secure material stability. As the standard of living increases, perspectives, priorities, and preferences are modified. That is to say, under the premise of material stability, the significance of non-material stability changes. People living at the margin of subsistence have other preferences and purposes in life than people receiving a regular salary and social security. Furthermore, higher material security alters the incentives for social affiliation. Social patterns that exist for security reasons are no longer necessary when income increases. Modern societies, for example, are usually linked with the breakup of the traditional family structure. That is to say, family, clan, or tribal affiliation becomes less important. More emphasis is on the individual. The birth rate decreases since couples have fewer children. In traditional societies, several generations often live under one umbrella, whereas the spatial distance between family members widens with modernity. Other social relationships, such as friends or colleagues, become more important. Therefore, the societal structure of generalized morality can rather be observed in modern societies.[29]

An increase in the living standard is accompanied by a change in values, norms, beliefs, attitudes, and convictions, as well as morality, habits, and codes of conduct. Since material stability is warranted from a certain level of income, the role of beliefs that are responsible for immaterial stability changes. Hence, attitudes concerning the individual, the family, women's work participation, minorities, materialism, and so forth change. With the collapse of familial and tribal boundaries, trust and respect concerning other people widens. Furthermore, even if an individual loses a part of their property, they still might not fear for their existence. Consequently, priorities in life change. Furthermore, increasing income levels are often accompanied by higher educational standards. Hence, people might be able to question traditional belief and value systems. They will realign informal institutions corresponding to their new preferences and needs.

However, trust depends on common norms and values, and if these are altered because of higher per capita incomes the level of trust will also adjust. We are trusting when we do not expect other people to cheat us, and thereby our expectations regarding other peoples' behaviors are decisive. Peoples' actions depend on their beliefs, attitudes, values, experiences, and so forth. Hence, if the common norms and values that are responsible for the level of trust change because of higher per capita income, trust will also adjust. An increase in the general level of trust alters the societal structure and generalized morality is thereby observable in modern societies.

The belief concerning control over one's life also becomes modified. A higher living standard contributes to an attitude of self-determination and self-confidence. People endued with property would rather that their wealth be traced back to their own decisions and activities. These individuals will also believe that they can shape their futures according to their own wishes. Of course, wealth can also be traced back to destiny such as, for example, in Weber's thesis on the Protestant work ethic. In this thesis, people thought God's chosen ones could be recognized by their material standards, and thereby people worked hard

[29] See, for example, Tabellini (2005, 2008a).

and accumulated capital to show to themselves and others that they belonged to the chosen ones. A high living standard will be preferred to be traced back to one's own efforts, and thereby will encourage further endeavor. Even in Weber's argument, people worked hard and invested to show that they are the chosen ones, and thereby their wealth could be traced back to their own efforts, even though they believed it was because of God's will.

Since the modernization that accompanies an increase in per capita income is associated with higher educational standards, a more rational and logical view of life and the world in general emerges. As a consequence, even religious doctrines and cultural traditions might need to adjust. Religious doctrines and traditions as well as conservative attitudes, values, and beliefs might be reconsidered and reinterpreted using this new knowledge (Mokyr, 2002).

Nevertheless, since humans are social beings, the non-material stability warranted through informal institutions cannot be completely replaced or altered. Several beliefs, values, and norms maintain since individuals need certain informal institutions for self-identification and self-orientation. Therefore, some informal institutions might not be changeable, independent of variations in living standards. Since informal institutions are sticky, an alteration takes time and only marginal change might be observable from one generation to the next. Informal institutions do not only impact per capita income, they also are influenced by higher living standards.

However, an increase in per capita income not only alters informal institutions but also formal institutions. We have already discussed this matter with reference to the model of Acemoglu, Johnson and Robinson (2005). Higher per capita incomes can shift the power allocation within a state. A group or person endued with appropriate resources is able to takeover de facto political power and, therefore, arrange institutions in a way that best fits their respective interests. If parts of the population gain de facto political power through economic growth and thereby higher per capita incomes, they will try to enforce their interests. However, radical changes in political and economic institutions are difficult to explain without the introduction of informal institutions. An increase in per capita income alters informal institutions, which then impact formal institutions. Hence, all three factors – per capita income and formal and informal institutions – influence each other. Thus, the basic settings of a society can jointly be responsible for the general concept of the state, the political system, and the structure of power. An autocratic government and a hierarchic system might enhance explicit cultural features such as disrespect, mistrust, resignation, a collective social structure and, hence, limited morality. In turn, these cultural characteristics again support the preservation of an authoritarian government and, in general, of the prevalent formal institutional structure. An increasing per capita income improves the level of informal institutions in the sense that people become more trustful and respectful, self-reliant, and confident. Apart from that, it could be correlated to higher educational standards, which are associated with more open-minded and educated individuals. These people might have the ability to question and criticize the predominant institutions, both formal and informal, and alter them. Therefore, in general, some level of physical and human capital is necessary to be able to understand the importance of a growth-promoting institutional framework.

Owing to their higher per capita incomes, individuals are able to enforce the institutions that fit their interests. Hence, they will question the current system and further enforce property rights and political participation. A democratic state might support growth-supporting informal institutions. Independent citizens who can freely participate in political, economic, and social processes might realize a higher level of trust, self-determination, and self-confidence.

The interplay between informal and formal institutions and the effect on economic growth is also mentioned by Persson and Tabellini (2008). They name the cultural and societal features that support democracy 'democratic capital'. Accordingly, democracy must be supported by the democratic attitudes and convictions of the citizens. Societies with no democratic tradition possess no accordant attitudes and are not persuaded by the ideas of democracy. Hence, democratic capital emerges through democratic experience. The longer democracy exists in a country, the stronger its democratic capital will be. That is to say, with the experience of democracy, people become more and more persuaded of its ideas and are prepared to plead and even fight for the preservation of democracy. Hence, certain attitudes and values might be more supportive of a political system than others, but a political system can also influence attitudes and values.

3.5 Deep determinants of growth

The aim of this study is to examine the effect of institutions on economic development. However, institutions are added to the explanatory variables because the variables that have been obtained in growth models so far have not helped explain the divergent processes of income levels and growth rates around the globe. That is to say, mainstream growth theory does not explain why the conventional factors of production – factor accumulation and technology – differ between countries. Or, more precisely, why countries are not able to use these conventional factors of production in a way that optimizes their growth performances. Factor accumulation and technology are called the proximate determinants of growth or the proximate causes of growth (Rodrik, 2003; Rodrik, Subramanian & Trebbi, 2004; Acemoglu, 2009, pp. 109–143). Hence, it must be examined which factors determine the proximate determinants of growth. If we know which variables determine factor accumulation and technology, we know why the proximate determinants differ and, eventually, we can seize the problem by the roots and help countries find a way out of the underdevelopment trap.

The theory of the deep determinants of growth states that the proximate determinants are endogenous and are determined by the deep determinants of growth. The deep determinants depict the pre-existing environment within which a country develops. Hence, the deep determinants are the basic conditions, which, at least for a certain period of time, must be taken as given. They are the underlying factors that shape a country's social, political, and economic development.

The deep determinants of growth are institutions, geography, and openness (Knowles & Weatherston 2006; Rodrik, 2003; Rodrik, Subramanian & Trebbi, 2004). Acemoglu (2009, pp. 109–143) speaks about the "fundamental causes of growth" instead of deep determinants. He defines these fundamental causes as luck or multiple equilibria, geography, culture, and institutions.

Since institutions are differentiated into informal and formal institutions, our analysis incorporates the fundamental causes of growth, which Acemoglu calls 'institutions' and 'culture'.

Of course, *geography* is a further determinant that affects factor accumulation and productivity. It makes a difference whether a country has access to the seaside and is located in a temperate climate zone, or whether it is embedded in inaccessible terrain and has to cope with climatic extremes such as droughts and heat or severe rainfall and cold. Moreover, its geographical position determines a country's resource endowment and is responsible for the disease environment.

However, the following analysis also includes *openness* as a deep determinant, since we follow the approach of Knowles and Weatherston (2006) and Rodrik, Subramanian & Trebbi (2004). The degree of a country's openness to international trade mainly depends on its geographical position, its institutions, and its history. Nevertheless, *openness* is defined as a deep determinant since we want to examine the level of current per capita income. Hence, we wish to find the underlying factors that determine the current proximate determinants. The level of *openness* influences factor accumulation and technology. Therefore, it will be included as a deep determinant of growth. However, *openness* is completely endogenous. It entirely depends on the remaining deep determinants, the proximate determinants, and per capita income (Dollar & Kraay, 2004).

Not only *openness* but also *institutions* and *geography* are at least partly endogenous.[30] Therefore, *Figure 3.1* demonstrates the connections between the

[30] Rodrik, Subramanian and Trebbi (2004) assume geography to be the only clear exogenous deep determinant of growth. From a theoretical point of view, this assumption is right since a country's geographical position, and thereby its environment, cannot be influenced by other factors. However, concerning the empirical analysis, geography is often pooled with ecology. Hence, ecological factors are described as geographical factors. This might not be wrong, since a country's ecological conditions depend on its geographical position. This, for exam-

proximate and the deep determinants of growth and per capita income. The proximate determinants are endogenous, that is to say, an analysis that only incorporates the proximate determinants of growth cannot express development processes since it does not consider the effects of the deep determinants and the reverse causality matters. A theoretical analysis that does not include the deep determinants of growth will not reproduce a real picture and thereby cannot examine real operations, since the assumed prerequisites are wrong. An empirical analysis that excludes the deep determinants will eventually suffer from an omitted variable bias. However, the empirical work knows methods to deals with this issue.[31]

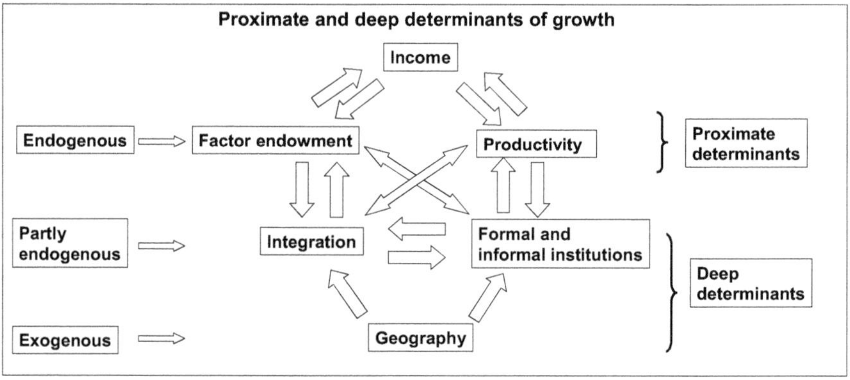

Figure 3.1: deep determinants of growth. Source: own illustration.

3.6 Methodical issues

The endogeneity and causality issues in institutional analysis depict a particular challenge for empirical work. Typically, an ordinary least squares (OLS) regression cannot be run because of a possible omitted variable bias and reverse causality. Institutions, as they are defined in this work, can be influenced by several factors, but we are not able to detect every determinant that might affect institu-

ple, is true regarding a country's disease burden. Growth regressions often use the risk of contracting malaria in a country as a proxy variable for geography. However, malaria risk is clearly endogenous. A higher per capita income decreases the risk of a malaria infection, since it is accompanied with improved health care and widespread vaccination. Therefore, geography is defined as partly endogenous. However, other geographical proxy variables are clearly exogenous.

[31] See, for example, Dollar & Kraay (2004); Easterly & Levine (2003); Sachs & Warner (1995).

tional quality. Hence, it is unavoidable that certain variables correlated with institutions are incorporated into the error term. That is, the coefficients are biased because of omitted variables.

The aim of the work is to estimate the effect of institutions on per capita income. As stated above, this effect is not unidirectional. Formal and informal institutions influence each other and income, which again has an impact on both kinds of institutions. Hence, the institutional coefficient of an OLS regression would not only estimate the unidirectional effect of, for example, informal institutions on income but also the feedback reaction from income to informal institutions.

However, the problem of endogeneity in growth empirics is commonly solved through instrumental variable estimation, that is, an instrumental variable must be found for each of the endogenous regressors. The detection of an adequate instrument can become tricky. An instrumental variable must possess two features: it has to be correlated with the appropriate endogenous variable and it must be uncorrelated with the disturbance. While the former can be tested, the fulfillment of the second feature, and thereby the relevance and accuracy of the regression result, relies on the researcher's intuition. Because causality is the main issue in the deep determinants analysis, a channel that transmits the effect of the particular endogenous variable in the right direction – and thereby from institutions to income and not vice versa – must be determined. It must be ensured that the instrumental variable does not influence the dependent variable directly, but only through its effect on the endogenous variable. If this requirement is fulfilled, the causality issue is solved and the estimated coefficient measures the effect of institutions on income.

3.6.1 Two stage least squares

The problems of omitted variable bias and reverse causality can be solved via an instrumental variable estimation.

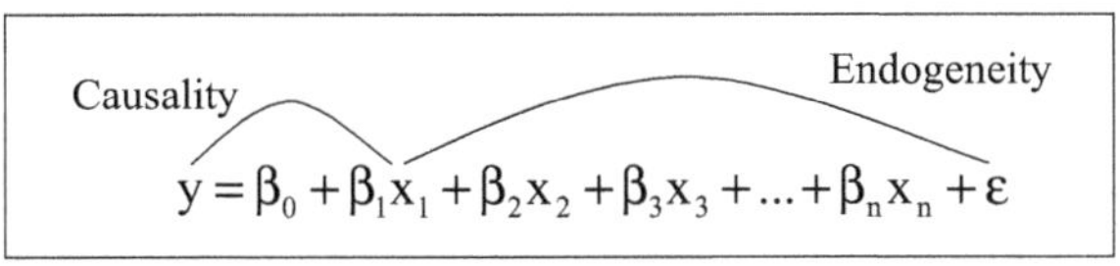

Figure 3.2: endogeneity and reverse causality. Source: own illustration.

As can be seen in *Figure 3.2,* endogeneity exists if an independent variable x_1 is correlated with an omitted variable included in the error term. Furthermore, the issue of reverse causality occurs if x_1 not only influences y, but if y also has a reverse impact on x_1. In the case of a single endogenous regressor we want to estimate the following equation:

$$y = \beta_0 + \beta_1 \mu + \beta_2 x_2 + \beta_3 x_3 + \ldots + \beta_n x_n + \varepsilon \tag{3.1}$$

with: y: dependent variable — μ: endogenous variable

x_i: exogenous variables — ρ: instrumental variable

ε: error term.

Hence, μ is assumed to be endogenous and influenced by y. If an OLS regression is run, β_1 and eventually the other coefficients would be biased. In addition, β_1 would measure the bilateral effect between μ and y instead of the unidirectional effect going from μ to y. Hence, to solve the problem of omitted variable bias and reverse causality, an instrumental variable for μ must be found. However, the instrument ρ must satisfy two premises:

1) to avoid omitted variable bias, it must not be correlated with the error term:

$$Cov(\rho_i, \varepsilon) = 0.$$

However, this precondition deters ρ from being an omitted variable included in the error term of the first-stage regression ε. Furthermore, the assumption declares that no direct correlation between y and ρ is allowed, thereby

$$Cov(y, \rho_i) = 0.$$

Therefore, the causality issue is solved since the direction of the effect goes from ρ to μ to y and not vice versa.

2) The instrumental variable must be correlated with the relevant endogenous variable:

$$Cov(\rho_i, \mu) \neq 0.$$

Applying the 2SLS method, two equations are estimated:

Second-stage regression: $$y = \beta_0 + \beta_1\hat{\mu} + \beta_2 x_2 + \beta_3 x_3 + \ldots + \beta_n x_n + \varepsilon, \qquad (3.2)$$

First-stage regression: $$\mu = \theta_0 + \theta_1\rho_1 + \theta_2 x_2 + \theta_3 x_3 + \ldots + \theta_n x_n + \upsilon, \qquad (3.3)$$

$$\Longrightarrow \hat{\mu} = \hat{\theta}_0 + \hat{\theta}_1\rho_1 + \hat{\theta}_2 x_2 + \hat{\theta}_3 x_3 + \ldots + \hat{\theta}_n x_n. \qquad (3.4)$$

Hence, first a regression on μ is run, including the instrumental variable ρ_1 and all exogenous independent variables x_i. This regression results in the fitted value $\hat{\mu}$. Then, $\hat{\mu}$ is used to estimate the coefficient of interest β_1. Since ρ_1 is not correlated with ε the problem of omitted variable bias is solved. However, ρ_1 is not correlated with y either – that is, there is no direct effect between the instrument and the dependent variable. Only an indirect effect between ρ_1 and y exists because ρ_1 influences $\hat{\mu}$, which is correlated with y. Hence, the transmission channel is unidirectional from ρ_1 to $\hat{\mu}$ to y. Therefore, β_1 measures the effect of $\hat{\mu}$ on y and not vice versa.

In the case of multiple endogenous regressors, at least one instrumental variable for each endogenous variable is needed. If fewer instruments than endogenous variables are available, the equation is underidentified and the regression cannot be run. However, if the number of instruments equates the number of endogenous variables, the equation is said to be exactly identified and the regression can be run. The same holds if the number of instruments exceeds the quantity of endogenous regressors – that is, if the equation is overidentified.

With multiple endogenous regressors μ_i, one first-stage regression for each endogenous variable must be run:

Second-stage regression:

$$y = \beta_0 + \beta_1\hat{\mu}_1 + \beta_2\hat{\mu}_2 + \ldots + \beta_n\hat{\mu}_n + \beta_{n+1}x_1 + \beta_{n+2}x_2 + \ldots + \beta_{n+m}x_m + \varepsilon \qquad (3.5)$$

First-stage regressions and fitted values:

$$\mu_1 = \theta_0 + \theta_1\rho_1 + \theta_2\rho_2 + \ldots + \theta_n\rho_n + \theta_{n+1}x_1 + \theta_{n+2}x_2 + \ldots + \theta_{n+m}x_m + \upsilon_1 \qquad (3.6)$$

$$\Longrightarrow \hat{\mu}_1 = \hat{\theta}_0 + \hat{\theta}_1\rho_1 + \hat{\theta}_2\rho_2 + \ldots + \hat{\theta}_n\rho_n + \hat{\theta}_{n+1}x_1 + \hat{\theta}_{n+2}x_2 + \ldots + \hat{\theta}_{n+m}x_m \qquad (3.7)$$

$$\mu_2 = \theta_0 + \theta_1\rho_1 + \theta_2\rho_2 + ... + \theta_n\rho_n + \theta_{n+1}x_1 + \theta_{n+2}x_2 + ... + \theta_{n+m}x_m + \upsilon_2 \quad (3.8)$$

$$\Longrightarrow \hat{\mu}_2 = \hat{\theta}_0 + \hat{\theta}_1\rho_1 + \hat{\theta}_2\rho_2 + ... + \hat{\theta}_n\rho_n + \hat{\theta}_{n+1}x_1 + \hat{\theta}_{n+2}x_2 + ... + \hat{\theta}_{n+m}x_m \quad (3.9)$$

$$\mu_n = \theta_0 + \theta_1\rho_1 + \theta_2\rho_2 + ... + \theta_n\rho_n + \theta_{n+1}x_1 + \theta_{n+2}x_2 + ... + \theta_{n+m}x_m + \upsilon_n \quad (3.10)$$

$$\Longrightarrow \hat{\mu}_n = \hat{\theta}_0 + \hat{\theta}_1\rho_1 + \hat{\theta}_2\rho_2 + ... + \hat{\theta}_n\rho_n + \hat{\theta}_{n+1}x_1 + \hat{\theta}_{n+2}x_2 + ... + \hat{\theta}_{n+m}x_m \quad (3.11)$$

However, instrumental variable estimation has its disadvantages, especially regarding the issues of instrument validity and instrument weakness. The validity of an instrumental variable depends on its correlation with the error term of the first-stage regression ε and, therefore, the compliance with assumption one. If the instrument is correlated with ε, it is not valid and an instrumental variable estimation cannot be conducted. The weakness of an instrumental variable is determined by its correlation with the endogenous variable μ_i. If μ and ρ are only sparsely correlated, the instrument is said to be weak.

An instrumental variable estimator (β_j) is consistent if assumptions one and two hold. If either condition fails, the instrumental variable estimator is inconsistent. However, even if the independent variable μ_i is endogenous so that instrumental variable estimation is necessary, the estimator β_j is never unbiased. Thus, especially in small samples, the bias in the instrumental variable estimator can be substantial.

If assumption one fails and the instrument ρ and the error term ε are sparsely correlated, this can lead to a large asymptotic bias of the instrumental variable estimator. However, weak instruments cause large standard errors of the instrumental variable estimator and large asymptotic variances.

Therefore, 2SLS should only be run if the relevant independent variable is clearly endogenous. In addition, a large sample size and instruments that are strongly correlated with the relevant endogenous variable provide for more precise estimates.[32]

3.7 Religion as an instrumental variable for institutions

In recent years, several studies have dealt with the impact of religion on economic development.[33] However, the idea that religion might influence economic growth is not new. As already exemplified, Weber discussed the issue in

[32] The section on instrumental variable estimation is based on the following literature: Wooldridge (2003); Stock & Watson (2003); Baum (2006); Baum, Schaffer & Stillman (2003); Murray (2006).

[33] See, for example, Barro & McCleary (2003); De Jong (2008); Guiso, Sapienza & Zingales (2003); Norris & Inglehart (2004); Platteau (2008); Tripp (2006).

1904/05 and established a connection between religious doctrines, human behavior, and economic growth. Weber emphasized the impact religion has on institutions respectively behavior. Hence, religious doctrines determine peoples' behaviors and thereby economic development. In Weber's case, the belief that a certain level of material wealth indicates the chosen ones and that idleness is a sin (as is luxury) led to an ethic of hard work and thereby capital accumulation and growth. Therefore, according to Weber, Protestants were economically more successful than Catholics. However, Weber's approach is not without controversy. Using the data of 452 counties of 19th century Prussia, Becker and Wößmann (2009) demonstrate that Weber was right about Protestantism leading to higher economic prosperity. However, the authors trace the Protestant economic success back to the high literacy rates of Protestants. Hence, to read the Bible Protestants had to become literate, which, according to human capital theories, fosters economic growth. The decisive transmission channel might not be a particular work ethic, but the accumulation of human capital through literacy. Using 'distance to Wittenberg' as an instrument for the share of Protestants in a county in 19th-century Prussia, Becker and Wößmann run instrumental variables regressions to estimate the effect of Protestantism on literacy. Applying a bounding analysis, they show that Protestantism has no effect on economic prosperity independent of its effect on literacy. However, the authors state that the human capital theory might be complementary to explanations emphasizing belief-based work effort and thrift. Nevertheless, they find the key channel of Protestant economic success to be literacy.[34]

Landes (1998), for example, emphasizes the positive growth effect of Protestantism and describes Catholicism and Islam as less supportive or even detrimental to growth. However, Noland (2003) empirically examined the connection between culture, religion, and economic performance and found no similar connection between religious affiliation in general and economic growth. Although approving the correlation between religion and culture, Noland detects no significant relation between culture and economic performance. However, Noland finds a connection between religion and economic performance, although no robust pattern concerning certain religious affiliations and growth is observable. In any case, Noland's results do not affirm a negative effect of Islam on economic development. Guiso, Sapienza and Zingales (2003) examine the effect religion has on economic attitudes. The authors model the impact of religion on informal institutions, since religious doctrines work through morals and attitudes. Hence, religion shapes informal institutions, which determine behavior, which influences economic performance on an aggregated level. However,

[34] Ekelund, Hébert & Tollison (2002) and Blum & Dudley (2001) also deal with the issue of the Protestant economic success by applying different approaches that partly support and partly refute Weber's thesis.

they are not only interested in religious affiliation but in the intensity of beliefs and whether the consulted person was brought up religiously. They use the WVS to measure the particular kind of religiosity. The religious variables are regressed on peoples' attitudes concerning cooperation, the government, working women, legal rules, thriftiness, and the market economy. They find that religious beliefs are generally correlated with growth-supporting attitudes. Accordingly, Christian religions are associated with attitudes that are more conducive to growth than others, whereas Muslims' attitudes are the most anti-market. Barro and McCleary (2003) studied the effect of church attendance and religious beliefs on economic outcome. However, they found that religious beliefs in general support growth. Nevertheless, church attendance seems to be less conducive to the growth rate, although the authors point out that the net effect has to be considered since church attendance might foster beliefs that are supportive of growth. They justify their results on the consideration that certain religious beliefs encourage specific individual behavior that supports growth. La Porta et al. (1997) examine the impact of trust on economic performance using the WVS data. However, they follow Putnam (1993) and argue that hierarchical religions discourage the formation of trust. To measure the impact of 'hierarchical religion' they take the percentage of the population being Catholic, Eastern Orthodox, and Muslim. The indicator is negatively correlated with trust. Running further regressions they demonstrate that "countries with more dominant hierarchical religions have less efficient judiciaries, greater corruption, lower-quality bureaucracies, higher rates of tax evasion, lower rates of participation in civic activities and professional associations, a lower level of importance of large firms in the economy, inferior infrastructures, and higher inflation" (p. 336f.). However, as is the case with every empirical study, general statements must be made consciously, since empirical results always depend on the particular data and methods applied. Noland (2003), for example, uses other data to measure religion and culture than Guiso, Sapienza and Zingales (2003) do, whereas Barro and McCleary (2003) again use other data sets on religion. Even though the data are used as a proxy for religion and culture, far-ranging differences in the results can be traced back to varying data sets. Therefore, the empirical results should be interpreted according to the particular data used, the regression method applied, and the corresponding theoretical foundation. Hence, it is possible that studies that seem to examine the same issue –for example, religion and economic performance – arrive at different conclusions. However, De Jong (2008) gives an overview concerning existing work on religion and economic performance. He critically reveals quantitative and qualitative approaches dealing with the topic and examines values, institutions, and governance as transmission channels. He also states that economic development might influence religiosity. He finds that the results of the studies considered differ concerning the way religion is measured, that no particular religion can be found to be more pro-growth than another, and that causality between values and economic performance can go both ways.

However, if religion does affect economic outcome, we would like to know whether religions exist that are more conducive to growth and development than others. If this was the case, it would explain parts of the differing development patterns around the world. Discussing religion as a growth-relevant determinant requires clear definitions of the main terms and transmission channels. It is important to define what is meant by religion since different understandings exist. It must be clarified whether one is examining the formal writings of the holy texts such as the Bible, Quran, or Torah, how religion is practiced, or even if the practices correspond to the religious texts. Furthermore, if only the formal holy texts or religious doctrines are being analyzed which are specified by a particular person and which might not correspond to the formal writings. Hence, if a political or religious leader exploits religion to force his interests, is this still called 'religion'? Do we still talk about a religion, when a certain interpretation is meant that might deviate from the original statements? The impact on individual behavior and thereby institutions is the same, no matter whether the individuals believe in a formal text or in the words of a preacher. However, as soon as the definition of religion is detached from a text, it is open to different interpretations. When examining religion from an institutional view, it is important to differentiate between what people believe and what they do. Hence, describing oneself as an adherent of a certain religion has no impact on institutions. The impact emerges when the person is persuaded of the religious doctrines and thereby acts according to the religious morals.

However, finding an exact definition of religion is not easy. Iannaccone (1998), for example, defines religion as: "any shared set of beliefs, activities, and institutions premised upon faith in supernatural forces" (p. 1466). Here, religion is defined as basic divine, spiritual, or supernatural doctrines and the according statements concerning morals and codes of conduct. However, religion is not equal to behavior. Hence, there must be a differentiation between the basic religious doctrines, which we call religion, no matter if they are written down or if they are common sense, and the convictions and the behavior with which humans implement religion. The statements of formal religious texts are not examined here, since this is the content of *religious economics* (Iannaccone, 1998, p. 1466). The emphasis is on whether and how people implement religious doctrines. Hence, the interpretations of religious texts or doctrines are incorporated that might be exploited by certain interest groups or political and religious leaders, as long as a connection to basic religious beliefs is observable. This might be a disputatious point. Anyway, since we are interested in the implementation of beliefs through behavior, it does not make sense to drop certain interpretations. We do not want to examine the motivation of a certain preacher, religious or political leader, or interest group. We are solely interested in the behavioral implementation of beliefs. Hence, the underlying motivation of the person or the group that passes on the beliefs is not essential. Beliefs become relevant as soon as people implement them. Since people believe in the particular interpretation and implement the morals and the corresponding behavior, it does not matter whether the statements can be traced back to an originally holy text or whether they are made by a particular person. However, statements should be attributable to a certain religion and individualistic spirituality and metaphysical thought are excluded, although the borders might be woolly. Therefore, the current definition of religion is a subjective matter and might be wrong from a religious studies point of view. However, this is why the current understanding of religion should be clearly defined.

However, the causality between religion and economic development seems clear when religion is defined as the formal writings of a holy text, since development or income cannot alter what has been written down. Nevertheless, if religion is defined as what people believe and how they act, then it might be influenced by higher incomes and thereby better living standards. Hence, the analysis of religion and economic development is depicted by the possibility of reverse causality. Religion might not only influence the growth rate, but religious beliefs might also be influenced by economic development. A higher per capita income changes perspectives and priorities in life. Coupled with education, it generates a more open-minded society, which reflects religious doctrines more critically. Hence, religious doctrines might become reinterpreted by individuals. Accordingly, what changes when income increases are not the basic religious doctrines per se, but peoples' preferences and priorities and, therefore, peoples' values, beliefs, and morals. Hence, basic religious statements are unchanged, but institutions change. Peoples' values, beliefs, and morals alter when living standards improve. The religious origin remains unchanged but becomes reinterpreted. In any case, besides asking what determines institutions and concluding that religion plays a crucial role, we could also ask how religion emerges. Answering this question, we are again confronted with reverse causality since religions might be the result of cultural value patterns and cultural differences (Hofstede, 1997).

The present hypothesis is that religion, defined as basic divine, spiritual, or supernatural doctrines, has no impact on economic outcome. Hence, we follow Weber (1904/05), Guiso, Sapienza and Zingales (2003), and Barro and McCleary (2003) and interpose the level of institutions between religion and economic performance. That is to say, we assume religion influences institutions but not, directly, economic performance.[35] Therefore, religious doctrines influ-

[35] Nevertheless, the achievements of Becker & Wößmann (2009) are considered as well. However, their results refer to the special case of the Protestant economic success and Weber's thesis of the Protestant work ethic. Furthermore, their findings do not mean that religion has generally no impact on behavior and economic prosperity.

ence peoples' behaviors provided the individuals are persuaded of the religion – that is, they believe. Then, people will behave according to the religious morals and their behaviors will influence economic outcome.

Religion defined as basic spiritual, divine, and supernatural doctrines, which identify and determine the religion, cannot be altered. Therefore, religion is taken as exogenous source of variation. To differentiate between religion and changeable religious beliefs religion is measured with data on the proportion of the population belonging to a certain religion. Hence, we do not use survey data that question whether people think they are religious. Religious affiliation data do not measure an individual's or a society's level of religiosity. We want to measure the underlying influence of religious doctrines. That is to say, we incorporate people who do not believe in God and do not attend religious services, but who, nevertheless, describe themselves as Protestants, Catholics, Muslims, and so on. These people belong to a religious group because of tradition, culture, or social pressure, or because it is 'usual', but not because they are convinced by the religious content. Hence, they implement religious norms and morals, but no longer connect their own behavior, attitudes, habits, and beliefs to religion.

An individual might describe themselves as not religious but belong to a part of the population belonging to a certain religion. We are interested in the deeper social and behavioral effects religion has on society. Hence, people who do not describe themselves as being religious (and all others) still behave according to particular religious morals because these morals have become a part of the society's culture. One could argue that all religions can be traced back to similar basic statements and, therefore, that all religions influence society in the same way. However, we will see if this is true when we regress religious affiliation on institutions.

The analysis so far demonstrates that the incorporation of religion into economics is a critical subject. However, the intention of the work at hand is not to emphasize the issue of religion and economics. Religion is going to be introduced as an exogenous factor of variation necessary for the instrumental variable estimation. The main intention of the current section is to justify the use of religious affiliation variables as instruments to introduce the topic of religion and economic development and to depict the approach's critical points. Nevertheless, we do not want to interfere with the topic any further. For the analysis at hand, religion is defined as basic divine, spiritual, and supernatural doctrines that identify a religion and determine human beliefs, values, morals, codes of conduct, and thereby human behavior. However, the divine, spiritual, and supernatural doctrines might be determined by culture. Since this has long happened, there is no connection to current culture aside from religion. Furthermore, even if religion is influenced by modern thought, its basic ideas such as its main doctrines and statements do not change. Hence, the basic religious statements are exogenous.

The current study is aware that the theoretical and empirical analysis of religion, institutions, and economic performance is mixed and no clear pattern is observable. Hence, the results of the forthcoming regression analysis and theoretical argumentation do not articulate general statements. All results, empirical and theoretical, must be considered under the particular assumptions and definitions made. As soon as we move beyond our definitions of religion and institutions, and as soon as we modify or extend the theoretical argumentation, the results might become indefensible. Hence, one should not generalize the forthcoming results, but consider them regarding the particular assumptions and definitions applied. It is important not to read more into the results than there is and not to misinterpret them.

Informal institutions are, inter alia, defined as a society's value system, beliefs, morals, and norms. In general, institutions are constraints humans impose on themselves to regulate their social interactions. Of course, this also applies to informal institutions. However, an interesting question is why particular informal institutions are implemented. That is to say, what determines the implementation of certain informal institutions? How do values, beliefs, norms, and morals emerge, and why do they differ between societies? Hence, which strategy do people apply when they place constraints on themselves? How do they justify the particular rules and constraints?

The origins of most of our values, beliefs, morals, and norms can be ascribed to religion and, therefore, depend on which religion has been, and still is, dominant in a particular region. Why, for example, do we speak of the Christian West or the Islamic countries? Why do we use religious terms to describe a group of countries or a region? The differences between these countries must exist in obvious areas such as social, cultural, or political life since it must affect us in some manner otherwise we would not care about it. Moreover, the difference must be attributed to religion since in other respects we would not use religious terms to describe the countries. Thus, religion seems to matter, and it matters so much that we classify countries according to their religious affiliations. In speaking of Christian, Islamic, or Buddhist countries, for example, we explicitly want to highlight their religious affiliations. Hence, we associate the prevalent religion with obvious features that differ between the countries. This can constitute particular conventions, values, morals, habits, attitudes, or behavior, as well as societal, political, legal, and economic differences. Thus, we are talking about different institutions. That is to say, religion has an impact on institutions. Since institutions influence economic development, religion has an indirect effect on the economy.

Concerning the analysis at hand, it is assumed that the religious environment affects institutions, which then influence per capita income. Religion cannot directly be correlated with income if we want to use it as an instrumental variable. However, applying our definition of religion as basic divine, spiritual, or supernatural doctrines, just being religious does not affect economic outcome. Religion cannot achieve anything as long as it is not implemented in peoples' attitudes, habits, and behaviors as well as in social, hierarchical, and political structures. Only then is an indirect influence on income possible. Over decades and centuries, religious doctrines have become a part of the prevalent culture. Although individuals, acting according to particular cultural norms and values, might no longer connect these features to religion, tracing the cultural properties back to their origins shows that religion is the starting point.

"The predominant religious cultural traditions in any society, such as the legacy of Protestantism and Catholicism in Western Europe, are expected to leave a distinct imprint upon the contemporary moral, beliefs and social attitudes that are widespread among the public in these nations" (Norris & Inglehart, 2004, p. 20). Even if religiosity declines, the prevalent religion has left its traces in culture. Hence, certain habits, morals, and norms can be attributed to religion, although the particular individual, who acts according to the rules, might not describe themselves as being religious.

Again, incentives play a role. Humans implement religious guidelines because they act from conviction, they fear punishment, or both; hence, their behavior corresponds to religious morality. Of course, this incorporates their economic behavior and, thus, being religious does not influence economic growth. Religious beliefs do not influence economic development until they become converted into norms, values, habits, and codes of conduct. Thus, just being Protestant does not affect economic development, because Protestantism must operate through its effect on human behavior, that is, through informal institutions.

However, the fact that formal and informal institutions are closely related to each other has led to the consideration that both kinds of institutions can be traced back to the same instrumental variable approach. Religious doctrines determine the general understanding of the state, the connection between secular and divine powers, and the role of the individual. Even modern states and democracies still implement religious statements in their constitutions. Hence, religious origins can also determine formal institutions. Certain religious beliefs can encourage property rights and, therefore, constraints on the executive, whereas others might inhibit it. The relationship between religion and formal institutions can best be seen in theocratic states, where religion claims terrestrial and religious power. But even in countries where state and religious power are separate, a basic attitude arising out of the religious background is prevalent. Originally, religious beliefs constituted worldviews and ideologies such as political ideologies, the general understanding of the state, and the societal system per se. Even if this is not the case and no general political ideology is prevalent in a society, certain cultural traits originating in religion support a particular political system through acquiescence and obedience.

Thus, using religious affiliation as an instrumental variable for formal institutions, we must assume that religion does not influence per capita income directly but only through institutions. As already elucidated, this is the case. Religion cannot achieve anything as long as it is not implemented in peoples' attitudes and behaviors as well as in social, hierarchical, and political structures.

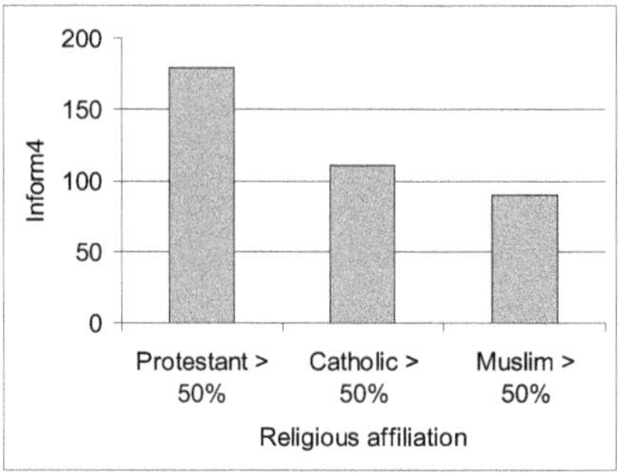

Figure 3.3: religious affiliation and informal institutions. Source: own illustration.

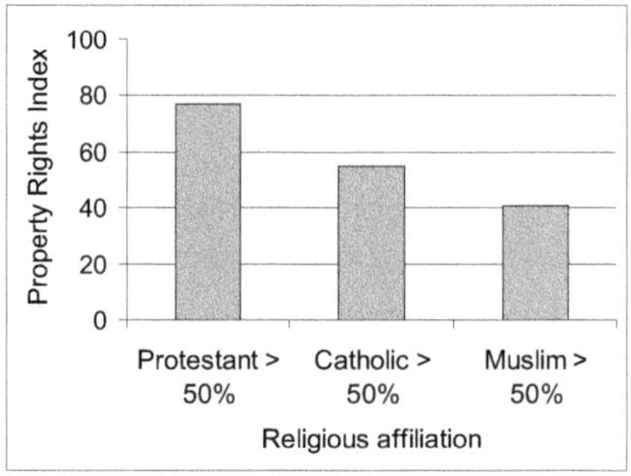

Figure 3.4: religious affiliation and formal institutions. Source: own illustration.

Figures 3.3 and *3.4* depict the relationship between the religious affiliation of the population and institutions. A high Protestant proportion of the population is accompanied by high levels of *inform4*, that is, growth-supporting informal institutions.[36] By contrast, countries with a high proportion of Muslim citizens realize a minor level of *inform4*, and thereby have growth-inhibiting informal institutions. However, *Figure 3.4* demonstrates the relationship between religious affiliation and the Freedom House property rights index 2000, which is scaled from 0 to 100, with 0 indicating unprotected and 100 completely protected property rights. A high Protestant proportion of the population is attended by a strong protection of property rights, whereas a high Muslim proportion of the population shows fewer protected property rights.[37] However, these Protestant and Muslim affiliations of the population are used as instrumental variables for informal and formal institutions, respectively. This is the case because we are looking preferably for unequal instruments. Since the current hypothesis is close to that of Weber on an argumentative level, Protestant affiliation is used to illustrate informal institutions, because Protestantism is said to alter norms and

[36] The indicator *inform4* is explained in more detail in part 3.8.1 of the current work.
[37] In Figures 7 and 8, countries with a Protestant, Catholic, and Muslim proportion of the population greater than 50 percent are included.

values in favor of economic growth. From a Western point of view, the differences in formal institutions that can be traced back to religion become particularly obvious in Islamic countries. Consider, for example, the political and legal systems, which often cannot be described as democratic or constitutional compared with Western standards. Hence, to note these differences, the Muslim affiliation of the population is used to illustrate formal institutions, that is, Protestant affiliation is assumed to be supportive of economic growth, whereas Muslim affiliation is said to be growth inhibiting (Guiso, Sapienza & Zingales, 2003; La Porta et al., 1999; Landes, 1998). More precisely, Protestantism and Islam are assumed to have different impacts on institutional development, and particular institutions then influence the growth rate. These statements will be tested within the empirical analysis. Of course, other religions should be considered, too. Thus, regressions including the Catholic affiliation of the population were run, although the intuitional justification is less clear, as are the empirical results. In any case, since several data sets had to be merged for the empirical analysis, insufficient observations remained to be able to run regressions with further religious affiliation variables. Therefore, our empirical analysis is restricted to proxies for Protestantism and Islam and, for the sake of completeness, Catholicism. Since it is expected that Protestantism and Islam, in particular, have different effects on institutions, and since both religions are widespread, this is not a disadvantage. However, when arguing that religion influences the development of institutions, we should be clear that we are talking about Protestantism and Islam and not religion in general.

3.8 Regression analysis: the impact of formal and informal institutions on per capita income

3.8.1 Data

My analysis follows Tabellini (2005) and Knowles and Weatherston (2006) with respect to their informal institutions index. Using data from the WVS, Tabellini composed an index of four cultural features. According to Tabellini: "Three of them are expected to encourage a positive and productive attitude towards market exchange, entrepreneurial activities, or the production of public goods … The fourth indicator is symptomatic of a more hierarchical society where individuals are less likely to take advantage of economic opportunities or to cooperate with each other" (Tabellini, 2005, p. 8f.). The measures are *trust*, *control*, *respect*, and *obedience*. As already illustrated, a high level of trust decreases transaction costs but increases the quantity of transactions and, accordingly, economic growth. In the WVS, *trust* is measured with the following question: "Generally speaking, would you say that most people can be trusted or that you can't be too careful in dealing with people?". Possible answers are "Most people can be trusted", "Can't be too careful", and "Don't know". The level of trust in a country is measured by the percentage of respondents who answered that "Most people can be trusted".

The second measure that favors economic development is *control*. The corresponding question in the WVS is: "Some people feel that they have completely free choice and control over their lives, while other people feel that what they do has no real effect on what happens to them. Please use this scale (from 1 to 10) where 1 means 'none at all' and 10 means 'a great deal' to indicate how much freedom of choice and control in life you have over the way your life turns out". As already explained, being persuaded of having control over one's own life supports growth and, thus, a high number for *control* is positively correlated with per capita income. To measure *control* I follow Knowles and Weatherston (2006) who used the percentage of respondents in a country who gave a score of 7–10 for the former question.

The last growth-supporting feature is *respect*. In the WVS, the corresponding question is: "Here is a list of qualities that children can be encouraged to learn at home. Which, if any, do you consider to be especially important? Please choose up to five." Respondents can decide between "good manners, independence, obedience, hard work, feeling of responsibility, imagination, thrift, saving money and things, determination and perseverance, religious faith, unselfishness, and tolerance and respect for other people". The variable *respect* is measured as the percentage of respondents in each country that mentioned "tolerance and respect for other people".

The fourth element of Tabellini's cultural indicator is *obedience*. This factor is not supportive of growth as it increases. The appropriate question in the WVS is again the one asking for important qualities in children. Hence, *obedience* is measured by the percentage of respondents answering that obedience is an important quality for children to learn. According to Tabellini, obedience without further reflection is a typical feature of hierarchical societies. Individualism is suppressed and obedience is more important than one's own opinion and personal responsibility. The suppression of individualism makes cooperation difficult and has negative effects on economic development (Tabellini, 2005, p. 11). Therefore, *respect* and *obedience* are used as proxies for the societal structure, resulting in generalized vs. limited morality. Accordingly, a country with a high level of *respect* and a low level of *obedience* is expected to realize generalized morality and vice versa.

Tabellini creates two indicators using the four cultural traits. He obtains the first by applying principal component analysis and the second by adding the three positive measures minus *obedience*. Here, it was decided to follow the second approach to create an indicator of informal institutions. Therefore, *trust*, *control*, and *respect* were added together, and *obedience* was subtracted. The resulting indicator is called *inform4*.

A proxy for formal institutions can reflect the interrelationship between formal institutions and growth. As already shown, property rights are usually assumed to be the main determinant of growth. Acemoglu and Johnson (2005), for example, emphasize the importance of property rights institutions. According to the authors, "property rights institutions are intimately linked to the distributions of political power in society because they regulate the relationship between ordinary private citizens and the politicians or elites with access to political power" (p. 951). Hence, their preferred measure of property rights is Polity IV's "constraints on the executive", which measures the extent of institutionalized constraints on the executive. Its scale ranges from "unlimited authority" (1) to "executive parity or subordination" (7). Following Acemoglu and Johnson, this means of measuring has two advantages, "first, it corresponds to the procedural rules constraining state action, and second, it highlights the close relationship between property rights institutions and political institutions" (p. 951). I follow Acemoglu and Johnson's approach and use Polity IV's "constraints on the executive" as a proxy for formal institutions in my regression analysis.

To allow for ecological conditions and geography, I use a measure of malaria risk. The variable is called *malfal94* and was first introduced by Gallup, Sachs and Mellinger (1998). It emerged from a variable called MAL94P, which depicts "the proportion of each country's population that live with risk of malaria transmission" (Sachs, 2003, p. 5). Malfal94 "multiplies the MALP94 index by an estimate of the proportion of national malaria cases that involve the fatal species, *Plasmodium falciparum*, as opposed to three largely non-fatal species of the malaria pathogen (*P. vivax, P. malariae, and P. ovale*)" (Sachs, 2003, p. 5). The measure was also used by Acemoglu, Johnson and Robinson (2001), Rodrik, Subramanian and Trebbi (2002), and Knowles and Weatherston (2006).

Openness is measured with data from the Penn World Tables 6.2. I use the variable *openk,* which represents exports plus imports divided by real GDP per capita in constant prices. The base year is 1996. The data from the Penn World Tables 6.2 are also used to measure per capita income. The corresponding variable is called *rgdpl*, which represents real GDP per capita in constant prices. Again, the reference year is 1996.

Figures 3.5 to *3.10* demonstrate the correlations between the measures of informal and formal institutions and per capita income. Accordingly, *trust, control,* and *respect* are positively correlated with GDP per capita, whereas *obedience* is negatively correlated with per capita income. This strengthens the hypothesis that generalized morality is correlated with higher living standards and that limited morality is accompanied by a lower per capita income. The causality cannot be determined according to the figures; however, they do explain that several feedback mechanisms exist and that the form of societal organization and GDP per capita interact. The figures demonstrate that levels of trust are lower in less developed economies, that people in poorer countries are less convinced of being in control of their lives, and that respect for other people is considered less important in low-income countries. Obedience, on the contrary, is considered more important than it is in high-income states, which indicates the hierarchical structures and prevalence of limited morality in less developed economies. The indicator *inform4* is positively correlated with GDP per capita, which also affirms the hypothesis of a connection between the form of societal organization – and thereby informal institutions – and wealth.

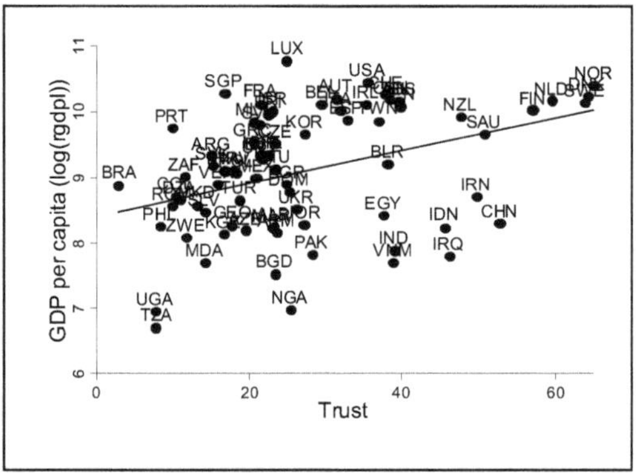

Figure 3.5: GDP per capita and trust. Source: own illustration.

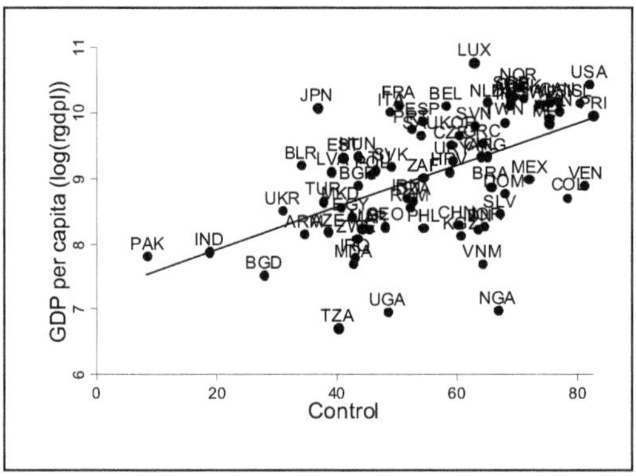

Figure 3.6: GDP per capita and control. Source: own illustration.

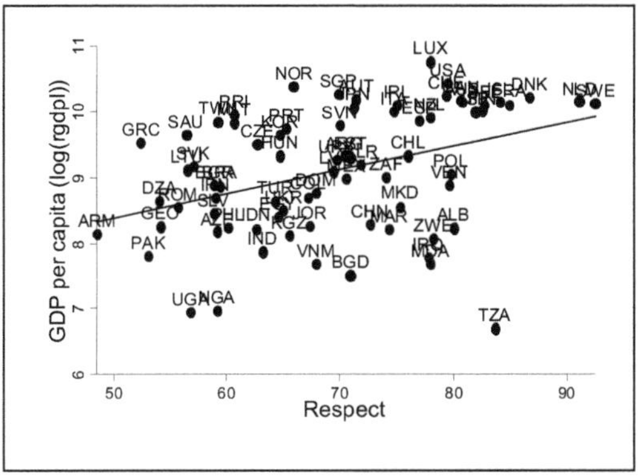

Figure 3.7: GDP per capita and respect. Source: own illustration.

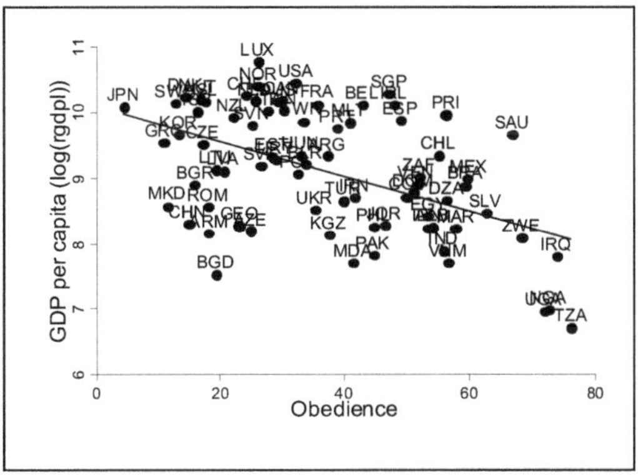

Figure 3.8: GDP per capita and obedience. Source: own illustration.

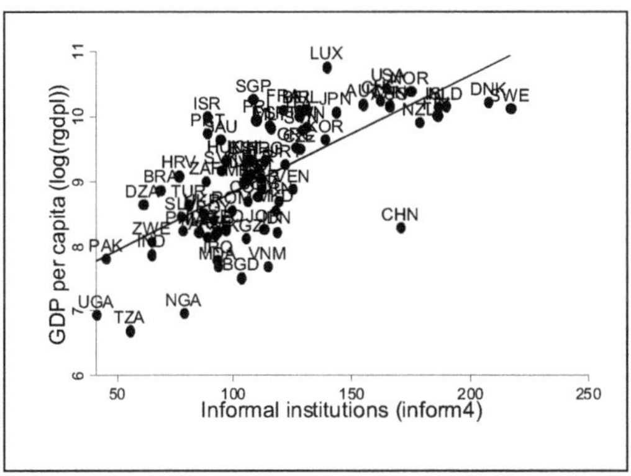

Figure 3.9: GDP per capita and inform4. Source: own illustration.

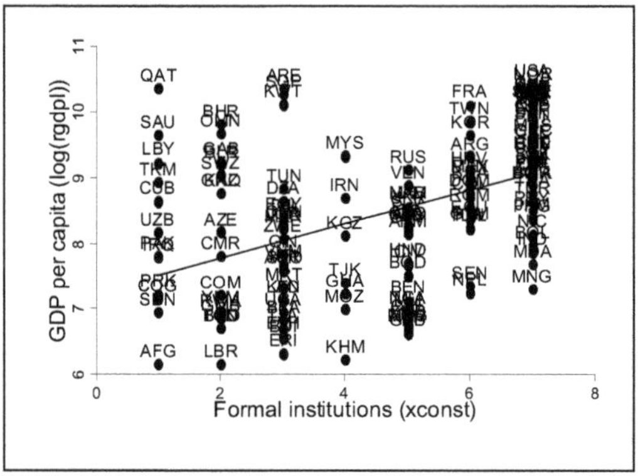

Figure 3.10: GDP per capita and xconst. Source: own illustration.

Furthermore, a correlation between *xconst* – that is, the indicator of formal institutions – and per capita income exists. However, the correlation might not seem that clear because of the scaling of *xconst* (the index is scaled with integers from one to seven) and because of a group of outliers in the upper left-hand corner. These countries are Bahrain, the UAE and Qatar, which exhibit relatively high per capita incomes, but underperform with respect to their levels of formal institutions. Indeed, these states are characterized by features that distinguish them from other countries with growth-supporting formal institutions. The mentioned Gulf states, for example, can afford a relatively high living standards for their indigenous populations because of their oil wealth; therefore, they are able to afford 'bad' institutions.[38] Thus, the positions of these outliers can be traced back to their resource wealth.

3.8.2 Regression approach

The aim of the regression approach is to measure the impacts of formal and informal institutions on per capita income. Hence, a regression is run that uses per capita income as a dependent variable and indices for formal and informal institutions as independent variables. As already elucidated, this kind of regression would lead to biased coefficients, since the error term would include further growth-relevant factors that are correlated with institutions. Therefore, we follow the deep determinants of growth approach, which defines institutions, geography, and openness as the deep determinants of growth. Hence, the deep determinants influence the proximate determinants – that is, factor accumulation and

[38] The term 'bad' institutions refers to institutions that are not supportive of economic growth.

technological progress – and, therefore, the deep determinants are the fundamental factors determining a country's economic development path.

However, there might still exist unknown factors influencing the deep determinants of growth. Furthermore, the deep determinants (even geography, depending on which proxy is used) depend on per capita income. Hence, a change in per capita income has an impact on institutions, on openness, and, eventually, on geography (for example, if a measure a disease burden is used as a proxy for geography). Therefore, instrumental variable regressions are run.

The equation to be estimated is:

$$y = \alpha + \beta_1 I + \beta_2 F + \beta_3 GEO + \beta_4 OPEN, \qquad (3.12)$$

where y indicates GDP per capita, I stands for informal and F for formal institutions, GEO denotes geography, and OPEN is openness.

Equation (3.13) corresponds to (3.12) with only the accordant proxies being inserted:

$$\log(rgdpl) = \alpha + \beta_1 \inf orm4 + \beta_2 xconst + \beta_3 malfal94 + \beta_4 openk. \qquad (3.13)$$

First, the equation is estimated via OLS. However, because the causality between institutions and per capita income is mutual, endogeneity is definitely an issue in the regression, and therefore OLS might not be an accurate estimation method. Therefore, the 2SLS method is used to solve the problem of unclear causality between institutions and per capita income. Consequently, the other regressors are assumed to be exogenous.

After instrumenting for formal and informal institutions, endogeneity could still be an issue in respect to geography and integration. A higher per capita income definitely lowers malaria risk. Better health care is affordable at the state and individual levels and vaccines are available for major parts of the population. Being aware of this issue, Sachs (2003) introduced an instrumental variable called 'malaria ecology' (ME) which "is built upon climatological and vector conditions on a country-by-country basis, and is therefore exogenous to public health interventions and economic conditions, [therefore] ME provides an ideal instrumental variable for malaria risk" (p. 7). Hence, *ME* is used as an instrument for malaria risk.

Concerning openness, it could be argued that richer countries are prone to open their economies because they are not protecting infant or other indigenous industries from competition on the world market. Hence, openness can lead to higher incomes, but higher incomes might also cause more openness. As in the former malaria case, this reverts to a well-established instrumental variable concerning openness and, therefore, the natural logarithm of the Frankel–Romer actual trade share is used (Frankel & Romer, 1999).

3.8.3 Regression results

Since the empirical analysis consists of different data sets, the number of included countries varies between 55 and 72. No differentiation is made between particular country groups such as OECD countries, developing countries, or former colonies since this would further decrease the sample size. Instead, all countries for which data are available are incorporated in each case. *Tables 3.1–3.5* as well as the data sources can be found at the end of the current chapter.

The first column in *Table 3.1* demonstrates the OLS regression results. A one percentage point increase in *inform4* leads to a 1.1 percentage point increase in per capita income. The result is significant at the one percent level. The coefficient on *xconst* is also significant at the one percent level. Accordingly, a one-score increase leads to a rise in per capita income of 13 percent. Of course, the coefficient on *malfal94* has a negative sign since an increase in malaria risk leads to a decline in income. *Openk* is significant at the five percent level and its coefficient is small, but at any rate a positive effect of openness on income becomes apparent.

Because the size of the coefficients can be misleading concerning the variables' relative impacts on income, the first column in *Table 3.2* presents the beta-coefficients of the OLS regression. When measured in standard deviations, *inform4* has the largest effect on per capita income compared with all included variables. Therefore, informal institutions seem to play a decisive role in explaining per capita income patterns.

Columns two and three in *Table 3.1* show the first- and second-stage regressions of a 2SLS estimation using *protestant* as an instrument for informal institutions. The remaining independent variables in this regression are assumed to be exogenous. The coefficient on *protestant* in the first-stage regression, which is significant at the one percent level, demonstrates the variables' correlation with *inform4*, which is a precondition for its use as an instrumental variable. The second-stage regression confirms the OLS results. The coefficient on *inform4* is significant at the one percent level. A one percentage point increase in *inform4* leads to a 1.2 percentage point rise in per capita income. A one-score increase of *xconst* on its scale from one to seven leads to a 12 percent or higher increase in per capita income.

Again, the beta-coefficients in column three of *Table 3.2* shed some light on the relation of the independent variables concerning their impacts on per capita income. A one standard deviation increase in *inform4* leads to an increase of 0.49 standard deviations in per capita income. The other variables' beta-coefficients are smaller than that.

Table 3.3 demonstrates further 2SLS results. In regression (4) we use *protestant* and *muslim* as instruments for *inform4* and *xconst*, respectively. *Protestant* is highly significant in the first-stage regression on *inform4*. As expected, *muslim* is negatively correlated with *xconst* and significant at the one percent level in the first-stage regression on *xconst*. Hence, a higher Protestant affiliation of the population enhances growth-supporting informal institutions, whereas a higher Muslim affiliation decreases the level of growth-supporting formal institutions. In the second-stage regression, all variables are significant at least at the five percent level. A one percentage increase in *inform4* leads to a rise in per capita income of 1.1 percentage points. If *xconst* increases by one score, per capita income rises by 17 percent. A look at the beta-coefficients in *Table 3.4* again demonstrates the superiority of *inform4*, which, when rising by one standard deviation, leads to a 0.44 standard deviation increase in per capita income.

Regression (5) demonstrates the case where we use *catholic* in place of *muslim* as an instrumental variable. Again, *protestant* is significant at the one percent level concerning *inform4*. *Protestant* and *catholic* are both significant in the first-stage regression on *xconst*. In the second-stage regression, *inform4* becomes insignificant, whereas the coefficient on *xconst* increases.

Regressions (6)–(8) show the 2SLS results when we use instrumental variables for all independent variables. Thus, regression (6) uses *protestant* as an instrument for *inform4*, *muslim* as an instrument for *xconst*, *me* as an instrument for *malfal94*, and *logfrankrom* as an instrument for *openk*. Regression (7) is consistent with regression (6), but it uses *catholic* instead of *muslim* as an instrument for *xconst*. Regression (8) also corresponds to regressions (6) and (7), but uses *catholic* and *muslim* as instruments for *xconst*. Hence, regressions (6)–(8) differ concerning the instrumental variables used to instrument for *xconst*. Apart from that they are equal. The first-stage regressions for *malfal94* and *openk* are listed in the continuation of *Table 3.3*. In any case, the instrumental variables *me* and *logfrankrom* are highly significant in each case.

In regression (6), *muslim* is used as an instrumental variable for *xconst*. Now, *protestant* is only significant on *inform4*, whereas *muslim* is significant and negatively correlated with *xconst*. All regressors of the second-stage regression are significant at least at the 10 percent level. A one percentage point increase in *inform4* leads to a 0.89 percentage point increase in per capita income. If *xconst* rises by one score, per capita income increases by 18.4 percent. Regarding the beta-coefficients in *Table 3.4*, a one standard deviation increase in *inform4* leads to a rise in per capita income by 0.37 standard deviations, which is nearly the same amount as the beta-coefficient on *xconst*.

In regression (7), *catholic* is again used instead of *muslim* as an instrumental variable for *xconst*, whereas all independent variables are assumed to be endogenous. However, *inform4* is significant at the 10 percent level. The coefficient on *xconst* again increases compared with regressions (1) and (3) in which *muslim* is used as an instrument, although the increase is not excessive. The most notable alteration occurs in the beta-coefficients table, where the coefficient on *xconst* increases by 0.47 standard deviations. Hence, when using *catholic* as an instrument for formal institutions, *xconst* gains more importance regarding its effect on per capita income and compared with the other regressors, whereas *inform4* becomes less significant.

Regression (8) is overidentified – that is, *protestant*, *muslim*, and *catholic* are used as instrumental variables. However, when *muslim* is incorporated, *catholic* is not significant in the first-stage regression on *xconst*. Instead, *muslim* is negatively correlated with *xconst* and significant at the one percent level. *Protestant* is also significant at the one percent level in the first-stage regression on *inform4*. All regressors are significant in the second-stage regression. A one percentage point increase in *inform4* leads to a 0.8 percentage point increase in per capita income. If *xconst* increases by one score, income rises by 19.6 percent. Regarding the beta-coefficients, the coefficient on *xconst* decreases by 0.37 standard deviations, but is still slightly higher than the coefficient on *inform4*. However, using *protestant*, *muslim*, and *catholic* as instrumental variables, the disturbing effect of *catholic* decreases. The coefficients on *inform4* and *xconst* are comparable to the ones using only *protestant* and *muslim* and, thus, the overidentified regression can be used as a test of robustness. If *catholic* has a significant effect that disturbs the relationship, the result would not be robust in comparison to the ones using *protestant* and *muslim*. Thus, the correlation between *protestant*, *muslim*, *xconst,* and *inform4* is stable. In any case, *catholic* does not seem to fit into the intuitive argument, and although Protestantism and Islam seem to influence institutions, this might not hold for all religions.

To confirm the results, tests were conducted to shed light on a few issues concerning instrumental variable estimation. The small sample size demonstrates a problem regarding 2SLS estimation as well as testing, but because we are working with country data and different data sets there is nothing we can do about that issue. Therefore, the tests can best be seen as an additional coverage, but they are not fully reliable and have to be considered with caution. Most assumptions and conclusions must be considered by relying on intuition.

A perpetual issue in empirical work is that of heteroskedasticity. Although heteroskedasticity does not affect the consistency of the instrumental variable coefficient estimate, it does affect the estimates of the standard errors. Therefore, the Pagan–Hall test was applied to regressions (4), (5), and (6) to detect possible heteroskedasticity in the 2SLS estimations. The results suggest that heteroskedasticity does not exist in the accordant regressions. However, caution is advisable concerning this outcome because the Pagan–Hall test statistic might not be useful when working with small sample sizes (Baum, Schaffer & Stillman, 2003, p. 14). Therefore, additionally, the White–Koenker test statistic was used, even though this test is usually not applied in instrumental variable estimation. However, again, the result suggests that no heteroskedasticity is prevalent.

Concerning the validity of the instruments, the Sargan test statistic was implemented, again only for the case of overidentification, since the test is not valid otherwise. However, the null hypothesis is not rejected and, thus, the instrumental variables are not correlated with the disturbance. Again, we cannot fully rely on the test statistic since the Sargan test might not be valid when all instruments share the same rationale (Murray, 2006, p. 117). Since three religious affiliation variables are used as instrumental variables, this definitely is the case and thereby the test only affirms our regression results but cannot be seen as evidence.

In the end, the Shea statistic to test for the issue of instrumental variable irrelevance was applied. Again, we achieved a positive result since the instruments for institutions are clearly relevant. To solve the problem of instrumental variable irrelevance, it is also useful to have a look at the first-stage regression results. The relevance is confirmed, since all instruments are highly significant in respect to the accordant endogenous regressors.

Table 3.5 demonstrates several tests of robustness. Yet again, regressions (6)–(8) were run including further independent variables. However, panel A incorporates dummy variables for English and French legal origin as additional regressors. The original regression results are robust. Again, *inform4* becomes insignificant when *catholic* is used as the sole instrumental variable for formal institutions. Moreover, the coefficient on *malfal94* further decreases. Interestingly, the coefficient on English legal origin is significant at the five percent level in all regressions.

Panel B includes a measure of population density (Sachs, 2003). Again, the original regression results are robust in respect to the inclusion of the additional regressors, whereas *pop100km* itself is insignificant.

In panels C, D, and E, the variables *coastline*, *temperature*, and *landlocked* from the Parker (1997) data set are added as exogenous regressors. All three factors are insignificant, and the results remain robust. The variables in panels C, D, and E depict geography measurements. Since they are not significant in contrast to *malfal94*, panel F examines what happens when *malfal94* is omitted, that is, when we do not control for geographical or ecological determinants. Still the results are robust. The main difference is depicted by *openk*, which is significant at the five percent level in all regressions and thereby there does not seem to be a high correlation between *malfal94* and our institutional measures.

The empirical analysis demonstrates that Protestantism and Islam have a significant influence on the quality of institutions. A high Protestant affiliation of the population is positively correlated with *inform4*. Accordingly, a high proportion of Protestant population accompanies growth-supporting informal institutions. *Muslim*, on the contrary, is negatively correlated with *xconst*. Therefore, a high proportion of Muslim population is accompanied by fewer constraints on the executive.

Figure 3.4 has already demonstrated the fact that countries with a high proportion of Muslim population possess less property rights. Since property rights are a decisive factor for economic growth, this could be one possible explanation for the low-growth performances of many Muslim countries. However, it has already been demonstrated that institutions influence each other and are influenced by further determinants. Hence, not all Muslim countries must underperform economically. This is even more the case, since our measure of religion (the proportion of the population belonging to a certain religion) might be disputed. The regression results demonstrate that countries with a high Muslim proportion of the population are accompanied by less constraints on the executive (measured with the variable *xconst* from the Polity IV data set).

The possible connections between religious affiliation and informal institutions have already been demonstrated. The hypothesis is that a certain religious affiliation encourages behavioral patterns that support or inhibit economic growth on an aggregated level. However, the regression results of the first-stage regressions for *inform4* demonstrate that *protestant* – that is, the protestant proportion of the population – is positively correlated with the proxy for informal institutions. That is to say, more Protestants in a country yield informal institutions that are more growth supporting, on an aggregated level, than are informal institutions in a country with a high Muslim proportion of the population.[39] Hence, the hypothesis that religious affiliation and institutional quality are somehow correlated is supported.

However, religion and its influence on economic development is not our main concern and so we will not pursue this issue any longer. Different religious affiliations are used as instrumental variables for formal and informal institutions. As the regression results show, the instruments are valid. Hence, an exogenous source of variation has been found and the endogeneity issue is solved.

---

[39] Again it must be mentioned that informal institutions, and thereby a society's value system and its culture, are not judged on a qualitative level. Hence, it is not argued that the value system or the culture of a Muslim society is 'bad', whereas the value system or the culture of a Protestant society is 'good'. It is just demonstrated that a Muslim society seems to develop informal institutions that are less supportive of economic growth compared with the informal institutions that emerge within a society with a majority of Protestant citizens.

Emphasis is on the influence of institutions on per capita income. The regressions demonstrate that the indicator of informal institutions is positively correlated with per capita income. Hence, informal institutions influence economic development. They can be growth supportive or growth inhibiting. The higher the levels of *trust*, *control*, and *respect*, and the lower the level of *obedience*, the better the economic growth. *Inform4* is significant at the one percent level in regression (4) and at the five percent level in regressions (6) and (8) (the regressions that include *catholic* as a single instrument for *xconst* are no longer considered since *catholic* cannot destroy the robust relationship between *protestant*, *muslim*, *inform4*, and *xconst*).

Formal institutions also have a significant impact on the level of per capita income. *Xconst* is significant at the five percent level in regressions (4), (6), and (8). The coefficient on *xconst* is somewhat difficult to interpret since *xconst* is measured on a scale from one to seven. However, an increase in *xconst* leads to a considerable rise in per capita income. Hence, constraints on the executive and, therefore, well-protected property rights are crucial for economic growth and high per capita incomes.

The beta-coefficients demonstrate the importance of the deep determinants of growth relative to each other. Accordingly, assuming that all independent variables are endogenous, malaria risk has the highest influence on per capita income. This is not a surprise since disease burden is well known to play a decisive role in economic development. A population suffering from malaria or other diseases cannot be as productive as a healthy population. However, disease burden is definitely an endogenous factor since a rise in per capita income allows improvements in health care, such as vaccination and medicine, for large parts of the population. Therefore, regressions (6), (7) and (8) use an instrumental variable to control for the reverse causality between malaria risk and income.

The beta-coefficients of regressions (6) and (8) demonstrate that informal and formal institutions both play a decisive role on the level of per capita income. However, regression (8) obtains a slightly higher beta-coefficient for *xconst* than for *inform4*. The beta-coefficients on openness are the lowest in all regressions.

The empirical results approve the theoretical reasoning. Both formal and informal institutions have a significant impact on per capita income. Religion influences institutions through its impact on human beliefs and human behavior, but religion has no direct effect on income. Hence, religious affiliation provides an exogenous source of variation, which is necessary to run 2SLS regressions. Since institutions are correlated with each other, with income, and with further growth-relevant determinants, an instrumental variable estimation is required.

The regression analysis tries to incorporate cultural traits into the growth analysis and examines whether the emergence of institutions can be traced back to religious origins. The assumption is that not only formal but also informal institutions influence economic growth. Theoretical and empirical analysis must consider the issues of endogeneity and reverse causality. Therefore, the transmission channels between informal and formal institutions and per capita income are examined. In the empirical analysis, several 2SLS regressions are run. The proportions of the population being Protestant or Muslim are used as instrumental variables. A high Protestant proportion of the population is correlated with growth-supporting informal institutions, whereas a high percentage of Muslim citizens is correlated with growth-inhibiting formal institutions. Moreover, the second-stage regressions demonstrate that informal and formal institutions have a crucial impact on per capita income.

The relevance of this result stems from the particular properties of informal institutions. In general, institutions are characterized by their stickiness, and thereby alterations take place slowly. Institutions that are particularly responsible for self-identification, that is, informal institutions, are even more resistant to change (Roland, 2005; Boettke, Coyne & Leeson, 2008). At the same time, these institutions are jointly responsible for economic development and are ambiguously correlated with formal institutions and income. Hence, an alteration in formal institutions that obviously hinders growth encounters several problems. First, formal and informal institutions are correlated and many formal institutions even originate in informal institutions. Therefore, when changing formal institutions the ambiguous transmission channels and prevalent informal institutions must be considered otherwise the change can lead to unexpected results. At best, the modification could worsen the situation or simply have no effect, because the prevalent culture might not match the formal transformations. Second, political or economic patterns, which in general are considered supportive of economic growth, do not do the job in countries with different societal and cultural origins, and thereby some institutions cannot be exogenously modified – that is, the transformation of institutions is constrained. Third, no true or right institutional structure exists, because the quality of institutions depends on their societal environment. Hence, institutions that might be judged as growth inhibiting in one country can be effective somewhere else. This holds for formal and informal institutions.

Of course, this means that a general pattern of growth that can be applied to every country does not exist. Although this conclusion might be depressing because it limits the scope for development economics, it has important political implications in that the implementation of standard Western institutions might not be helpful in certain cases. Thus, in the majority of cases externally imposed institutions that are not rooted in the historical and cultural environment will not be accepted.

Table 3.1: regression results

Table 3.1			
	OLS Regression: Dependent Variable is GDP per capita 2000	2SLS Regression: First-Stage Regression for inform4	2SLS Regression: Second-Stage Regression for logrgdpl
	logrgdpl	inform4	logrgdpl
inform4	0.0109712*** (0.0019954)		0.012326*** (0.0033731)
xconst	0.1301642*** (0.0388388)	3.182979* (1.886719)	0.1218325*** (0.0437352)
malfal94	-1.216108*** (0.2801185)	-46.61603*** (13.02763)	-1.158406*** (0.3064585)
openk	0.0031212** (0.0011989)	0.013975 (0.0585996)	0.003085** (0.0012155)
protestant		0.8527801*** (0.139111)	
N	73	72	72
R-sq	0.6989	0.5417	0.6972
adj. R-sq	0.6812	0.5143	0.6792
Standard errors in parentheses * p<0.10, ** p<0.05, *** p<0.01			

Table 3.2: regression results

Table 3.2			
Beta-Coefficients			
	(1)	(2)	(3)
	OLS Regression: Dependent Variable is GDP per capita 2000	2SLS Regression: First-Stage Regression for inform4	2SLS Regression: Second-Stage Regression for logrgdpl
	logrgdpl	inform4	logrgdpl
inform4	0.431*** (0.00200)		0.485*** (0.00337)
xconst	0.254*** (0.0388)	0.157* (1.887)	0.236*** (0.0437)
malfal94	-0.326*** (0.280)	-0.318*** (13.03)	-0.310*** (0.306)
openk	0.176** (0.00120)	0.020 (0.0586)	0.173** (0.00122)
protestant		0.540*** (0.139)	
N	73	72	72
R-sq	0.699	0.542	0.697
adj. R-sq	0.681	0.514	0.679
Standard errors in parentheses * p<0.10, ** p<0.05, *** p<0.01			

Table 3.3: regression results

Table 3.3					
Second-Stage Regression: Dependent Variable is log GDP per capita 2000					
	(4)	(5)	(6)	(7)	(8)
	logrgdpl	logrgdpl	logrgdpl	logrgdpl	logrgdpl
inform4	0.0110657*** (0.0039334)	0.0060033 (0.0048982)	0.0088514** (0.0036032)	0.0074439* (0.0038851)	0.0083195** (0.0035529)
xconst	0.1701662** (0.0749776)	0.364313*** (0.114528)	0.1843526** (0.0789653)	0.2490486** (0.1073546)	0.1958257** (0.0779052)
malfal94	-1.116845*** (0.3076477)	-0.949904** (0.3873074)	-1.67678*** (0.4386155)	-1.60776*** (0.4660777)	-1.66728*** (0.4399537)
openk	0.0031156** (0.0012227)	0.0032386** (0.0014964)	0.0037304* (0.0020363)	0.0039139* (0.0021822)	0.0034932* (0.0020212)
N	72	72	55	55	55
R-sq	0.6942	0.5419	0.7479	0.7231	0.7461
adj. R-sq	0.6760	0.5145	0.7277	0.7010	0.7258
First-Stage Regression for inform4					
	inform4	inform4	inform4	Inform4	inform4
protestant	0.8670299*** (0.134401)	0.950064*** (0.1366442)	0.958102*** (.1652765)	1.073868*** (0.1708423)	0.873540*** (0.1932181)
muslim	-0.1786212** (0.0915166)		-0.2148313* (0.112025)		-0.292980** (0.1450689)
catholic		0.058028 (0.0822803)		0.0567608 (0.1061688)	-0.1132904 (0.1330707)
malfal94	-52.37387*** (12.24637)	-53.1000*** (12.56179)			
me			-2.828471** (1.102847)	-2.940639** (1.150023)	-2.95732** (1.116203)
openk	-0.005205 (0.0589431)	0.0149562 (0.0596696)			
logfrankrom			1.613699 (4.889369)	0.9411052 (5.038896)	1.871671 (4.912235)
R-sq	0.5479	0.5257	0.5421	0.5112	0.5487
adj. R-sq	0.5209	0.4974	0.5054	0.4721	0.5027
First-Stage Regression for xconst					
	xconst	xconst	xconst	xconst	xconst
protestant	0.0132785* (0.0067509)	0.031027*** (0.007739)	0.009939 (0.0076016)	0.031890*** (0.0090671)	0.0109815 (0.0089475)
muslim	-0.031136*** (0.0045969)		-0.03154*** (0.0051524)		-0.03058*** (0.0067178)
catholic		0.019568*** (0.00466)		0.019145*** (0.0056347)	0.0013966 (0.0061622)
malfal94	-2.011171*** (0.6151319)	-2.02049*** (0.7114536)			
me			-0.0992628* (0.0507237)	-0.0959334 (0.0610348)	-0.0976744* (0.0516891)
openk	-0.0034739 (0.0029607)	0.0003524 (0.0033795)			
logfrankrom			0.0731941 (0.2248785)	-0.0271093 (0.2674277)	0.0700139 (0.2274758)
R-sq	0.5312	0.3748	0.5268	0.3274	0.5273
adj. R-sq	0.5032	0.3375	0.4889	0.2735	0.4790
Standard errors in parentheses * *p*<0.10, ** *p*<0.05, *** *p*<0.01					

Table 3.3: continuation regression results

Continuation 1 Table 3.3: First-Stage Regressions for malfal94 and openk					
	(4)	(5)	(6)	(7)	(8)
First-Stage Regression for malfal94					
	malfal94	malfal94	malfal94	malfal94	malfal94
protestant			-0.0002708 (0.0011411)	-0.0004137 (0.0011435)	-0.0000772 (0.0013427)
muslim			0.0003133 (0.0007734)		0.0004921 (0.0010081)
catholic				-0.0000263 (0.0007106)	0.0002593 (0.0009247)
malfal94					
me			0.049746*** (0.007614)	0.050013*** (0.0076972)	0.050041*** (0.0077568)
openk					
logfrankrom			-0.061459** (0.0337559)	-0.0604866* (0.033726)	-0.0620498* (0.0341363)
N					55
R-sq			0.4954	0.4937	0.4962
adj. R-sq			0.4550	0.4532	0.4448
First-Stage Regression for openk					
	openk	openk	openk	openk	openk
protestant			-0.0804346 (0.2505681)	0.0717136 (0.2570871)	-0.1952616 (0.2933571)
muslim			-0.284334 (0.1698359)		-0.3904517* (0.2202536)
catholic				0.0727887 (0.159765)	-0.1538373 (0.2020371)
malfal94					
me			4.285681** (1.671976)	4.132947** (1.730579)	4.110717** (1.694697)
openk					
logfrankrom			39.49943*** (7.412546)	38.60958*** (7.582637)	39.84973*** (7.458096)
N					
R-sq			0.4151	0.3849	0.4219
adj. R-sq			0.3683	0.3357	0.3630
Standard errors in parentheses * $p<0.10$, ** $p<0.05$, *** $p<0.01$					

Table 3.3: continuation regression results

Continuation 2 Table 3.3: Tests					
	(4)	(5)	(6)	(7)	(8)
First-stage F-value (inform4)			14.80	13.07	11.92
First-stage F-value (xconst)			13.91	6.08	10.93
Partial R-squared (inform4)			0.5421	0.5112	0.5487
Partial R-squared (xconst)			0.5268	0.3274	0.5273
Shea Partial R-squared (inform4)			0.3593	0.3394	0.3721
Shea Partial R-squared (xconst)			0.3122	0.1855	0.3229
Pagan-Hall (*p*-value)			0.1592	0.1486	0.1170
Sargan (*p*-value)					0.40526
White-Koen. (*p*-value)			0.0715	0.0913	0.0640

Table 3.4: regression results

Table 3.4 Beta-Coefficients Second-Stage Regression: Dependent Variable is log GDP per capita 2000					
	(4)	(5)	(6)	(7)	(8)
	logrgdpl	logrgdpl	logrgdpl	logrgdpl	logrgdpl
inform4	0.435*** (0.00393)	0.236 (0.00490)	0.367** (0.00360)	0.308* (0.00389)	0.345** (0.00355)
xconst	0.330** (0.0750)	0.706*** (0.115)	0.345** (0.0790)	0.467** (0.107)	0.367** (0.0779)
malfal94	-0.299*** (0.308)	-0.254** (0.387)	-0.457*** (0.439)	-0.438*** (0.466)	-0.454*** (0.440)
openk	0.175** (0.00122)	0.182** (0.00150)	0.207* (0.00204)	0.217* (0.00218)	0.194* (0.00202)
N	72	72	55	55	55
R-sq	0.694	0.542	0.748	0.723	0.746
adj. R-sq	0.676	0.515	0.728	0.701	0.726
Standard errors in parentheses * $p<0.10$, ** $p<0.05$, *** $p<0.01$					

Table 3.5.1: regression results

Table 3.5.1			
Panel A			
	(6)	(7)	(8)
	logrgdpl	logrgdpl	logrgdpl
inform4	0.0094889** (0.0045785)	0.0075245 (0.0050173)	0.0087682* (0.0044858)
xconst	0.1945928** (0.0819317)	0.2846951** (0.1116936)	0.203846** (0.0805763)
malfal94	-2.228658*** (0.5376502)	-2.152575*** (0.579737)	-2.183146*** (0.529676)
openk	0.0043812** (0.00216)	0.0046514* (0.0023407)	0.0041055* (0.0020983)
english	0.6565551** (0.2660942)	0.6754848** (0.2893617)	0.6219092** (0.2613492)
french	0.2283765 (0.2455269)	0.2316959 (0.2653676)	0.1969592 (0.2411923)
N	55	55	55
R-sq	0.7418	0.6990	0.7482
adj. R-sq	0.7095	0.6614	0.7168
Panel B			
	(6)	(7)	(8)
	logrgdpl	logrgdpl	logrgdpl
inform4	0.008841** (0.0036417)	0.0075162* (0.0039005)	0.0082946** (0.0035883)
xconst	0.1838067** (0.0809815)	0.2504497** (0.1111879)	0.1952384** (0.0799616)
malfal94	-1.674253*** (0.4522285)	-1.620561*** (0.4793294)	-1.665716*** (0.4536114)
openk	0.0037066* (0.0021968)	0.0040206 (0.0024029)	0.0034688 (0.0021836)
pop100km	0.0134323 (0.2512838)	-0.061855 (0.2870537)	0.0233186 (0.2518145)
N	55	55	55
R-sq	0.7483	0.7214	0.7466
adj. R-sq	0.7226	0.6930	0.7207
Panel C			
	(6)	(7)	(8)
	logrgdpl	logrgdpl	logrgdpl
inform4	0.0087755** (0.0037577)	0.0074503* (0.0040522)	0.0083239** (0.0037303)
xconst	0.1825715** (0.08044)	0.2490132** (0.107262)	0.1949644** (0.0793047)
malfal94	-1.694253*** (0.4687028)	-1.607031*** (0.4981968)	-1.674253*** (0.4695803)
openk	0.0039155* (0.0020308)	0.0039045* (0.0021287)	0.0037504* (0.0020275)
coastline	1.11e-06 (7.01e-06)	-5.41e-08 (7.48e-06)	1.02e-06 (7.04e-06)
N	55	55	55
R-sq	0.7483	0.7232	0.7467
adj. R-sq	0.7227	0.6949	0.7209

Table 3.5.2: regression results

Table 3.5.2			
Panel D			
	(6)	(7)	(8)
	logrgdpl	logrgdpl	logrgdpl
inform4	0.00891**	0.0076644*	0.0084437**
	(0.0035609)	(0.0038069)	(0.0035162)
xconst	0.1734568**	0.2311892**	0.1836091**
	(0.0784331)	(0.1061646)	(0.0774783)
malfal94	-1.704199***	-1.641676***	-1.701954***
	(0.4393179)	(0.4643527)	(0.4414064)
openk	0.4393179	0.0032403	0.0028494
	(0.0019907)	(0.002126)	(0.0019823)
landlocked	0.3485095	0.3279966	0.3469645
	(0.2550788)	(0.2661393)	(0.2562887)
N	55	55	55
R-sq	0.7588	0.7403	0.7565
adj. R-sq	0.7342	0.7138	0.7316
Panel E			
	(6)	(7)	(8)
	logrgdpl	logrgdpl	logrgdpl
inform4	0.0115617**	0.0108259*	0.0106079**
	(0.0052573)	(0.0054342)	(0.0050568)
xconst	0.1886492**	0.2597326**	0.2002203**
	(0.0842191)	(0.1190618)	(0.0819711)
malfal94	-1.902622***	-1.893423***	-1.86252***
	(0.5216246)	(0.5522283)	(0.5131576)
openk	0.0039582*	0.0042222*	0.0036705*
	(0.0022113)	(0.00243)	(0.0021558)
temperature	0.0232571	0.0299827	0.0201449
	(0.0238961)	(0.0282988)	(0.0232954)
N	55	55	55
R-sq	0.7185	0.6833	0.7249
adj. R-sq	0.6898	0.6509	0.6969
Panel F			
	(6)	(7)	(8)
	logrgdpl	logrgdpl	logrgdpl
inform4	0.0097821**	0.0074649	0.0089669**
	(0.0042433)	(0.0046714)	(0.0041732)
xconst	0.2011776**	0.3036175**	0.2230783**
	(0.0942365)	(0.1273722)	(0.0919103)
openk	0.0067656**	0.006862**	0.0061272**
	(0.002712)	(0.0028934)	(0.0026432)
N	56	56	56
R-sq	0.6325	0.5886	0.6319
adj. R-sq	0.6113	0.5649	0.6106

Table 3.6: data definitions and sources

control	Percentage of respondents who chose a score of 7–10 in response to the question 'Some people feel they have completely free choice and control over their lives, while other people feel that what they do has no real effect on what happens to them. Please use this scale were 1 means "none at all" and 10 means "a great deal" to indicate how much freedom of choice and control you feel you have over the way your life turns out.' Accessed at www.worldvaluessurvey.org on October 27, 2009.
trust	Percentage of respondents who answer that 'Most people can be trusted' to the question 'Generally speaking, would you say that most people can be trusted or that you need to be very careful in dealing with people?' (other possible answers are 'Can't be too careful' and 'Don't know'). Accessed at www.worldvaluessurvey.org on October 27, 2009.
respect	Percentage of respondents who mention 'Tolerance and respect for other people' when asked the following question: 'Here is a list of child qualities that children can be encouraged to learn at home. Which, if any, do you consider to be especially important? Please choose up to five.' Possible answers are: 'Independence, hard work, feeling of responsibility, imagination, tolerance and respect for other people, thrift, saving money and things, determination and perseverance, religious faith, unselfishness, obedience.' Accessed at www.worldvaluessurvey.org on October 27, 2009.
obedience	Percentage of respondents who mention 'Obedience' when asked the following question: 'Here is a list of child qualities that children can be encouraged to learn at home. Which, if any, do you consider to be especially important? Please choose up to five.' Possible answers are: 'Independence, hard work, feeling of responsibility, imagination, tolerance and respect for other people, thrift, saving money and things, determination and perseverance, religious faith, unselfishness, obedience.' Accessed at www.worldvaluessurvey.org on October 27, 2009.
inform4	Sum of *trust*, *respect* and *control* minus *obedience*.
xconst	Extent of institutionalized constraints on the executive. The variable ranges from a score of (1) 'Unlimited authority' to (7) 'Executive parity or subordination'. Source: Jaggers and Marshall (2005); accessed at http://www.systemicpeace.org/polity/polity4.htm on October 27, 2009.
malfal94	Proportion of each country's population that live with the risk of malaria transmission multiplied by an estimate of the proportion of malaria cases that involve *Plasmodium falciparum*. Source: Sachs (2003); accessed at http://www.earth.columbia.edu/articles/view/1040 on October 27, 2009.
openk	Exports plus imports divided by rgdpl. Source: Heston, Summers and Aten (2006); accessed at http://pwt.econ.upenn.edu/ on October 27, 2009.
rgdpl	Real GDP per capita (Laspeyres). Source: Heston, Summers and Aten (2006); accessed at http://pwt.econ.upenn.edu/ on October 27, 2009.
me	Instrumental variable for malaria risk. Source: Sachs (2003); accessed at http://www.earth.columbia.edu/articles/view/1040 on October 27, 2009.
logfrankrom	Natural logarithm of the Frankel–Romer predicted trade share. Source: Hall and Jones (1999); accessed at http://elsa.berkeley.edu/~chad/datasets.html on October 27, 2009.

protestant	Percentage of the population being Protestant. Source: La Porta et al. (1999); accessed at http://mba.tuck.dartmouth.edu/pages/faculty/rafael.laporta/publications.html on October 27, 2009.
muslim	Percentage of the population being Muslim. Source: La Porta et al. (1999); accessed at http://mba.tuck.dartmouth.edu/pages/faculty/rafael.laporta/publications.html on October 27, 2009.
catholic	Percentage of the population being Catholic. Source: La Porta et al. (1999); accessed at http://mba.tuck.dartmouth.edu/pages/faculty/rafael.laporta/publications.html on October 27, 2009.
french	Dummy variable for French legal origin. Source: La Porta et al. (1999); accessed at http://mba.tuck.dartmouth.edu/pages/faculty/rafael.laporta/publications.html on October 27, 2009.
english	Dummy variable for English legal origin. Source: La Porta et al. (1999); accessed at http://mba.tuck.dartmouth.edu/pages/faculty/rafael.laporta/publications.html on October 27, 2009.
pop100km	Share of the national population living within 100 km of the coast. Source: Sachs (2003); accessed at http://www.earth.columbia.edu/articles/view/1040 on October 27, 2009.
latitude	Latitude in absolute degrees. Source: Parker (1997); accessed at http://faculty.insead.edu/parker/resume/personal.htm on October 27, 2009.
coastline	Coastline length in kilometers. Source: Parker (1997); accessed at http://faculty.insead.edu/parker/resume/personal.htm on October 27, 2009.
landlocked	Dummy variable for landlocked. Source: Parker (1997); accessed at http://faculty.insead.edu/parker/resume/personal.htm on October 27, 2009.

4. Institutions and economic development in the MENA region

4.1 Introduction

The first part of this dissertation project deals with the general impact of institutions on economic development. However, the second part aims to demonstrate the significance of the general findings with a case study on the Arab region.

It was demonstrated empirically that informal and formal institutions influence the level of per capita income. The significance and complexity of the institutional system lead to several connections and feedbacks between institutions themselves and institutions and other factors, which make institutional change a complex and difficult task. However, to demonstrate the relevance of these results, a case study is carried out on a region that differs from the economically successful countries of the Western hemisphere in two respects: first, the Arab region exhibits a worse economic growth performance than Western industrialized countries and, second, the Arab region exhibits different institutions compared with Western states. Therefore, it will be examined whether the economic performance of Arab countries correlates with its institutional quality and, hence, whether the general findings of the first part of the study can be applied to real world developments.

Furthermore, the institutional development of the Arab region is examined. It was argued that institutional emergence and development exhibit a dynamic process. Nevertheless, several institutions are inertial and marginal change is hardly observable in a human's lifetime. This means that history and path dependence play important roles in institutional development. Historical events that occurred in ancient times can still impact the current institutional environment through several transmission channels, complementarities, institutional inertia, and path dependence. Therefore, it will be examined whether accidents in Arab history influenced institutional quality in the long run.

In particular, those institutions characterized as being growth relevant in the first part will be examined concerning their implementation in the Arab world. Property rights, the rule of law, political participation, civil liberties, business regulations, and the levels of trust, control, and the concept of generalized and limited morality in the Arab region will be examined inter alia. However, corresponding to the results of the previous empirical analysis, institutional quality in the Arab region should be crucial for its economic development. Hence, institutions in the Arab region should be growth inhibiting rather than growth supporting.

Nine years after the terror attacks of 09/11/2001, public discussion about differences between the Islamic world and the Western hemisphere continues.

However, differences can be observed in cultural and religious as well as economic patterns. Therefore, GDP per capita and thereby living standards differ significantly. Thus, it is an obvious question to ask whether a connection between different cultures and the corresponding development patterns exists. Hence, can Arab economic backwardness be traced back to its culture and the corresponding institutions, and is the institutional quality of the West responsible for its economic success?

However, first a regional definition is necessary. The above passage mentioned the Islamic world and the Arab region, which are not equal. Of course, Islam is the main religion and a determining cultural factor of the Arab region. However, Islam is also widespread in parts of Europe, Asia, and Sub-Saharan Africa. Indonesia, for example, exhibits the world's most populous Muslim majority. Islam is the state religion not only in Middle Eastern and North African countries, but also in Bangladesh and Malaysia, for example. Islamic states, that is, states in which Islam builds the ideological foundation for political and societal life in general, are, inter alia, Afghanistan, Brunei, and Pakistan. Hence, Islam and 'Arabic' should not be equalized. However, the aim of the dissertation project is not to examine the effects of a particular religion on economic development. Instead, culture as an institution is emphasized. Culture does not merely consist of religious features. Geographical proximity, language, traditions, and a shared morality are also binding determinants. In fact, the Arab language plays an important role in Arab culture and identity. Arabic is the language in which the Quran was originally written. It connects a region ranging from North-Western Africa through West Asia. Islamic countries in Eastern Europe or South-East Asia can exhibit significantly different cultural influences to Arab countries, although they share the same religion. Relevant factors such as history, geographical proximity, language, and so forth differ decisively compared with Arab countries.

However, in the current study the region that is culturally and historically described as 'Arabic' is emphasized. This region is usually called MENA, that is, the countries of the Middle East and North Africa. The corresponding countries are, in some way, connected through history, culture, language, and, of course, Islam. The World Bank defines MENA as Algeria, Bahrain, Djibouti, Egypt, Iran, Iraq, Jordan, Kuwait, Lebanon, Libya, Morocco, Oman, Qatar, Saudi Arabia, Syria, Tunisia, the UAE, West Bank and Gaza, and Yemen. Iran is included although Arabic is not its official language. Nevertheless, other cultural and historical determinants justify its inclusion. This is even more the case since other countries in which Arabic is the official state language are excluded from in the definition.[40] Particular countries can be added to an African rather than an Arab culture even though Arabic is one of the official state languages.

Hence, to draw a clear borderline between the Arab region and its neighboring regions is difficult. The current study, however, adopts a more pragmatic approach. That is to say, the broadest definition of MENA corresponds to the World Bank's definition. Since data on one or other relevant country are usually missing, the analysis will not always include all countries in question. An historical analysis, on the contrary, emanates from a broader definition of the Arab region. Depending on the observed period, the 'Arab region' depicts the corresponding area at that time. Since a culture does not stop at a certain borderline, behind which a new culture begins, the current study does not have a strict definition of the MENA region but incorporates countries for which an inclusion seems to make sense.

Furthermore, it should be emphasized that the countries of the MENA region are not assumed to be identical. On the contrary, Arab countries exhibit great heterogeneity in many respects. Even cultural determinants, and thereby traditions, codes of conduct, habits, and so on, might differ. Nevertheless, differences are not as large as they are between MENA, and, for example, Western industrialized states. Despite its internal heterogeneity, MENA depicts one cohesive cultural area. Its main similarities are based on history, religion, language, and societal organization.

Some MENA countries vary significantly regarding their economic performances. This is the case because the MENA region includes resource-poor countries with large indigenous populations as well as oil-rich states with small indigenous populations, such as the UAE, Qatar, or Bahrain. For example, 2006 per capita income in Yemen accounted for USD 551.37, whereas per capita income in the UAE amounted to USD 25,192.33.[41] Thus, economically, MENA should not be treated as a homogeneous group, even though many dependencies and complementarities inhibit a clear separation. According to the World Bank classification, the MENA countries can be separated into three groups:

- RPLA (resource-poor, labor-abundant economies): Djibouti, Egypt, Jordan, Lebanon, Morocco, Tunisia, West Bank and Gaza;
- RRLA (resource-rich, labor-abundant economies): Algeria, Iran, Iraq, Syria, Yemen;
- RRLI (resource-rich, labor-importing countries): Bahrain, Kuwait, Libya, Oman, Qatar, Saudi Arabia, the UAE.

---

[40] These countries are Chad, Comoros, Eritrea, Israel, Mauritania, Somalia, and Sudan. Some of these countries possess two or more official state languages.
[41] GDP per capita in constant 2000 US dollars; data retrieved July 2, 2009, from the World Bank WDI database.

4.2 Arab economic performance

Figure 4.1 demonstrates the per capita income development of the MENA region compared with high-income country groups since 1965.[42] The high-income country groups exhibit constant growth in GDP per capita over the whole period. By comparison, per capita income in the MENA region has on average stagnated since 1965. Hence, per capita income divergence is observable between the MENA region and high-income country groups. Neither the convergence of per capita income levels nor the convergence of the per capita income growth rates occurs. The predictions of the neoclassical growth model, however, seem not to apply to the Arab countries on average. MENA countries, although poor compared with high-income countries, do not benefit from their potential to catch up. On the contrary, they are falling further behind high-income countries in per capita income levels.

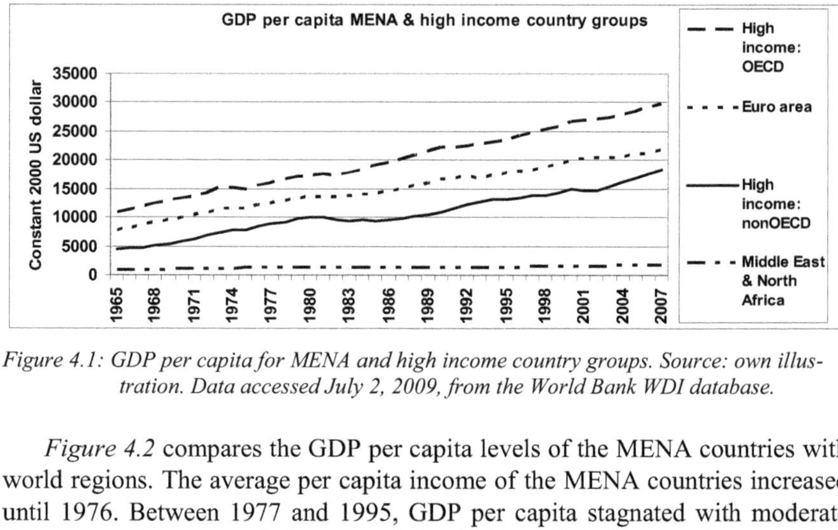

Figure 4.1: GDP per capita for MENA and high income country groups. Source: own illustration. Data accessed July 2, 2009, from the World Bank WDI database.

Figure 4.2 compares the GDP per capita levels of the MENA countries with world regions. The average per capita income of the MENA countries increased until 1976. Between 1977 and 1995, GDP per capita stagnated with moderate decreases and increases in between. After 1995, a slight increase is observable. Since 2000, income divergence is also observable between MENA and Europe and Central Asia. East Asia, however, started at a significantly lower income level than MENA in 1965, but its GDP per capita has increased constantly and will probably catch up to the MENA countries in the near future. Sub-Saharan Africa and South Asia have considerably lower per capita income levels than the

[42] GDP per capita in constant 2000 US dollars; data retrieved July 2, 2009, from the World Bank WDI database. The World Bank classification of the country groups can be found in Appendix B.

MENA region during the whole period. However, since GDP per capita stagnated in Sub-Saharan Africa for more than 40 years, South Asia at least realized moderate growth.

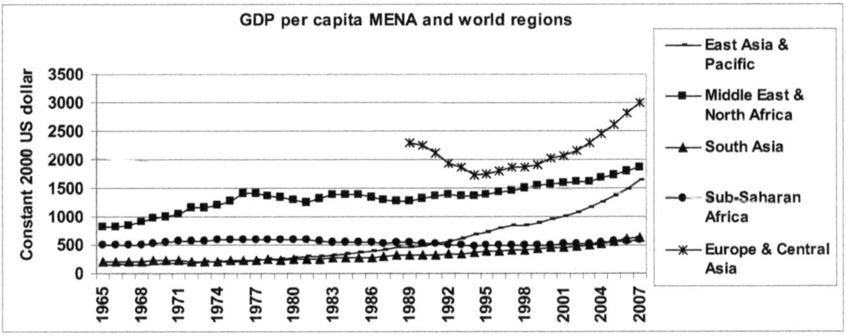

Figure 4.2: GDP per capita for MENA and world regions. Source: own illustration. Data accessed July 2, 2009, from the WDI database.

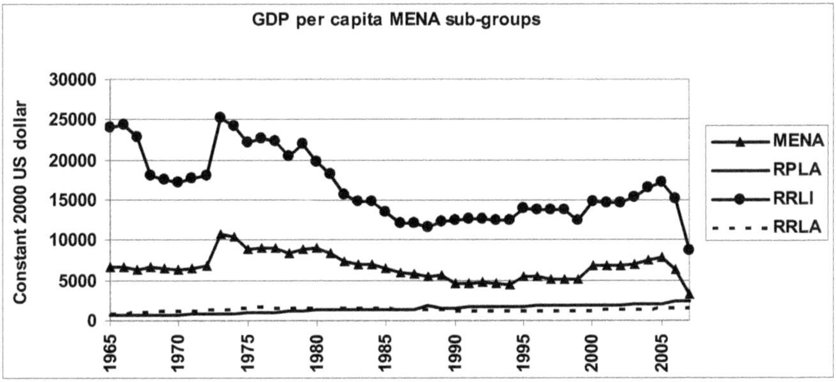

Figure 4.3: GDP per capita for the MENA subgroups. Source: own illustration. Data accessed July 2, 2009, from the WDI database.

Figure 4.3 demonstrates GDP per capita in constant 2000 US dollars for MENA and its three subgroups in the period between 1965 and 2007. However, data are not available for every country at all points in time. Therefore, at any point in time, the available GDP per capita data were added and divided by the corresponding number of countries. For example in 1965, data on eight countries were available. Between 1999 and 2005, data on 18 countries were available, and so on. Hence, at some points in time, average GDP per capita is calculated for only a few countries, whereas at others it is calculated for almost all

MENA countries. Of course, this method is unusual and distorts the results. However, it is the only way to achieve a long run data series for the MENA subgroups. Some highs and lows might, therefore, be exaggerated since the data points might depend only on a few countries that experienced extreme values at that time.

The oil boom at the beginning of the 1960s led to a sharp increase in average per capita incomes in the RRLI countries and, hence, in the region on average. Further increases occurred in 1973 and 1974. This reflects the fact that MENA's, and especially the Arab oil producers', income levels depend mainly on developments on international oil markets. However, since the mid-1970s GDP per capita in the MENA region declined dramatically, which can be attributed to the even more dramatic decline in the RRLI countries and the almost stagnant development in the RRLA and RPLA countries. The RRLA countries realized a moderate increase in GDP per capita between 1965 and 1977. Afterwards, per capita income remained stagnant. The average per capita income of the RPLA countries remains at very low levels during the whole period. However, despite a short decline at the end of the 1980s, income steadily increased from 539.37 US dollars in 1960 to 2389.95 US dollars in 2007. Nevertheless, since we are observing a time span of almost 50 years, the increase in per capita income of the RPLA countries is moderate indeed. Since the 2000s, MENA's GDP per capita has increased slightly. The decline after 2005 must be considered carefully since data on several high- and middle income countries were not available for 2006 and 2007.[43] However, although income has increased since the mid-1990s, it has never reached the high levels of the oil boom period.

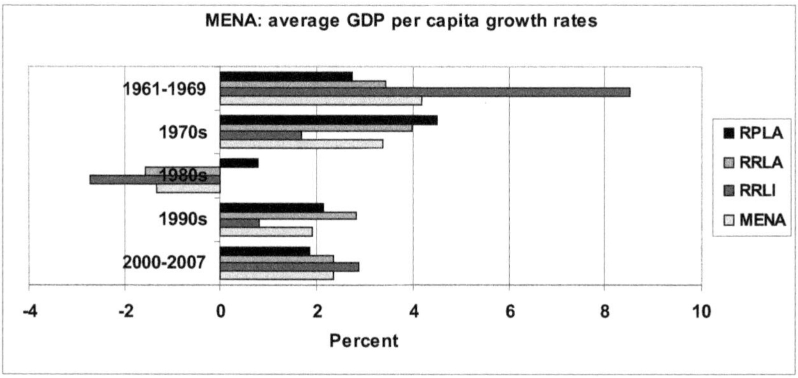

Figure 4.4: MENA average GDP per capita growth rates. Source: own illustration. Data accessed July 2, 2009, from the WDI database.

[43] Bahrain (2006 & 2007), Kuwait (2007), Oman (2007), Qatar (2006 & 2007), the UAE (2007).

Figure 4.4 demonstrates the development of per capita income growth rates from 1961 to 2007. GDP per capita growth rates are highly volatile because of the region's dependence on oil prices.[44] However, MENA average growth rates peaked in 1972. In the 1980s, growth rates deteriorated and became negative on average. In the 1990s, a marginal recovery occurred. However, growth rates remained volatile and reached an average level of 3.05 percent in 2007.

MENA belongs to the group of world regions that has been unable to catch up to industrialized countries in recent decades. While the industrialized world has exhibited constant growth over the past 50 years, MENA has nearly stagnated, at least since 1980. The higher growth rates at the beginning of the 2000s can almost completely be traced back to high energy prices on world markets.

Compared with less developed regions, MENA's growth performance might look less alarming at the first glance. However, MENA's moderate growth depicts a severe problem, since almost no progress has been observable for decades. Although the region of East Asia and the Pacific started from a significantly lower level of per capita income in the 1960s, it now exhibits higher growth rates and will overhaul the MENA average income levels soon. Apart from that, only Sub-Saharan Africa and South Asia perform worse than MENA. However, MENA will face enormous social and economic problems if its growth performance does not improve dramatically in the near future (Cornelius & Schwab, 2003; Sala-i-Martin & Artadi, 2003; Yousef, 2004).

4.3 Economic development in the second half of the 20th century

After the Great Depression of the 1930s and the consequent breakdown of the international economic order the role of the state was expanded, not only in MENA countries, but on a worldwide level. The development model, which was enforced in the MENA countries from the 1940s until the 1970s, involved state planning, import substitution, agrarian reform programs, the nationalization of

[44] The enormous growth rates of the RRLI countries at the end of the 1960s are down to Oman, which exhibited growth rates of 61.58 percent and 76.56 percent in 1967 and 1968, respectively. However, even without Oman the RRLI countries' growth rates accounted for 2.38 percent in 1967, 9.36 percent in 1968, 4.39 percent in 1969, and 7.61 percent in 1970. The sharp decline in 1989 as well as the increase in growth rates in 1990 in the RPLA countries can be traced back to developments in Lebanon, where 15 years of civil war came to an end in 1990. The data record for Lebanon starts in 1989, where the GDP per capita growth rate is quoted as –42.88 percent. Lebanese growth rates then increased to 24.27 percent in 1990 and 34.62 percent in 1991. Data retrieved July 2, 2009, from the World Bank WDI database.

private and foreign assets, the state provision of education, housing, and health care, food subsidies, centralized trade unions, and the establishment of authoritarian political regimes (Yousef, 2004, p. 92). Emphasis was placed on physical capital accumulation. Infrastructure was expanded through large public investments and health and social security systems were implemented. Many social indicators were notably improved. For example, infant mortality declined, life expectancy increased, school enrolment levels improved, and literacy rates increased. Workers were provided with lifelong job guarantees in the public sector or in state-owned firms. This development strategy relied on a strong public sector and physical capital accumulation. The private sector as well as human capital was not equally promoted. Nevertheless, in the 1960s the MENA region exhibited an average growth rate of GDP per worker of six percent, which accounted for some of the highest growth rates worldwide (Yousef, 2004).

However, in MENA the general trend to centralize economic planning met the problematic phase of nation building, which occurred after the colonial powers had withdrawn. All that remained were nation states whose borders had been drawn arbitrarily and which were suddenly reigned by the weak governments appointed by the colonial powers. This opened space for political insecurity and instability, which, in turn, led to the implementation of elaborate control and security apparatuses. Political, intellectual, and labor movements were monitored and opposition in one form or another was oppressed. In many Arab states, the military was strongly involved in politics, which was justified by the permanent threat of political insecurity.

A further decisive factor that shaped the development of the MENA region in the second half of the 20th century was the large-scale exploration of oil after the Second World War. The oil revenues afforded the particular development of the Arab countries, even if they were not endowed with natural resources themselves.

Oil revenues were crucial in several ways:

1) Oil revenues were distributed among Arab countries, even among the non-oil countries, through a complex system of rents and workers' remittances. Hence, resource-poor countries also benefited from oil exploitation. Workers of the RPLA countries were employed in the oil industries of resource-rich economies and sent home significant amounts of remittances. Jordan, for example, received workers' remittances and the compensation of employees amounting to 25 percent of GDP in 1976 and 22 percent of GDP on average between 1976 and 1986. Remittances still play an important role for the RPLA and RRLA countries. Yemen, for example, obtained an average of 21 percent of its GDP as workers' remittances between 1990 and 2000. West Bank and Gaza received an average of 18 percent of GDP between 1994 and 2005, and Lebanon received an average of 19 percent of GDP in the period

between 2000 and 2007. Jordan also received high workers' remittances between 1995 and 2007, an average of 22 percent of GDP. Egypt obtained workers' remittances amounting to an average of 11 percent of GDP between 1978 and 1994. Afterwards, Egyptian remittances declined to an average of four percent of GDP between 1995 and 2007.[45]

2) The redistribution of oil revenues to MENA citizens occurred via public sector employment and subsidies (for example, subsidies for fuel, electricity, food, health, and education). Hence, oil revenues made an efficient private sector unnecessary. The incomes permitted the state to finance social security systems and employ its citizens. According to Yousef (2004, p. 96): "The welfare gains also helped to cement an "authoritarian bargain," with citizens of the Middle East effectively trading restrictions on political participation in exchange for economic security and the public provision of social services and welfare". That is to say, the people of the MENA region sold their political rights in exchange for jobs and subsidies. Oil revenues enabled the perpetuation of authoritarian governments and additionally, large security and military apparatuses could be financed (Askari, 2006). Furthermore, stable revenues from oil exploration enabled income distribution, the allocation of social security, further governmental services, and public goods without the establishment of a system of income taxation. Hence, most MENA countries do not have an efficient tax system.

The deployment of oil revenues and the interventionist-redistributive development system led to growth rates of approximately six percent per worker per year in the 1960s (Yousef, 2004). However, although the one-dimensional growth strategy that relied on physical capital accumulation, oil revenues, and foreign aid ensured temporary economic success, it had serious consequences in the long run.

In the 1980s, declining oil prices and increasing international competition revealed the weaknesses of the development strategy. The economic performance of the oil exporting economies largely depends on developments in international oil markets. Hence, the decrease in energy prices at the beginning of the 1980s led to a decline in demand for migrant labor. The falling oil prices also affected resource-poor states, whose balances of payments depended on workers' remittances employed in oil-rich states. Declining oil prices and decreasing remittances meant that the states had trouble financing public sector wages and subsidies. Hence, public debts increased strongly and macroeconomic balances eroded in the 1980s.

Furthermore, the highly regulated business environment in MENA countries, the well-protected state-owned enterprises, and the large bureaucratic sector inhibited private and foreign investment and prevented the development of

[45] Data retrieved July 2, 2009, from the World Bank WDI database.

competitive, export-oriented industries. As a result, physical capital accumulation fell by 75 percent per worker in the 1980s (Yousef, 2004). The RRLI countries exhibited an average growth rate of GDP per capita of –2.7 percent between 1980 and 1989. Growth in the RRLA economies also became negative (–1.6 percent on average). The RPLA countries only grew by 0.8 percent per year during the 1980s.[46] Furthermore, total factor productivity (TFP) growth in the region declined and became negative (Sala-i-Martin & Artadi, 2003; Yousef, 2004). Decreasing growth rates met an increasing working age population and, therefore, yielded high unemployment rates. MENA experienced one of the worst growth performances worldwide in the 1980s.

In the mid-1980s, most MENA countries undertook policy reforms to stabilize their economies. Therefore, subsidies and public expenditures were reduced and exchange rate regimes were reformed. In fact, in the early 1990s, debt levels had decreased, inflation was under control, and economic performance had been stabilized in most MENA countries. However, despite macroeconomic successes reform efforts were insufficient and not qualified to solve the structural deficiencies. Additionally, external factors such as volatilities in oil prices and agricultural production led to a weak economic performance of the MENA countries in the 1990s in general with average GDP growth rates of 4.44 percent (RRLA), 4.40 percent (RPLA), and 5.10 percent (RRLI).[47]

Although the 1990s brought a slight recovery, the general trend of GDP per capita in the period between 1975 and 2000 was downwards. In the 2000s, especially the RRLI countries, exhibited increasing growth rates, mainly after 2003/2004. Although some countries further conducted economic reform efforts, for example Saudi Arabia, the improved growth rates of the oil exporters can again be traced back to developments on the energy markets. The RPLA countries further achieved moderate but constant growth rates in the 2000s. Data for 2008/2009 and thereby for the period of the worldwide financial crisis are not yet available.

4.4 Total factor productivity

One of MENA's most significant problems, however, is the general inefficiency of its economy. Despite high investment in physical capital accumulation in the 1960s and 1970s, TFP growth in the region declined steadily. According to Sala-i-Martin and Artadi (2003, p. 29), average TFP growth between 1975 and 2000

[46] GDP per capita in constant 2000 US dollars. Data retrieved July 2, 2009, from the World Bank WDI database.

[47] GDP per capita in constant 2000 US dollars. Data retrieved July 2, 2009, from the World Bank WDI database. The RRLA country group excludes Iraq and the RPLA country group excludes West Bank and Gaza.

was negative for Algeria, Bahrain, Jordan, Kuwait, Lebanon, Morocco, Qatar, Saudi Arabia, and the UAE. Egypt, Oman, Syria, and Tunisia realized positive TFP growth during the period, although the average TFP growth rates per year were below two percent. Yousef (2004, p. 97) demonstrates average TFP growth per laborer in the MENA region between 1960 and 2000. Accordingly, the region exhibited an average TFP growth of 3.4 percent in the 1960s, –1 percent in the 1970s, –1.5 percent in the 1980s, and –0.2 percent in the 1990s. Only Sub-Saharan Africa performed equally bad. South Asia, Latin America and the Caribbean, and the OECD countries exhibited only one decade of negative TFP growth during this period, and East Asia and the Pacific showed positive TFP growth rates throughout (Yousef, 2004).

Hakura (2004) calculates TFP growth for some MENA countries using the growth accounting method. She finds that TFP growth in the observed MENA countries declined by an average of one percent per year between 1980 and 2000. The decline of the non-oil countries in her study (Egypt, Jordan, Morocco, Syria, Tunisia) accounts for –0.15 percent, whereas the decline in oil countries (Algeria, Iran, Kuwait) is –1.86 percent per year.

The Arab Human Development Report 2002 calculates the labor productivity of the MENA region as a percentage of the North American level in constant 1985 US dollars. Accordingly, industrial labor productivity per worker in the MENA region deteriorated from 32 percent of the North American level in 1970 to 25 percent in 1980 and 19 percent in 1990 (p. 87f.). Therefore, the MENA region must improve its general economic efficiency to generate growth and employ its increasing working age population (Dyer & Yousef, 2007; Yousef, 2004).

4.5 Investment

Because of its disappointing growth performance, one would expect investment rates in the MENA region to be low. However, this is not true. The gross fixed capital formation as a percentage of GDP is higher than in most other observed regions in the 2000s, apart from East Asia and Pacific and South Asia. Nevertheless, *table 4.1* shows that gross fixed capital formation as a percentage of GDP declined from 30.48 in 1983 to 21.92 in 2000. Since 2001 a slight recovery is observable.

Public expenditures account for a large part of general investment. Private indigenous investment as well as foreign direct investment (FDI) is hampered by the regulatory environment, inefficient bureaucracies, and political instability and insecurity. FDI inflows are not only desirable because of the potential increase in physical capital, FDI also implies a transfer of knowledge, skills, and technology. Hence, regulations restricting FDI flows limit a country's possibility to accumulate capital as well as technology and knowledge.

Table 4.1: gross fixed capital formation as a percentage of GDP. Source: own illustration. Data accessed July 2, 2009, from the WDI database.

Gross fixed capital formation as a percentage of GDP			
	1980s	1990s	2000–2007
East Asia and Pacific	28.27	31.86	34.08
Euro area	21.87	20.90	20.59
OECD	22.34	21.15	20.42
Latin America and Caribbean	20.15	18.93	18.49
MENA	26.93	23.27	22.94
South Asia	19.63	21.90	26.01
Sub-Saharan Africa	20.12	17.03	17.86

The investment environment in the MENA region can be depicted with data on *Investment Freedom* from the Index of Economic Freedom 2009 (*figures 4.5* and *4.6*). This variable measures a country's investment climate regarding foreign and internal capital flows. Hence, it can be examined whether a special code exists that determines laws and procedures on FDI, how far the government encourages FDI, whether restrictions on access to foreign exchange exist, whether foreign and domestic firms are treated equally, whether capital transactions are restricted, and whether FDI is allowed in all industries (Miller & Holmes, 2009, p. 446).

Except for Jordan, Morocco, and Tunisia, all MENA countries exhibit scores equal to or below 50. Although the investment climate in Bahrain, Kuwait, Libya, Oman, Saudi Arabia, Syria, and Yemen improved between 1999 and 2009, it deteriorated in Jordan, Lebanon, Morocco, Qatar, and Tunisia and stagnated in the remaining countries. The average level of *Investment Freedom* in MENA countries amounted to 42 in 1999 and 43 in 2009. Hence, almost no improvement is observable on average in the region. The selected advanced economies exhibited an average level of *Investment Freedom* of 64 in 1999 and 72 in 2009.

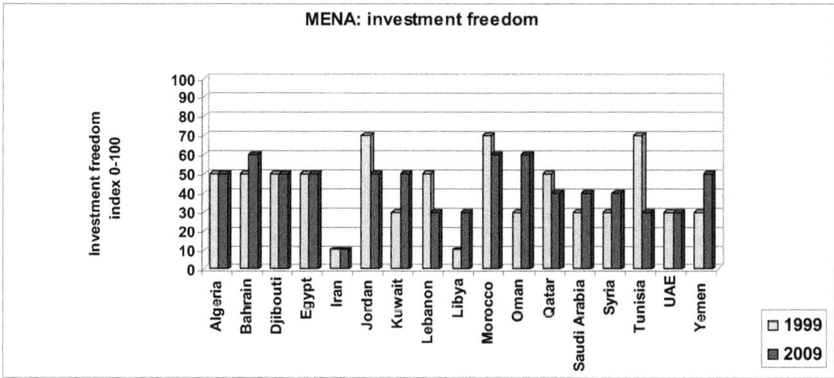

Figure 4.5: investment freedom in the MENA region. Source: own illustration. Data accessed March 10, 2010, from the Heritage Foundation [online], Index of Economic Freedom 2009.

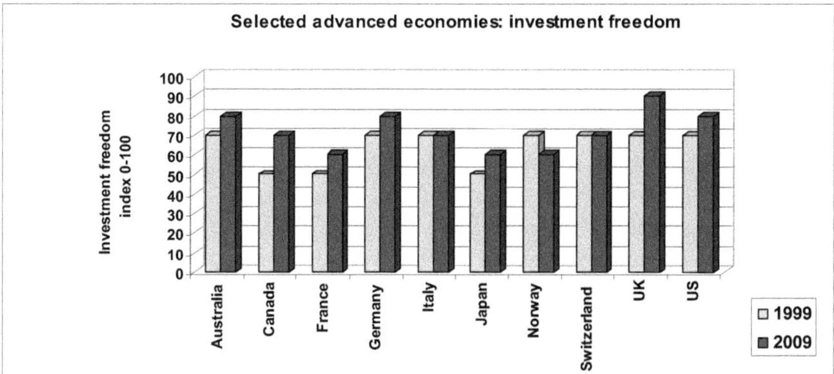

Figure 4.6: investment freedom in advanced economies. Source: own illustration. Data accessed March 10, 2010, from the Heritage Foundation [online], Index of Economic Freedom 2009.

Figure 4.7 demonstrates average FDI inflows in millions of US dollars at current prices. MENA FDI inflows have almost stagnated at a low level since 1973. However, after 2003 all MENA countries, but especially the RRLI and RPLA countries, have exhibited an increase in FDI inflows. Nevertheless, the development of FDI inflows is disappointing compared with the selected advanced economies, which exhibited averages of 1,952 million US dollars between 1973 and 1979, 6,705 million US dollars in the 1980s, 18,745 million US dollars in the 1990s, and 48,908 million US dollars between 2000 and 2007.[48]

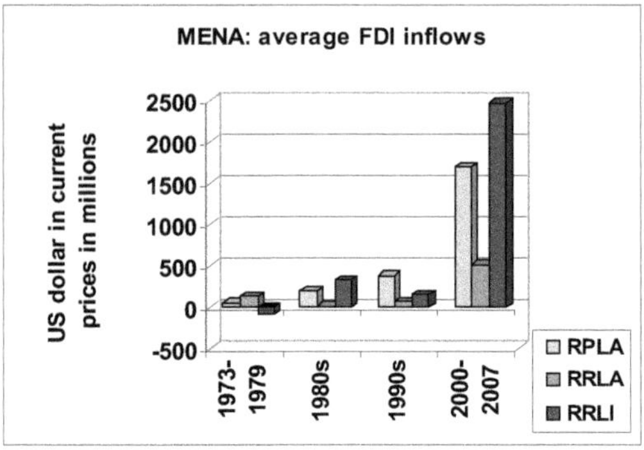

Figure 4.7: MENA average FDI inflows. Source: own illustration. Data accessed July 2, 2009, from the WDI database.

4.6 Public sector

The public sector plays a dominant role in MENA countries. Public investment is high, the state owns most of the firms and thereby is the main employer. *Figure 4.8* presents the government share of the RGDPL of the MENA countries and advanced economies between 1979 and 2003.[49] As can be seen, the MENA country groups exhibit higher government shares of real GDP per capita compared with the advanced economies (except for RRLI in the 1970s). The RRLA countries realized their highest government shares between 1980 and 1995. Even after 1995, the share remained at over 27 percent of real GDP per capita. The RRLI countries possessed a moderate government share until 1980. Then, the government share increased and culminated in 1991 with 32 percent of GDP per capita. After 1991, the RRLI government share declined significantly to under 20 percent. Unfortunately, the data do not cover the years after 2003. The government share of real GDP per capita of the RPLA countries has been above 25 percent since 1970. Development has been relatively constant compared with other MENA country groups. Only in 1991 was a sharp increase observable, which can be traced back to events in Lebanon. However, after 1994 the gov-

[48] US dollars in current prices.

[49] RGDPL is real GDP per capita generated by using the Laspeyres method. The data are taken from the Penn World Tables 6.2 (Heston, Summers & Aten (2006); accessed at http://pwt.econ.upenn.edu/ on October 27, 2009).

ernment share of RPLA countries decreased and remained slightly above 20 percent.

Sala-i-Martin and Artadi (2003) show that the private-to-public investment ratio in the 1980s and 1990s was significantly lower in the MENA region compared with OECD countries and East Asia. The Arab oil countries, however, exhibited the worst ratios with 1.4 in the 1980s and 1.7 in the 1990s. The Arab non-oil economies realized a ratio of private-to-public investment of 1.8 in the 1980s and 3.0 in the 1990s. By comparison, the ratio of the OECD countries accounted for 5.7 in the 1980s and 6.6 in the 1990s. In East Asia, the ratio rose from 4.8 in the 1980s to 5.1 in the 1990s. Hence, although improvements in the ratio of private-to-public investment are observable over time, the MENA countries perform worse than the OECD economies and East Asia, which, by the way, also improved their ratios between the 1980s and 1990s.

Furthermore, Yousef (2004, p. 103) demonstrates that, in the 1990s, government employment as a percentage of total employment was highest in the MENA region with just below 18 percent compared with the OECD economies, Eastern Europe and the former USSR, Sub-Saharan Africa, and Latin America. Of course, government wages as a percentage of GDP were also highest in the MENA region with just below 10 percent in the 1990s.

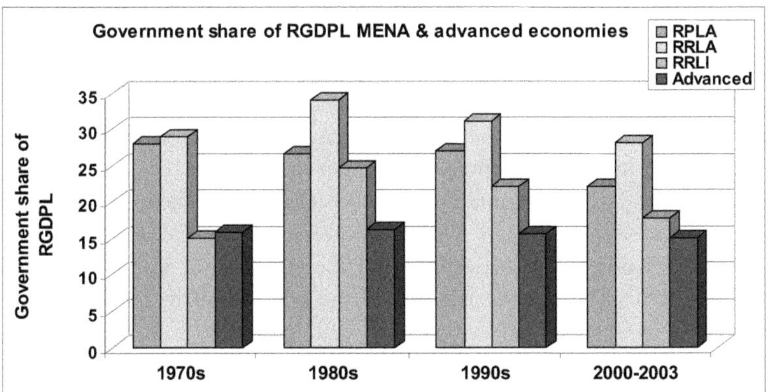

Figure 4.8: government share of RGDPL. Source: own illustration. Data accessed October, 2009, [online] from the Penn World Tables 6.2.

4.7 Demography and education

A decisive development factor is MENA's demography. In 2007, the total population of the MENA region accounted for 319,586,985 people compared to 102,600,124 people in 1960.[50]
[51]

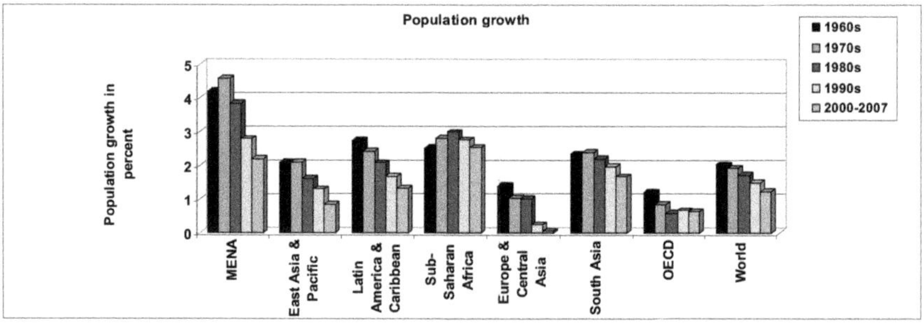

Figure 4.9: population growth. Source: own illustration. Data accessed July 2, 2009, from the World Bank WDI database.

Figure 4.9 demonstrates the average population growth rates from 1960 to 2007. Between 1960 and 1979, MENA exhibited an average population growth rate of 4.4 percent per year and thereby obtained the highest population growth rates worldwide. Although population growth has declined since 1980, MENA still lies above other world regions and the world average. Only Sub-Saharan Africa has exhibited higher population growth rates since 1994. Given that MENA realized its highest population growth rates in the 1960s and 1970s, and that growth rates have remained above two percent since then, the MENA labor markets are under enormous pressure. The percentage of the working age population (aged 15–64) in the MENA region increased from 52.5 in the 1960s to 63.9 in the 2000s. Thirty-one percent of the population in the MENA region were aged 0–14 in 2007 and this group will gradually join the working age population in the forthcoming years. According to the Arab World Competitiveness Report 2002–2003, the total population of the MENA region will amount to 470 million in 2025 and 654 million in 2050 (UNFPA, 2003, p. 36).[52] Yousef (2004) calculates that to meet the present and forthcoming labor supply, the 2004 level of employment must double within two decades or that, within the next 15 years, as many new jobs must be created as was done in the past 50 years (p. 102).

---

[50] The calculation for 2007 excludes Iraq because of data unavailability.
[51] The calculation for 1960 excludes West Bank & Gaza because of data unavailability.
[52] The definition of the MENA region might vary slightly in this report compared with the definition of the current study.

However, economic decline and increasing public debt in the 1980s hit the public sector as the main employer. Furthermore, the disappointing economic performance of the 1980s and 1990s led to a decrease in labor exports to the Gulf states. Hence, unemployment in the labor-abundant countries grew and, at the same time, workers' remittances declined. Therefore, the public sectors were unable to employ the workers that usually would have worked in the Gulf states and sent home parts of their wages. More and more educated first-time job-seekers became unemployed, since the public sector could no longer absorb the enormous quantity of labor supply. Furthermore, the development of the private sector as an alternative employment strategy had been oppressed systematically since the 1950s. Hence, unemployment in the MENA region has increased significantly since 1980.

Although the education systems of the MENA countries improved in the second half of the 20th century, it could not keep up with educational progress in other developing regions. Nevertheless, literacy rates improved from 58 percent of the adults in 1990 to 73 percent in 2007. Secondary net school enrolment accounted for 60 percent in 2000 and 67 percent in 2005.

However, despite progress in enrolment rates the main problem of the MENA education system is its quality. MENA education systems do not provide pupils and students for the relevant labor markets. It has focused on training young people for public sector jobs instead of encouraging other skills. Hence, a significant mismatch between labor markets and educational output exists. Therefore, reforms in the MENA education system will play a crucial role regarding the challenge of demographic development and unemployment. To deal with the worsening job crisis, the MENA countries have to extend their private sectors. The public sector has not been able to absorb the increasing labor force in the past and will be even less able to create the necessary amount of new jobs in the future. However, such an encouragement of the private sector must be accompanied by severe improvements in the quality of education. A strong private sector can only emerge if an appropriately educated labor supply is available (UNDP, 2002, pp. 51–63; UNDP, 2003, pp. 51–68; Yousef, 2004).

Private sector enlargement must also be accompanied by several other improvements: the quality of education has to be improved; business regulations have to be reduced; FDI must be attracted; the financial sectors must be developed and the banking system must be reformed; red tape and corruption have to be combated; investments in R&D must increase to improve TFP growth and the general efficiency of the economies; trade barriers have to be abolished; and diversification must be pursued to end the oil dependence.

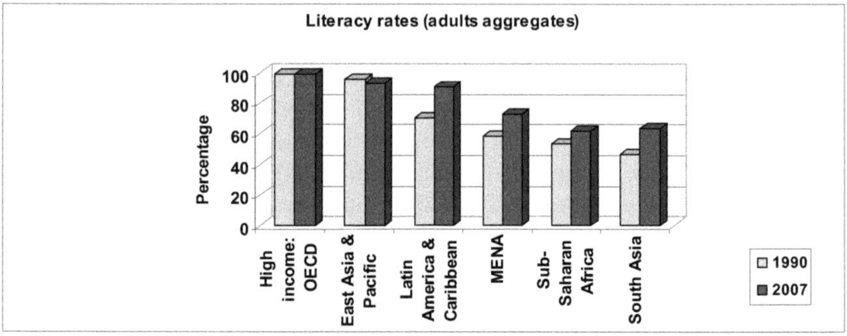

Figure 4.10: literacy rates (adults). Source: own illustration. Data accessed July 2, 2009, from the World Bank WDI database.

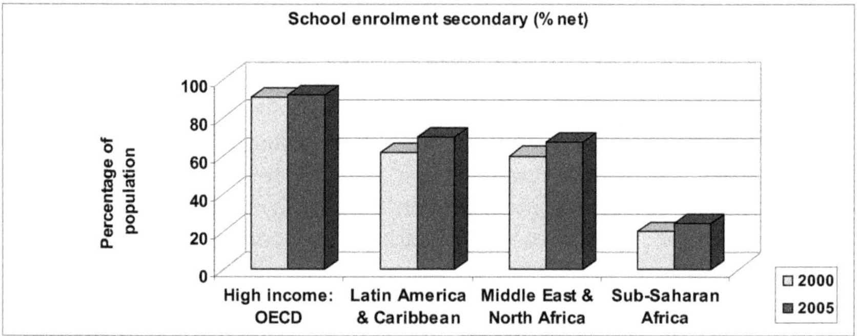

Figure 4.11: secondary school enrolment. Source: own illustration. Data accessed July 2, 2009, from the World Bank WDI database.

4.8 Business environment

Business regulations belong to the institutional environment of a state. The restrictions present formal constraints humans impose on themselves to regulate their interactions. As already explained in the general part on institutions, these restrictions might not be efficient. They can be shaped by the interests of certain groups and are influenced by a set of institutional and non-institutional factors. Hence, a country's business environment can be growth supporting or growth inhibiting. In general, more regulations disturb market forces and result in less efficiency. However, some regulations are necessary to constrain the actions of individuals in favor of general freedom. Nevertheless, too many and inefficient constraints prevent market participants from investing and resources from being efficiently allocated. Therefore, a free business environment with as few as possible restrictions is supposed to foster growth. According to the hypothesis of growth-inhibiting institutions in the Arab region, the business regulations in the MENA region should be many and more inefficient compared with regulations in the advanced economies.

Figures 4.12 and *4.13* demonstrate the business freedom index from the 2009 Index of Economic Freedom by the Heritage Foundation. The index incorporates data on starting a business (number of procedures, time in days, costs as a percentage of per capita income, minimum capital as a percentage of per capita income); data on obtaining a license (number of procedures, time in days, costs as a percentage of per capita income); and data on closing a business (time in years, costs as a percentage of estate, recovery rate in cents in the dollar).[53]

A score of 100 depicts the freest business environment, whereas zero describes the least free and most regulated business environment.

Arab countries, especially Djibouti and Libya, perform poorly with a business freedom index in 2009 of 20 and 38, respectively. However, the MENA countries in general have lower scores than the advanced economies. The MENA average is 66 in 2000 and 65 in 2009, compared with an average of 76 in 2000 and 88 in 2009 in the advanced countries. Furthermore, the advanced countries' average business freedom index improved in the period from 2000 to 2009, whereas the business environment in several MENA countries deteriorated. Hence, the business environment in the MENA region is more regulated and less supportive of growth than the business environment in the advanced economies.

Table 4.2 uses data from the World Bank's WDI database to analyze business regulations in more detail. It demonstrates the time required to start up a business in days in 2008, the time in days required to register property in 2008, and the time required to enforce a contract in days in 2008. Again, the available data for the MENA region are compared with a set of advanced economies. On average, it takes 23 days to start up a business in the MENA region and 12 days on average in the advanced economies. However, not all Arab countries perform poorly concerning this index. In Bahrain, Egypt, and Qatar it takes less than 10 days to start up a business. However, Algeria (24 days), Djibouti (37 days), Iran (47 days), Iraq (77 days), Kuwait (35 days), and West Bank and Gaza (49 days) exhibit the worst results.

[53] A detailed description of the derivation of the index can be found on the Heritage Foundation's homepage at http://www.heritage.org/index/Business-Freedom.aspx [accessed at 10 March 2010].

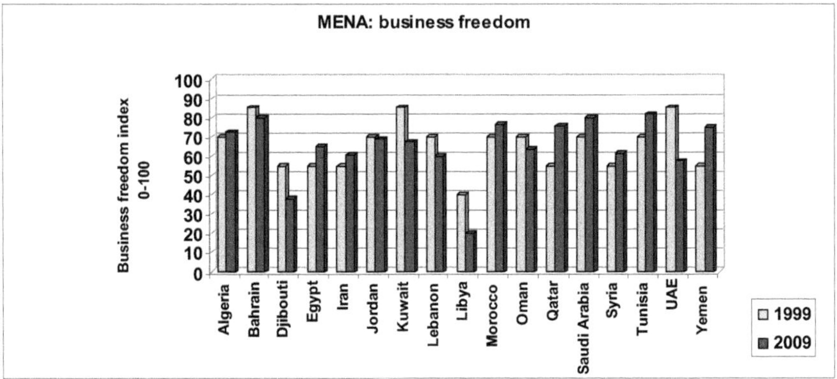

Figure 4.12: MENA business freedom. Source: own illustration. Data accessed March 10, 2010, from the Heritage Foundation [online], Index of Economic Freedom 2009.

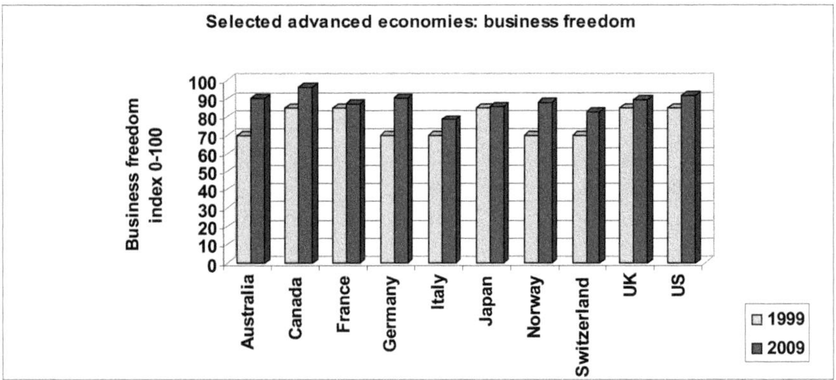

Figure 4.13: advanced economies business freedom. Source: own illustration. Data accessed March 10, 2010, from the Heritage Foundation [online], Index of Economic Freedom 2009.

Concerning the time required to register property, the performance of the Arab countries is mixed. For example, the registration of property takes eight days in Iraq, two days in Saudi Arabia, and six days in the UAE. However, one should also consider the data on the existence and security of property rights in these countries. Furthermore, even though the registration of property might take little time, not every citizen in the country might be able to register property or, even if registered, property might not be secure. Since the methodology applied to generate the data is untraceable, the numbers should be considered carefully. Nevertheless, in 2008 it took 32 days on average to register property in the

MENA region, according to the WDI data. The results for the advanced economies are somewhat biased by the data score of France. However, including France, it took an average of 28 days to register property in the advanced economies in 2008. Excluding France, the average was 17 days.

Some MENA outliers can be detected concerning contact enforcement. These are Djibouti (1225 days), Egypt (1010 days), and Syria (872 days). The advanced economies also exhibit an outlier, Italy, with 1210 days. On average, it takes 678 days to enforce a contract in MENA compared with 422 days in the advanced economies (312 days without Italy). Concerning business regulation, the MENA region performs worse than the advanced economies, at least regarding the data and variables considered.

4.9 Financial sector

The development of the financial sectors in MENA countries varies. Nevertheless, financial sectors still underperform and are not able to support sustainable economic growth. The banking sectors in the MENA region are still dominated by public ownership and low access to banking services. This is even true for the GCC (Gulf Cooperation Council) countries where severe regulations hinder intra-GCC and international investments in the banking sector. For example, the state and other GCC countries own 65 percent of the banking system in Dubai and Abu Dhabi. Nevertheless, new financial centers have been implemented in the Gulf states, such as the Dubai Financial International Center. However, these centers are special financial zones, within which special regimes are applied. The financial zones are thought to attract Western and Asian financial institutions and are not connected to the indigenous banking system (World Bank, 2008, p. 59).

However, improvements of the banking sector have been observable in countries such as Egypt, Lebanon, Jordan, Tunisia, Syria, and Morocco. This is because privatization in the banking sector has been enforced, banks are opening branches in neighboring countries, and GCC countries are investing in the countries' banking sectors.

Since the beginning of the 2000s, bank deposits, the M2-to-GDP ratio, and bank credits to the private sector have increased (World Bank, 2008, p. 58). Nevertheless, access to banking services is still restricted and small-to-medium private enterprises find it difficult to obtain credit. Access to financing was mentioned as one of the most problematic factors for doing business in the MENA

Table 4.2: MENA business regulations. Source: own illustration. Data accessed July 2, 2009, from the World Bank WDI database.

Days required to start up a business in 2008				Days required to register property in 2008				Days required to enforce a contract in 2008			
MENA		Advanced Ec.		MENA		Advanced Ec.		MENA		Advanced Ec.	
Algeria	24	Australia	2	Algeria	51	Australia	5	Algeria	630	Australia	395
Bahrain	9	Canada	5	Bahrain	31	Canada	17	Bahrain	635	Canada	570
Djibouti	37	France	7	Djibouti	40	France	113	Djibouti	1225	France	331
Egypt	7	Germany	18	Egypt	72	Germany	40	Egypt	1010	Germany	394
Iran	47	Italy	10	Iran	36	Italy	27	Iran	520	Italy	1210
Iraq	77	Japan	23	Iraq	8	Japan	14	Iraq	520	Japan	316
Jordan	14	Norway	10	Jordan	22	Norway	3	Jordan	689	Norway	310
Kuwait	35	Sweden	15	Kuwait	55	Switzerland	16	Kuwait	566	Switzerland	417
Lebanon	11	Switzerland	20	Lebanon	25	UK	21	Lebanon	721	UK	404
Morocco	12	UK	13	Morocco	47	US	12	Morocco	615	US	300
Oman	14	US	6	Oman	16			Oman	598		
Qatar	6			Qatar	16			Qatar	570		
Saudi Arabia	12			Saudi Arabia	2			Saudi Arabia	635		
Syria	17			Syria	19			Syria	872		
Tunisia	11			Tunisia	39			Tunisia	565		
UAE	17			UAE	6			UAE	607		
West Bank and Gaza	49			West Bank and Gaza	63			West Bank and Gaza	700		
Yemen	13			Yemen	19			Yemen	520		
Average	*23*	*Average*	*12*	*Average*	*32*	*Average*	*27*	*Average*	*678*	*Average*	*422*

region in the 2007 Arab World Competitiveness Report.[54] The report uses survey data from the World Bank's Opinion Survey, which is conducted for the yearly Global Competitiveness Report. Foreign and indigenous enterprises operating in the MENA countries are asked for their particular business environments. In eight of the 12 MENA countries, access to financing is described as the first or second most problematic factor for doing business.[55] In the remaining four MENA countries, access to financing is rated as the sixth or seventh most problematic factor.[56]

The development of stock markets in the MENA region has improved over the past decade. Stock markets exist in nearly all MENA countries and especially the Gulf states invest in other Arab countries' stock markets, such as Jordan or Egypt. For example. MENA market capitalization increased from approximately 73,000 million US dollars in 1994 to approximately 883,000 million US dollars in 2006. During the same time span, the value traded increased from circa 10,500 million US dollars to 1,684,000 million US dollars, and the number of listed firms grew from 1089 in 1994 to 1571 in 2006 (World Bank, 2008, p. 62f.). Although change is apparent, obscure legal restrictions, constraints on capital accounts, and restraints on capital outflows and foreign capital inflows inhibit further capital market integration. However, more reform efforts can be expected, since all MENA countries want to benefit from the high existing liquidity released by the oil boom in 2004–2006.

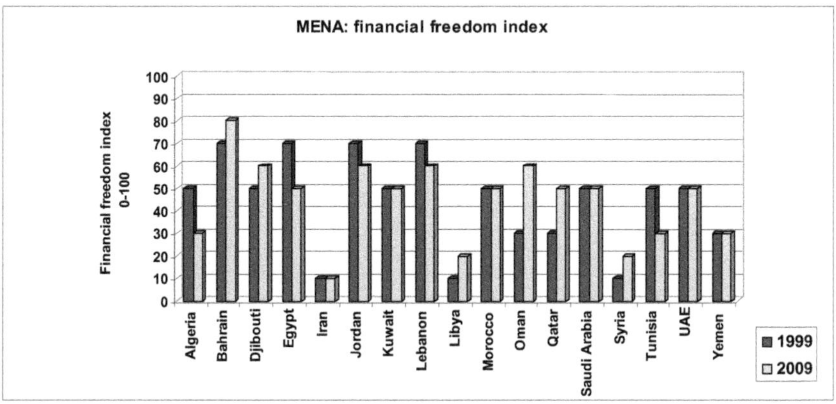

Figure 4.14: MENA financial freedom. Source: own illustration. Data accessed March 10, 2010, from the Heritage Foundation [online], Index of Economic Freedom 2009.

[54] See the country profiles of the 2007 Arab World Competitiveness Report (Drzeniek Hanouz, El Diwany & Yousef, 2007, p. 150 ff.).
[55] Algeria (1), Egypt (1), Morocco (1), Tunisia (1), Jordan (2), Libya (2), Qatar (2), Syria (2).
[56] Bahrain (7), Kuwait (6), Oman (6), UAE (6).

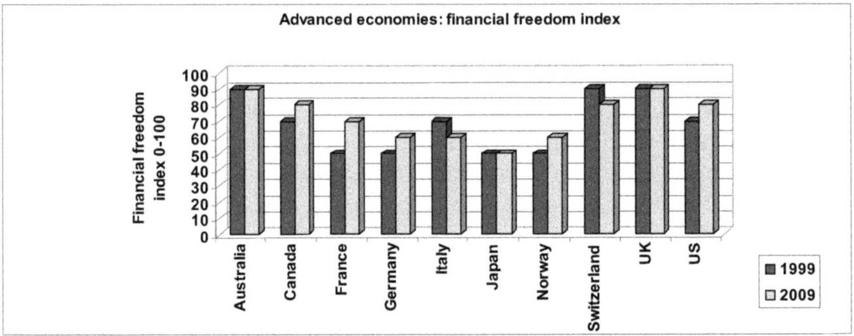

Figure 4.15: advanced economies financial freedom. Source: own illustration. Data accessed March 10, 2010, from the Heritage Foundation [online], Index of Economic Freedom 2009.

Figure 4.14 depicts financial freedom in the MENA countries, a measure taken from the 2009 Index of Economic Freedom. The variable incorporates "the extent of government regulation of financial services; the extent of state intervention in banks and other financial services; the difficulty of opening and operating financial services firms (for both domestic and foreign individuals); and government influence on the allocation of credit" (Miller & Holmes, 2009, p. 447). Financial freedom is measured on a scale from 0–100, with 0 indicating no financial freedom and 100 indicating full financial freedom. Accordingly, it varies widely between MENA countries. Nevertheless, only Bahrain exhibits a score greater 60 (more particularly, 80) in 2009. Apart from Djibouti, Jordan, Lebanon, and Oman, who exhibit scores of 60, the remaining countries obtain 50 or less. Furthermore, on average no improvements are observable in the period between 1999 and 2009. In both years, the MENA countries realized an average level of 44. By contrast, selected advanced economies realized an average score of 68 in 1999 and 72 in 2009.

In general, the financial sectors of the MENA countries are unfit to promote the necessary support for persistent economic growth. However, Creane et al. (2007) find that the MENA region in general must improve its institutional quality and foster non-bank financial development to achieve higher financial sector efficiency. Accordingly, in particular, government interventions must be reduced and the quality of the legal system improved.

4.10 Trade

Tariffs have significantly reduced over the past decade in most MENA countries. Nevertheless, substantial differences between MENA countries remain. MFN tariffs are a severe problem, since they benefit less efficient partner countries.[57] Furthermore, intraregional trade is partly hampered by trade complementarities. Although intraregional trade has expanded, it remains low compared with all other world regions except for South Asia. Although improvements in official tariff rates have occurred in recent years, non-tariff barriers remain a key obstacle. Quantity restrictions, regulatory restrictions, and customs restrictions are widespread in the region. *Figure 4.16* demonstrates the levels of trade freedom in the MENA countries. The variable *trade freedom* is taken from the Index of Economic Freedom. It is a "composite measure of the absence of tariff and non-tariff barriers that affect imports and exports of goods and services" and it is based on "the trade-weighted average tariff rate and non-tariff barriers" (Miller & Holmes, 2009, p. 442). It can be seen that trade freedom in many MENA countries has improved significantly since 1999. The average trade freedom changed from a scale of 57 in 1999 to 71 in 2009. However, selected advanced economies exhibited an average of 79 in 1999 and of 85 in 2009. Hence, large differences in the freedom of trade still exist between the two country groups.

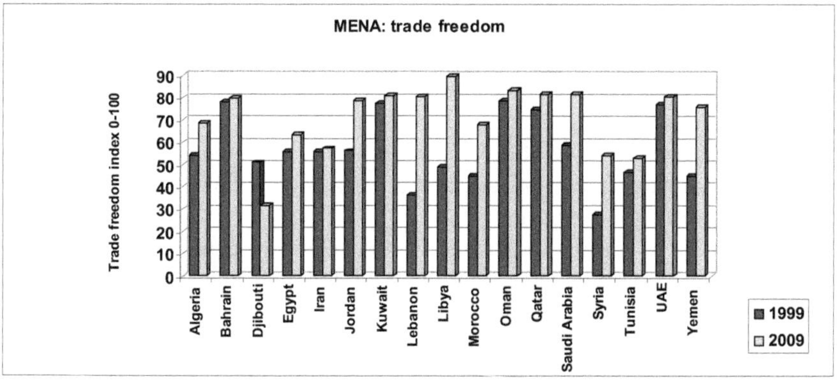

Figure 4.16: MENA trade freedom. Source: own illustration. Data accessed March 10, 2010, from the Heritage Foundation [online], Index of Economic Freedom 2009.

[57] MFN tariff: most favored nation tariff.

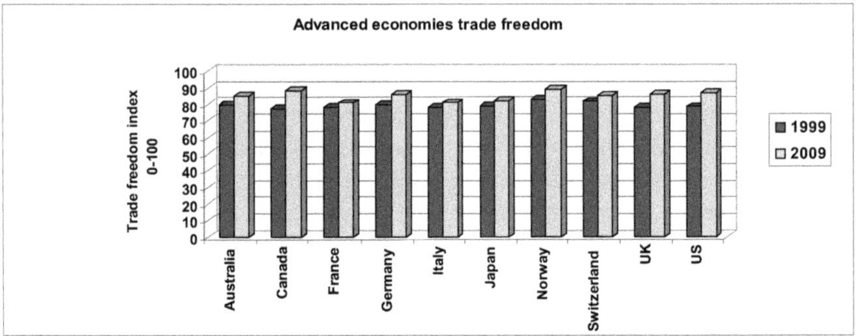

Figure 4.17: advanced economies trade freedom. Source: own illustration. Data accessed March 10, 2010, from the Heritage Foundation [online], Index of Economic Freedom 2009.

4.11 Corruption and red tape

In corruptive regimes, efficient economic activity is inhibited. Foreign and indigenous investment and thereby growth are negatively hit by high levels of corruption (Asiedu & Freeman, 2008; Mauro, 1995). Furthermore, corruption and red tape are interdependent and have to be jointly considered (Guriev, 2004). Although theories of efficient corruption exist, corruption is always a second best solution, since the best strategy would be to abolish the distortions and inefficiencies themselves (Aidt, 2003).

The concentration of political power, lack of governmental and bureaucratic transparency, a large public sector, and a weak rule of law constitute an environment favorable for corruption.

Freedom from corruption in the MENA region is demonstrated in *figure 4.18*. The variable is also taken from the 2009 Index of Economic Freedom and is measured on a scale from 0–100, with zero indicating very corrupt governments and 100 indicating very little corruption. The score is derived from Transparency International's Corruption Perceptions Index for 2007 (Miller & Holmes, 2009, p. 450).

Corruption depicts a severe problem in the MENA region. The average score deteriorated between 1999 and 2009, from 45 to 37. Only two countries, Qatar and the UAE, achieved a score higher than 50. Still both countries exhibit relatively low scores with 60 in the case of Qatar and 57 in the case of the UAE. The selected advanced economies exhibited an average score of 78 in both 1999 and 2009.

Hence, improvements in combating corruption could generate significant efficiency gains in the MENA region. However, as already indicated, corruption is usually accompanied by red tape and thereby large, inefficient bureaucracies, authoritarian regimes, and by a weak rule of law. Hence, the abolishment of corruption in the MENA region requires deeper structural and institutional reforms.

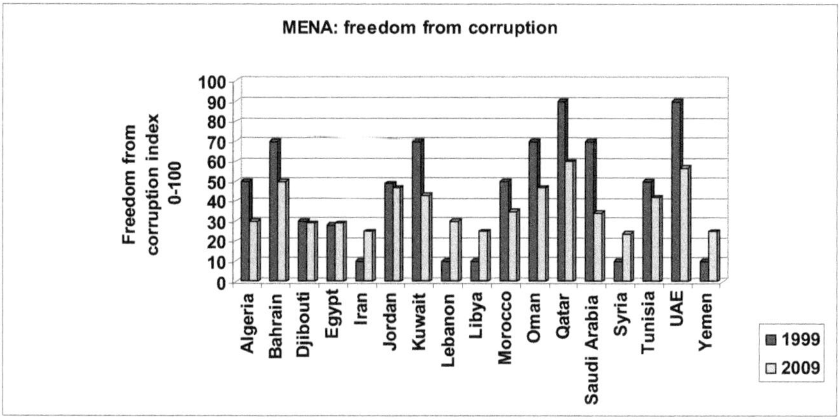

Figure 4.18: MENA freedom from corruption. Source: own illustration. Data accessed March 10, 2010, from the Heritage Foundation [online], Index of Economic Freedom 2009.

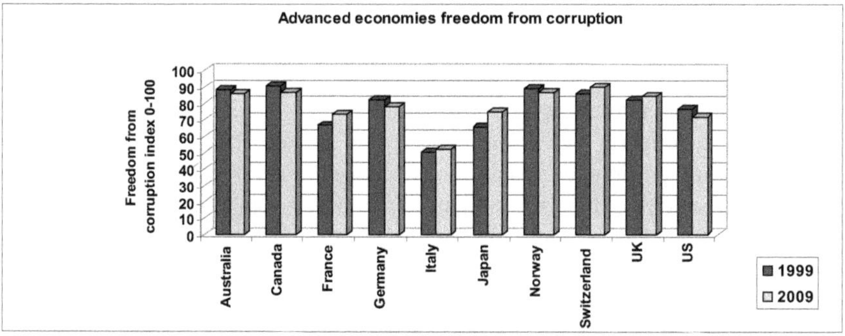

Figure 4.19: advanced economies freedom from corruption. Source: own illustration. Data accessed March 10, 2010, from the Heritage Foundation [online], Index of Economic Freedom 2009.

4.12 Political and legal Institutions

Political and legal institutions mark the main direction of a country's economic performance. These constraints have a direct effect on investment in physical and human capital and on production and, therefore, directly influence productivity and growth. A growth-inhibiting formal institutional environment makes economic success impossible. Whether an institution supports or inhibits growth depends on several factors and the interplay with other institutions. Nevertheless, some institutions can be described as growth supportive since without them efficient factor allocation is impossible. One growth-supportive formal institution is the implementation of property rights. Property rights ensure optimal individual utility maximization. Clearly defined ownership offers incentives to invest and allows the owner of an asset to charge the optimal price. Furthermore, with property rights an asset can be used as collateral, create new capital and thereby can be optimally applied (De Soto, 2000). The institution of property rights involves the implementation of further institutions. Property rights can only be enforced if the rule of law is implemented and if an independent judiciary exists otherwise the government or private interest groups are able to expropriate the owner of an asset. That is to say, the implementation of secure property rights needs some kind of separation of powers. However, the division of powers usually incorporates a form of political participation, which restrains governmental authority and prevents the enforcement of interests required by a certain interest group or minority. Furthermore, political freedom and civil liberties must be implemented to optimize growth. Both institutions allow for the optimal use of an asset. Human and physical capital can only then be optimally applied when the owner is in complete control and has the freedom to use his asset in a way that maximizes his utility.

Therefore, property rights, the rule of law, an independent judiciary, political freedom and participation, and civil liberties are supposed to be growth supportive. Nevertheless, even these institutions underlie institutional complementarities and dependencies. Missing traditions of property rights and the rule of law can inhibit their formal implementation. Hence, it is possible that the informal institutional environment does not match the mentioned formal institutions and thereby their implementation does not result in optimal growth. That is to say, without property rights, an independent judiciary, and political participation and freedom the growth rate cannot be maximized. Countries that nevertheless realize high growth rates might still underperform compared with a situation in which the particular institutions are implemented. Hence, if the enforcement of property rights, an independent judiciary, and political freedom is not possible because of the complementarities and dependencies of the institutional system, the country is stuck in an institutional trap. External institutional change might not help either for the reasons analyzed in chapters two and three. Therefore, the political and legal institutional environment can be responsible for economic backwardness. Economic institutions that hinder growth usually arise from certain political and legal institutions.

4.12.1 Property rights

The protection of property rights is measured with data from the 2009 Index of Economic Freedom by the Heritage Foundation (Miller & Holmes, 2009). The corresponding property rights index (freedom eight) measures "the degree to which a country's laws protect private property rights and the degree to which its government enforces those laws. It also assesses the likelihood that private property will be expropriated and analyses the independence of the judiciary, the existence of corruption within the judiciary, and the ability of individuals and businesses to enforce contracts" (Miller & Holmes, 2009, p. 449). A score of 100 depicts perfectly protected property rights, whereas a score of zero describes a situation in which property rights are missing and all property is owned by the state.

Figure 4.20 demonstrates the property rights index scores for the available MENA countries in 1999 and 2009, and *Figure 4.21* displays the index for certain advanced economies. The MENA countries exhibit considerably lower levels of property rights. Property rights are nearly missing in Iran and Libya, and Bahrain and Jordan are the only countries exhibiting a property rights score marginally greater than 50 in 2009. Furthermore, the level of the index deteriorated in Algeria, Djibouti, Egypt, Jordan, Kuwait, Lebanon, Morocco, Saudi Arabia, and the UAE in the period from 1999 to 2009. The average score for the 10 MENA countries accounted for 52 in 1999 and 38 in 2009. The advanced economies, on the contrary, exhibited an average score of 86 in 1999 and 82 in 2009. Hence, in the MENA countries the legal systems are highly inefficient and influenced by governmental interest groups, corruption is extensive, ownership is weakly protected, and expropriation is common (Miller & Holmes, 2009, p. 449). The bad scores that MENA countries exhibit in the property rights index already indicates one of the region's serious growth issues. Without improvements in the implementation and protection of property rights, growth rates will not approach their optimal level.

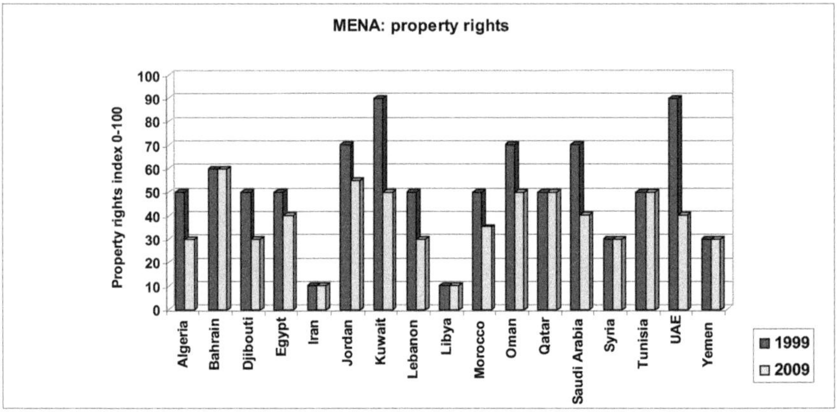

Figure 4.20: MENA property rights. Source: own illustration. Data accessed March 10, 2010, from the Heritage Foundation [online], Index of Economic Freedom 2009.

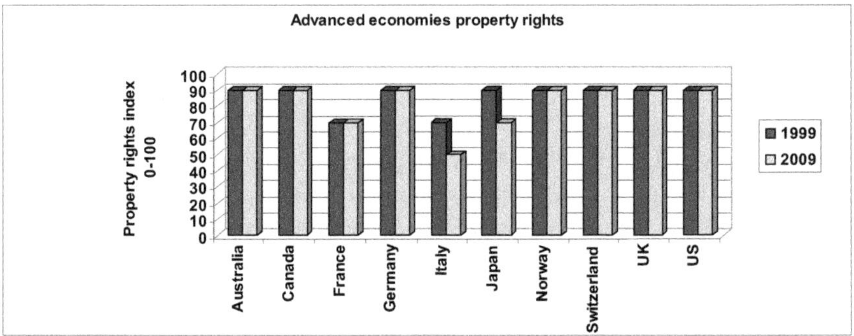

Figure 4.21: advanced economies property rights. Source: own illustration. Data accessed March 10, 2010, from the Heritage Foundation [online], Index of Economic Freedom 2009.

4.12.2 Constraints on the executive and democracy

Political and legal institutions are first examined using Polity IV data.[58] In the general empirical analysis in section one, *xconst* was used as a proxy for property rights and the accordant political and legal institutions that must accompany

[58] Data available online at: http://www.systemicpeace.org/polity/polity4.htm [accessed 2 July 2009].

secure ownership. Therefore, we will examine which levels of *xconst* for MENA countries.

Xconst reflects "the extent of institutionalized constraints on the decision-making powers of chief executives, whether individuals or collectives" (Marshall & Jaggers, 2007, p. 23). The variable is measured on a score from (1) 'Unlimited Authority' to (7) 'Executive Parity or Subordination'. In (1), the authority is unconstrained and no independent judiciary exists, whereas (7) depicts a state of separation of powers; accountability groups have equal or more authority than the executive.

However, public and private actors must be constrained to implement property rights, political freedom, and civil rights otherwise the government or private interest groups might expropriate the owner of an asset and restrain her or his freedom. Hence, an independent judiciary, which cannot be influenced by political powers or other public or private interest groups, must exist. By measuring the constraints on the executive, we also measure whether expropriation is possible or not and whether separation of powers and an independent judiciary are implemented. *Xconst* concentrates on constraints on the executive; thus, private expropriation is not reflected. Nevertheless, *xconst* incorporates whether checks and balances and an independent judiciary are realized. If these institutions exist in a state, they also regulate relationships between private actors. Hence, governmental and private constraints regarding expropriation are at least indirectly included.

Furthermore, the forms of government in the MENA countries are examined. However, the official notations of political systems in the MENA region do not necessarily reflect reality in the countries. For example, in the CIA World Factbook, some MENA countries are described as republics.[59] This might be true regarding their official descriptions, but these countries are far from realizing political freedom, political participation, civil liberties, division of powers, and so on. Corruption, oppression, nepotism, and authoritative governance are still prevalent in many states, although the official denotation might promise something else. Therefore, a measure from the Polity IV data set is used to examine the character of the MENA countries' political systems. Polity IV contains a measure of democracy (*democ*) and a measure of autocracy (*autoc*). Democracy is defined as a mixture of three elements: "the presence of institutions and procedures through which citizens can express effective preferences about alternative policies and leaders. [...] the existence of institutionalized constraints on the exercise of power by the executive. [...] the guarantee of civil liberties to

[59] The CIA World Factbook, online available at: https://www.cia.gov/library/publications/the-world-factbook/ [accessed 10 September 2010]. Examples: People's Democratic Republic of Algeria; Arab Republic of Egypt; Republic of Iraq; Lebanese Republic; Syrian Arab Republic; Tunisian Republic; Republic of Yemen.

all citizens in their daily lives and in acts of political participation" (Marshall & Jaggers, 2007, p. 13). The indicator is derived from certain coded variables – "Competitiveness of Executive Recruitment", "Openness of Executive Recruitment", "Constraint of Chief Executive", and "Competitiveness of Political Participation" (Marshall & Jaggers, 2007, p. 14) – and is scaled from 0–10, with zero indicating no democracy and 10 indicating strong democracy.

Autocracies "sharply restrict or suppress competitive political participation. Their chief executives are chosen in a regularized process of selection within the political elite, and once in office they exercise power with few institutional constraints" (Marshall & Jaggers, 2007, p. 14). The autocracy indicator is derived from codings of the variables "Competitiveness of Executive Recruitment", "Openness of Executive Recruitment", "Constraints of Chief Executive", "Regulation of Participation", and "Competitiveness of Participation" (Marshall & Jaggers, 2007, p. 15). *Autoc* is also scaled from 0–10 with zero indicating no autocracy and 10 indicating strong autocracy.

The variable *polity2* now combines the democracy and autocracy indicators into one score. It is calculated by subtracting the autocracy score from the democracy score and enables the classification of countries on a scale from strongly democratic (+10) to strongly autocratic (–10).

Table 4.3 demonstrates the average *xconst* and *polity2* scores for the MENA countries between 1990 and 2007.[60] *Table 4.4* depicts the *xconst* and *polity2* scores for 2007, the last year for which data are available. All countries exhibit low levels of *xconst*, with a region average of 2.31. None of the MENA countries realizes a score of four or higher. This implicates that substantial limitations on the executive do not exist in any the MENA countries. The authority is either unlimited (1) or a moderate limitation including an independent judiciary exists (3). (2) is defined as an intermediate category. However, the fact that in (3) an independent judiciary exists does not indicate that a Western standard rule of law or constitution is implemented. The standards towards which the judiciary is oriented can differ completely from Western standards.

The average *polity2* scores are negative for all MENA countries, indicating that the states are closer to autocracy than to democracy. Of course, Qatar and Saudi Arabia exhibit –10, since both countries are hereditary monarchies.[61] However, Bahrain, Kuwait, Libya, Oman, Syria, and the UAE are also close to the categorization of being strongly autocratic with average scores of –7 and less. Nevertheless, the 2007 scores show improvements compared with the averages, at least for Algeria and Djibouti and, slightly, for Bahrain, Egypt, and

[60] Iraq and Lebanon are excluded because of data unavailability. The average polity2 score for Kuwait is calculated from 1991–2007, and the average polity2 score for Yemen is calculated for 1993–2007.

[61] In the case of Qatar the correct notation is 'Emirate'.

Syria. On the contrary, the score for Iran worsened significantly compared with the average.

The implementation of political rights and civil liberties in MENA countries is further analyzed with data from the Freedom in the World 2009 Survey by Freedom House. *Table 4.5* reveals the scores for political rights and civil liberties, as well as the categorization in free (F), partly free (PF), and not free (NF) MENA countries for 1980 and 2008 compared with selected advanced economies in *Table 4.6*. Political rights (PR) and civil liberties (CL) are rated on a scale from 1–7, with one indicating the most possible freedom and seven indicating the least possible freedom.

None of the MENA countries is categorized as free. Eleven countries are rated not free in 2008, and seven countries are rated partly free.

Table 4.3: MENA average xconst and polity2, 1990–2007. Source: own illustration. Data accessed 27 October, 2009, [online] from the Polity IV project.

	Average 1990–2007	
Country	**xconst**	**polity2**
Algeria	3.11	–2.44
Bahrain	1.83	–8.44
Djibouti	2.50	–2.44
Egypt	3.00	–5.50
Iran	3.17	–2.50
Jordan	3.00	–2.28
Kuwait (1991–2007)	2.88	–7.12
Libya	1.00	–7.00
Morocco	2.89	–6.56
Oman	1.94	–8.72
Qatar	1.00	–10.00
Saudi Arabia	1.00	–10.00
Syria	1.89	–8.11
Tunisia	2.67	–3.67
UAE	3.00	–8.00
Yemen (1993–2007)	2.00	–2.33
Average	*2.31*	*–5.94*

Table 4.4: MENA xconst and polity2, 2007. Source: own illustration. Data accessed 27 October, 2009, [online] from the Polity IV project.

	2007	
Country	**xconst**	**polity2**
Algeria	5	2
Bahrain	2	–7
Djibouti	3	2
Egypt	3	–3
Iran	2	–6
Jordan	3	–3
Kuwait	3	–7
Libya	1	–7
Morocco	3	–6
Oman	2	–8
Qatar	1	–10
Saudi Arabia	1	–10
Syria	3	–7
Tunisia	2	–4
UAE	3	–8
Yemen	2	–2

Table 4.5: MENA political freedom. Source: own illustration. Data accessed 21 March, 2010, [online] from Freedom House, Freedom in the World Comparative and Historical Data 2009.

	1980			*2008*		
Country	**PR**	**CL**	**Status**	**PR**	**CL**	**Status**
Algeria	6	6	NF	6	5	NF
Bahrain	5	5	PF	5	5	PF
Djibouti	3	4	PF	5	5	PF
Egypt	5	5	PF	6	5	NF
Iran	5	5	PF	6	6	NF
Iraq	6	7	NF	6	6	NF
Jordan	6	6	NF	5	5	PF
Kuwait	6	4	PF	4	4	PF
Lebanon	4	4	PF	5	4	PF
Libya	6	7	NF	7	7	NF
Morocco	4	4	PF	5	4	PF
Oman	6	6	NF	6	5	NF
Qatar	5	5	PF	6	5	NF
Saudi Arabia	6	6	NF	7	6	NF
Syria	5	7	NF	7	6	NF
Tunisia	6	5	PF	7	5	NF
UAE	5	5	PF	6	5	NF
Yemen				5	5	PF
Yemen, N.	6	5	NF			
Yemen, S.	6	7	NF			

Table 4.6: Advanced economies political freedom. Source: own illustration. Data accessed 21 March, 2010, [online] from Freedom House, Freedom in the World Comparative and Historical Data 2009.

	1980			*2008*		
Country	**PR**	**CL**	**Status**	**PR**	**CL**	**Status**
Australia	1	1	F	1	1	F
Canada	1	1	F	1	1	F
France	1	2	F	1	1	F
Germany				1	1	F
Germany, E.	7	7	NF			
Germany, W.	1	2	F			
Italy	1	2	F	1	2	F
Japan	1	1	F	1	2	F
Norway	1	1	F	1	1	F
Switzerland	1	1	F	1	1	F
UK	1	1	F	1	1	F
US	1	1	F	1	1	F

4.12.3 Good governance

Individuals are able to optimize their utility when they are free to live their lives according to their own desires. Hence, freedom is an important factor for utility maximization. Therefore, freedom should only be constrained to prevent individuals from violating others. Hence, some form of societal organization – that is, some form of governance – must exist otherwise individuals harm each others' freedoms. Good governance, therefore, depicts a form of governance that ensures the highest possible individual freedom, which only hinders the violation of other individuals and their properties. Kaufmann, Kraay and Mastruzzi (2009) define governance as "the traditions and institutions by which authority in a country is exercised" (p. 5). According to the Arab Human Development Report 2002, "governance can be seen as the exercise of economic, political and administrative authority to manage a country's affairs at all levels. It comprises the mechanisms, processes and institutions through which citizens and groups articulate their interests, exercise their legal rights, meet their obligations and mediate their differences" (p. 105). Good governance is characterized through policies that offer the most possible individual freedom in a society and thereby enable optimal economic growth. Therefore, good governance promotes political freedom, civil liberties, and the rule of law. It is participatory, transparent, accountable, and effective. Regulations are enacted when individual freedom harms others.

Hence, political and legal institutions are determinants of governance. Almost every study that deals with Arab economic growth performance mentions governance, and thereby formal institutions, as the main obstacle for economic growth. The Arab Human Development Report 2004, for example, solely deals with freedom, governance, and its components in the Arab world. This section examines determinants of good governance, and thereby political and legal institutions, in the MENA region. According to this study's hypothesis, institutions are the main determinants of economic growth. Hence, we would expect Arab formal institutions to be less growth supportive than the institutions in more advanced economies. As we will see, the hypothesis proves to be right.

Kaufmann, Kraay and Mastruzzi (2009) measure six worldwide government indicators (WGI). These are calculated using 441 individual variables taken from 35 varying sources by 33 different organizations. All variables are based on survey data.[62] Governance is measured on a scale between –2.5 and 2.5 with higher scores describing more efficient and thereby more growth-supportive outcomes.

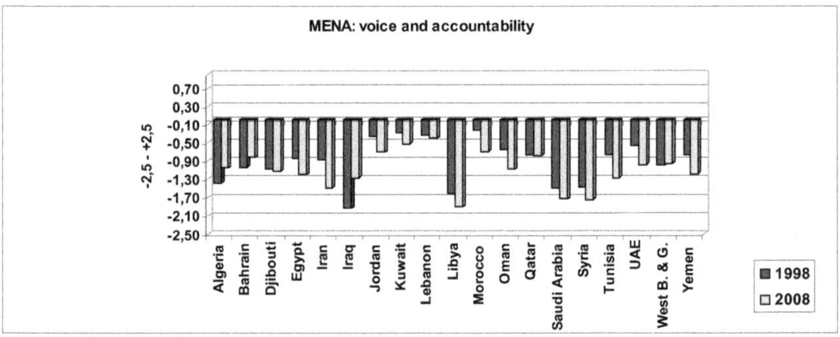

Figure 4.22: MENA: voice and accountability. Source: own illustration.

[62] A detailed description of the methodology and data sources can be found in Kaufmann, Kraay and Mastruzzi, 2009, pp. 5–25.

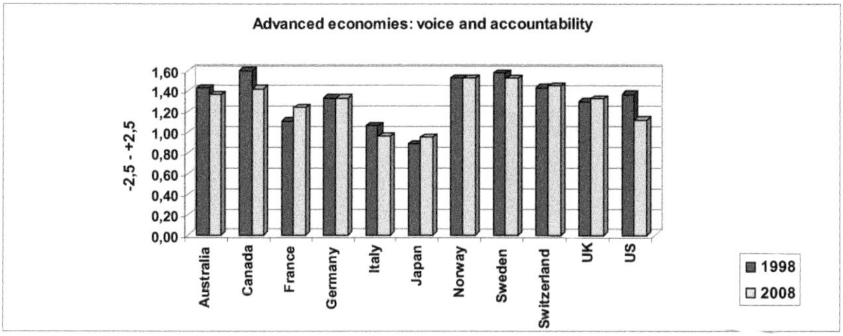

Figures 4.23: advanced economies: voice and accountability. Source: own illustration.

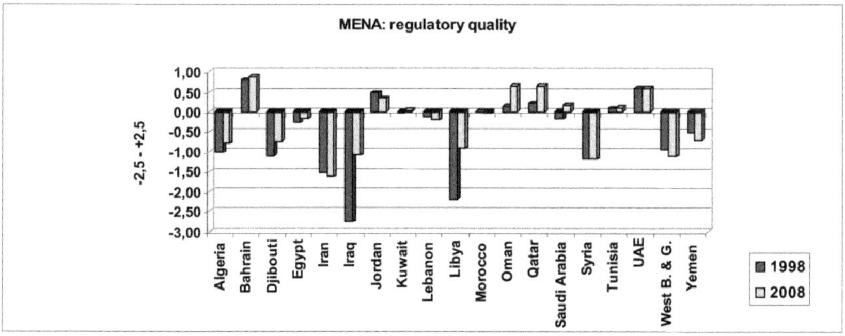

Figure 4.24: MENA: regulatory quality. Source: own illustration.

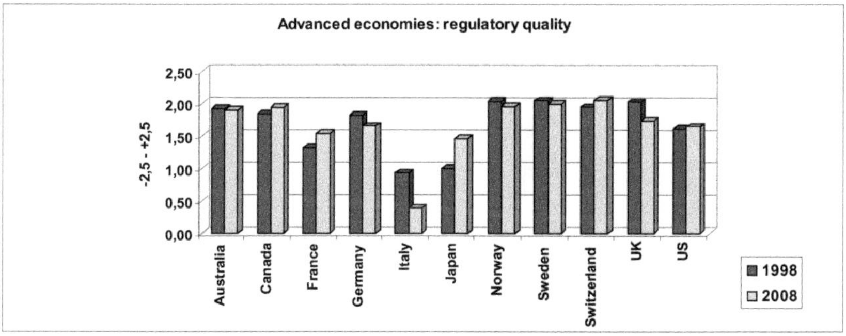

Figure 4.25: advanced economies: regulatory quality. Source: own illustration.

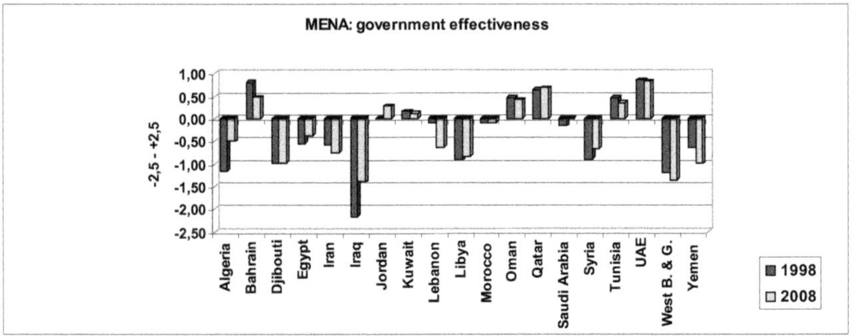

Figure 4.26: MENA: government effectiveness. Source: own illustration.

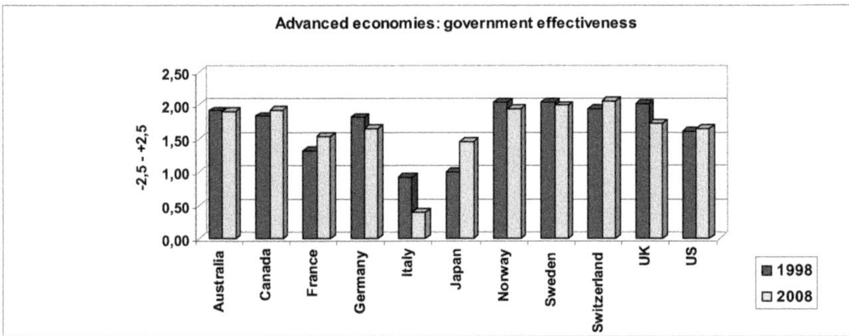

Figure 4.27: advanced economies: government effectiveness. Source: own illustration.

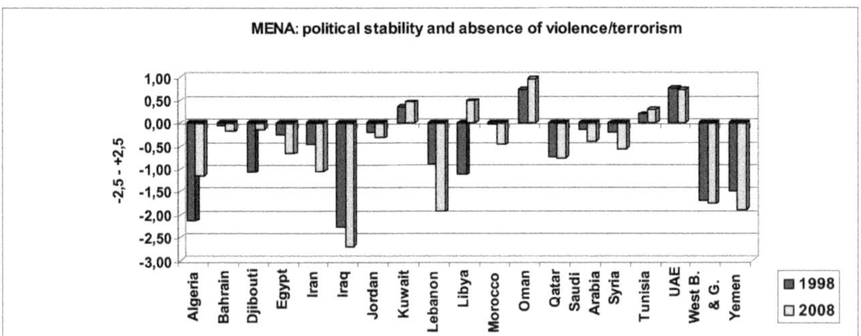

Figure 4.28: MENA: political stability and absence of violence/terrorism. Source: own illustration.

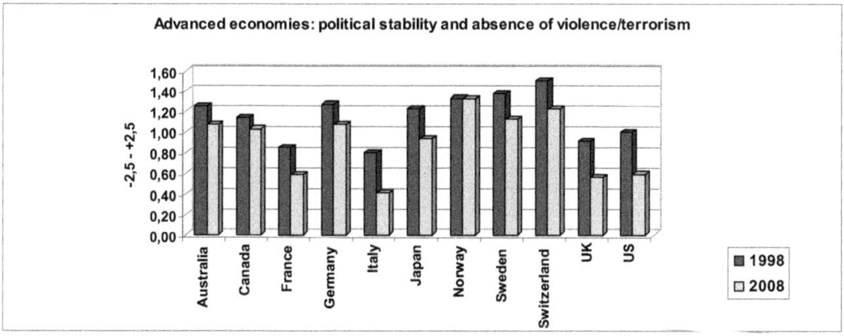

Figure 4.29: advanced economies: political stability and absence of violence/terrorism. Source: own illustration.

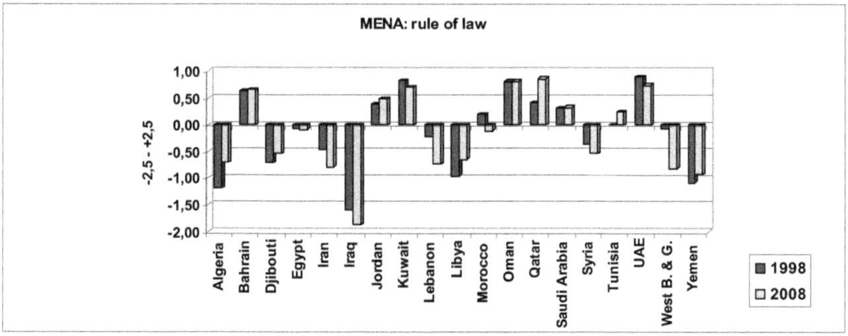

Figure 4.30: MENA: rule of law. Source: own illustration.

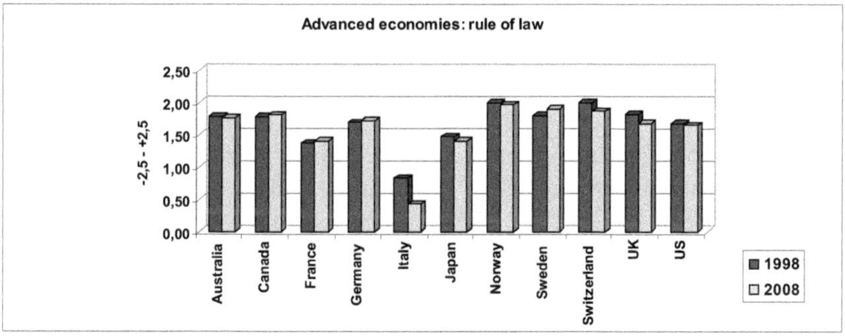

Figure 4.31: advanced economies: rule of law. Source: own illustration.

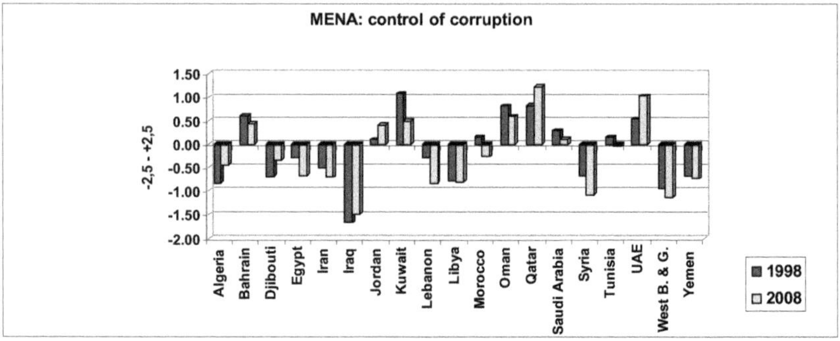

Figure 4.32: MENA: control of corruption. Source: own illustration.

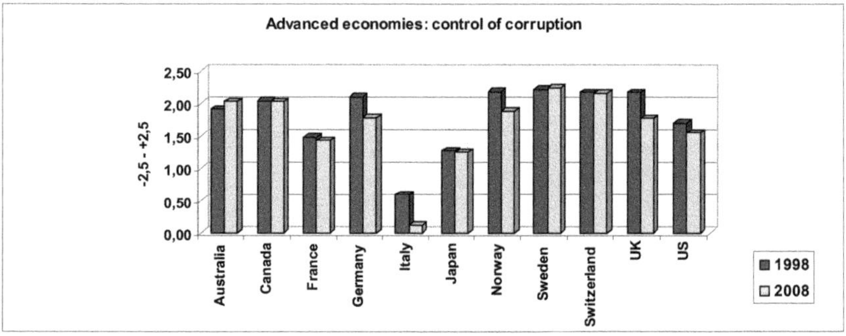

Figure 4.33: advanced economies: control of corruption. Source: own illustration.

Figures 4.22–4.33 compare the WGI for the incorporated MENA countries with the selected advanced economies.[63] The MENA countries perform significantly worse than the selected advanced economies. Concerning *Voice and Accountability*, all MENA countries exhibit negative values; the average in 2008 amounts to –1.10. Hence, political participation, freedom of expression, and freedom of association are almost not given and the press is not free. On the contrary, all of the selected advanced economies exhibit values greater 0.9, with an average score of 1.27 in 2008. Kuwait, Libya, Oman, Qatar, Tunisia, and the UAE are the only Arab states who realized positive values for *Political Stability*

[63] Worldwide Government Indicators (Kaufmann, Kraay and Mastruzzi, 2009), data accessed at 8 August, 2009, [online] from Governance Matters VIII: Aggregate and Individual Governance Indicators 1996-2008.

& Absence of Violence/Terrorism in 2008, although none of them achieved a score greater than one. Iraq received the lowest score.[64] The averages for the MENA countries are –0.47 in 1998 and –0.49 in 2008. Improvements took place in Algeria, Djibouti, and Libya. However, the situation of political stability is still poor in these countries. In general, political instability, violence, and terrorism show significant threats to the region. The advanced economies achieve averages of 1.13 in 1998 and 0.88 in 2008. Of course, the increasing threat of terrorism since 9/11/2001 led to a deterioration in the index in the advanced economies in general. Concerning *Government Effectiveness*, MENA countries perform significantly worse than the selected advanced economies. The averages account for –0.32 in 1998 and –0.29 in 2008 in MENA and 1.65 in 1998 and 1.63 in 2008 in the advanced countries. Bahrain, Jordan, Kuwait, Oman, Qatar, Tunisia, and the UAE at least achieve positive scores in 2008, but all countries remain below a score of one. Hence, the quality of public services and government commitment are low in MENA countries and political pressure is prevalent. The same is true for *Regulatory Quality* on which MENA countries achieve an average of –0.27 in 2008. However, a slight improvement from an average of –0.50 in 1998 is observable. Nevertheless, private sector development is inhibited by the regulatory quality and the inability of governments to implement sound policies. The advanced economies achieve averages of 1.32 in 1998 and 1.47 in 2008. MENA countries perform equally bad regarding *Rule of Law* and *Control of Corruption.* However, the implementation of the rule of law is an indispensable step to greater economic growth. The rule of law clarifies that every entity in a state has to abide to the laws, even the political power. Hence, it must be implemented to establish property rights. Only then can laws protecting property rights be applied to inhibit private as well as governmental expropriation. Furthermore, the rule of law is necessary to enforce political freedom and civil liberties, which can only be protected if every entity, even the state itself, accepts them. Of course, an independent judiciary is necessary to enforce the laws against private and governmental violators. MENA countries perform poorly on the *Rule of Law* indicator, although great variations exist within the region. The average amounts to –1.08 in 1998 and –0.93 in 2008; hence, very slight improvement is observable over the decade. The averages of the selected advanced economies account for 1.64 in 1998 and 1.57 in 2008. On *Control of Corruption,* MENA countries exhibit an average of –0.15 in 1998 and –0.22 in 2008 compared with an average of the advanced economies of 1.76 in 1998 and 1.60 in 2008. Corruption inhibits efficient economic activity. Hence, it must be assumed that the economic performance of the MENA countries is significantly hampered by the high levels of corruption.

---

[64] Iraq, however, achieved a score of –2.69. It is not traceable how this value is achieved since the lower bound is defined to be –2.5.

However, the improvements or deteriorations in the levels of the WGI between 1998 and 2008 have to be considered cautiously. In 1998, significantly fewer data sources were used to create the WGI. Hence, although the same data sources were used for the 1998 and 2008 indicators, additional data sources were applied in 2008. Therefore, comparability is restricted. This might partly explain the deteriorations in many indicators in the MENA countries over the decade. Nevertheless, several indicators in the MENA countries might in fact have worsened.

It is conspicuous that even though all MENA countries perform relatively poorly on the WDI, large variations within the region exist. Bahrain, Jordan, Kuwait, Oman, Qatar, and, to a lesser extent, Tunisia exhibit relatively good governance compared with the rest of the region. However, the 'best' MENA countries still perform poorly regarding the quality of governance compared with the advanced economies.

Of course, data analysis must always be critically considered. Although all the mentioned studies measure institutions in one way or another, data sets are composed in different ways and various methods are applied. The outcome depends on the data sources, previous definitions, codings, weightings, and so forth. Therefore, the analyses of data sets might differ even though they are supposed to measure similar institutions. Hence, the judgment concerning a certain country might differ according to whether Polity IV, Freedom House, the 2009 Index of Economic Freedom, or the WGI by Kaufmann, Kraay and Mastruzzi (2009) was applied. This is the case since the definitions of, for example, democracy and autocracy differ or since constraints on the executive, the regulatory environment, the rule of law, the quality of bureaucracy, and governmental efficiency are measured differently according to varying criteria. Furthermore, the construction of the indicators and categorizations can often not be completely reconstructed. Objectivity is not always assured; therefore, the data sets might be influenced by the opinions of the preparing entities and sponsors. The conclusions drawn in this study refer merely to the particular definitions and data sets. Nevertheless, although the detail of a particular country analysis might differ in some cases, the general implications are universal. Hence, authorities in MENA countries are not constrained. Often small elites are in power and political participation is restricted. Several chief executives are not assigned via popular vote, but within small circles of the political elite or by hereditary right. This might be the case even if officially a popular vote is run. Often, no independent judiciary exists and no Western standard rule of law. Governments are generally inefficient, private sector development is inhibited, and large bureaucracies and red tape are prevalent. Corruption, bribery, and nepotism are widespread. Property rights are not secure and, hence, efficient economic activity is inhibited.

Furthermore, the MENA region exhibits some of the worst indicators of political freedom and civil rights worldwide. None of the countries are categorized as free. That is to say, political and legal institutions are not implemented in a way that supports growth.

4.13 Informal institutions

The first part of this dissertation project also emphasized informal institutions – that is, beliefs, attitudes, morals, norms, habits, codes of conduct, conventions, and culture in general. The hypothesis was that informal institutions differ between societies since cultures vary. Informal institutions determine an individual's behavior. If certain cultural features hold for the whole society, almost every individual acts accordingly and thereby the informal institutions influence aggregated societal behavior. However, nearly all human behavioral patterns have an impact on an individual's economic life. Therefore, informal institutions that are implemented in society affect its aggregated economic performance. One example is the attitude towards the female labor force in traditional, hierarchical societies (limited morality). Some individuals are convinced that women should not participate in the job market, but instead raise children and maintain the house. Since this is the majority's opinion, the female labor force is also sparse on an aggregated level. Hence, the economies abdicate one half of their workforce and thereby one half of their human capital.

In chapter three of the dissertation project, the variables *trust*, *control*, *respect*, and *obedience* were analyzed and it was demonstrated that these informal institutions influence the level of per capita income. These particular variables will now be examined for the MENA countries. Again, a regression analysis is not possible because of data limitations. Thus, descriptive statistics will be applied. Since the societal structure is decisive for economic development, further variables that allow inference on societal organization are observed. The examination of the informal institutions of the MENA region is considered to provide the weakest evidence because of the issues already mentioned; measurement error and data limitations.

4.13.1 Trust

WVS question text: "Generally speaking, would you say that most people can be trusted or that you need to be very careful in dealing with people?" Possible answers: 1) Most people can be trusted; 2) Can't be too careful; 3) Don't know.

The variable *trust* is defined as the percentage of the respondents of a particular country answering that most people can be trusted. *Figure 4.34* demonstrates the results for the available MENA countries and selected advanced economies. The connection between trust and per capita income in the particular countries is depicted.[65] *Trust* varies greatly between the MENA countries, with Algeria exhibiting a level of trust of only 10.80 percent compared with Saudi Arabia, which realizes a level of trust of 50.50 percent. In the advanced economies, *trust* varies between 21.40 percent in France and 41.00 percent in Switzerland, with Norway being an outlier (64.80 percent). The average level of trust in the MENA countries is 34.39 percent and the average level of trust in the advanced economies is 37.63 percent. Hence, the country averages do not vary and no general trend can be singled out. However, concerning the explanatory content of *trust*, no pattern between the MENA countries and the advanced economies helps explain the differences in economic development. Hence, no conclusions on *trust* and its impact on economic development in the MENA region can be drawn.

4.13.2 Control

WVS question text: “Some people feel they have completely free choice and control over their lives, while other people feel that what they do has no real effect on what happens to them. Please use this scale where 1 means "none at all" and 10 means "a great deal" to indicate how much freedom of choice and control you feel you have over the way your life turns out”.

Control is measured by adding the percentages of scores 7–10 for each country. *Figure 4.35* demonstrates the results for *control*. The available MENA countries realize an average level of control of 51.84 percent. The selected advanced economies exhibit an average of 65.30 percent. Thus, the advanced economies exhibit higher scores of *control*, with only France, Italy, and Japan possessing levels comparable to the MENA countries. Hence, six of the nine advanced economies exhibit higher levels of *control* than the MENA countries. The results for the MENA countries vary, with Egypt exhibiting a level of *control* of 42.80 percent and Jordan 65.10 percent.

---

[65] GDP per capita is measured in constant 2000 US dollars. GDP data were accessed July 2, 2009, from the World Bank WDI database. The WVS was conducted between 1995 and 2003. Therefore, per capita incomes do not date from the same year. For example, Algeria’s per capita income dates from 2002, Australia’s per capita income dates from 1995, etc. Hence, the levels of per capita income cannot be directly compared. Instead, only the connection between per capita income and the level of trust in the particular country is demonstrated. Furthermore, the levels of trust can be compared, since it is assumed that informal institutions change only marginally over time. Iraq is omitted since no data on per capita income is available for the particular year. Great Britain is also omitted because the WDI provide data for the United Kingdom, while the WVS data correspond to Great Britain. This note applies to all WVS indicators in this section.

The results are not clear, but a pattern is more recognizable than in the case of *trust*. The attitude concerning control over one's own life varies between MENA countries. Nevertheless, most advanced economies exhibit higher levels of *control* than MENA countries. Therefore, it can be concluded that people in MENA countries, Italy, France, and Japan are rather persuaded by predetermination. Per capita incomes in France, Italy, and Japan are higher than in MENA countries. However, this observation does not disturb our hypothesis since per capita incomes are not solely determined by one's attitude concerning destiny. It could be the case that the people of MENA countries invest less than people in selected advanced economies because of their attitude concerning predestination. However, as mentioned in Chapter 3, this reveals nothing regarding causality. Both per capita income and *control* influence each other, but the result is not convincing.

4.13.3 Respect and obedience

WVS question text: "Here is a list of qualities that children can be encouraged to learn at home. Which, if any, do you consider to be especially important? Please choose up to five".

Respect is defined as the percentage of the population of a country that considers "tolerance and respect for other people" to be important. *Obedience* is the percentage of the population of a country that considers "obedience" to be important.

Figures 4.36 and *4.37* show the results. On average, 63.43 percent of the population in the MENA countries state that "tolerance and respect for other people" is especially important compared with 77.29 percent in the advanced economies. Apart from Norway (65.90 percent), the advanced economies exhibit significantly higher levels of *respect* than the MENA countries do.

The same pattern is observable for *obedience*. In the MENA countries, more than 40 percent of the population chose obedience to be an important child quality. Regarding the advanced economies, France realizes the highest score with 35.60 percent. On average, 55.70 percent of the MENA population regards obedience as an important child quality compared with an average of 27.14 percent in the advanced economies.

In terms of *respect* and *obedience*, a difference between MENA countries and advanced economies is observable. In chapter three, *respect* and *obedience* were used as proxies for the general structure of the society. Hence, the two variables were used as proxies for generalized and limited morality, or rather modern and traditional societies. It was argued that high levels of *respect* depict a society in which emphasis is placed on the individual and trust and respect are shown to anybody, independent of group affiliation and hierarchy. On the contrary, high levels of *obedience* indicate a traditional, conservative society in which hierarchy and authority are considered important. Independence, logical reasoning, rationality, and the challenging of orders are undesirable. Consequently, collectivism is superior to individualism.

Therefore, it seems that MENA countries correspond to more traditional, conservative societies, where limited morality is prevalent. Hence, the societal structures of MENA countries are less growth supportive compared with the advanced economies that exhibit high levels of respect and low levels of obedience.

In addition, other properties exist that suggest the structure of the society. *Respect* and *obedience* are merely proxy variables. Since no regression analysis is run because of data limitations, the analysis might not be evidence enough to demonstrate that the MENA countries belong to traditional, conservative societies. Therefore, further indicators from the WVS will be considered.

Traditional societies and limited morality are inter alia characterized through the importance of the family, clan, or tribe as well as through more conservative attitudes towards the labor market participation of women, children and familial cohabitation, and gender equality in general. Usually, traditional societies exhibit low rates of women labor force participation and high birth rates. Often, families – that is, children, parents, grandparents, and eventually further relatives – live together in one house or at least close to each other. Furthermore, women are not treated the same as men; they receive less education; become married young; raise children; run the household; work on the fields; and so on but do not participate in the labor market or in political life.

Therefore, several questions from the WVS are analyzed, which deal with topics such as gender equality, the labor market participation of women, and familial structures. Thus, conclusions can be drawn regarding the structure of the society. The results are demonstrated in *Figures 4.38–4.44*. On average, 40.94 percent of the respondents from MENA countries live with their parents compared to an average of 14.49 percent in selected advanced economies. This suggests a traditional societal structure in the MENA countries where close relatives live together. In modern societies, familial structures are fractured and parents and their adult children live apart from each other.

An average of 89.90 percent of respondents from the MENA countries think that women should not have children without having a stable relationship with a man. In the selected advanced economies, 39.52 percent on average disapprove of women being single mothers. Furthermore, on average, 76.27 percent of the population in MENA countries hold that a woman needs to have children to be fulfilled compared with 33.70 percent on average in the advanced economies. According to an average of 50.86 percent of the MENA respondents, divorce is hardly ever justifiable. In the advanced economies, only 18.19 percent on average think that divorce is hardly ever justifiable.

Hence, it seems that in MENA countries family bonds are stronger than in advanced economies and that a more conservative attitude concerning the role of women is prevalent. This is proved by the fact that on average 40.89 percent of the respondents from the MENA countries agree that university education is more important for boys than for girls compared with 11.34 percent in the advanced economies. In addition, an average of 77.79 percent of the respondents in MENA countries holds that men make better political leaders than women compared with 25.48 percent in the advanced economies. Furthermore, on average, 79.78 percent of MENA respondents agree that politicians who do not believe in God are unfit for public office. In the selected advanced economies, only 15.64 percent share this opinion.

However, apart from *trust*, all variables show differences between the MENA countries and the selected advanced economies. In particular, the variables indicating the societal structure vary between MENA and advanced states. This indicates that society in MENA countries is more conservative and traditional and thereby exhibits limited morality. Chapters two and three examined the correlation between generalized and limited morality and economic growth. It was concluded that a traditional societal structure and limited morality inhibit economic growth. Hence, the form of societal organization of the MENA countries is one factor that is responsible for its disappointing economic performance. Women are discriminated concerning education and labor market participation. Hence, half of the region's workforce, and thereby half of its human capital, lies idle. Furthermore, a conservative belief and value system fosters collectivism and limited morality.

Hence, the MENA region's societal organization differs from most Western industrialized economies. Its institutional environment is less growth supportive. According to the equilibrium view of institutions, the Arab region's form of societal organization and its belief and value systems can be contingent on its history and environment. However, the transition from a traditional to a modern society is a process which every economy passes through at a certain point in time. The problem with societal transition is that it implies informal institutional change and that the form of change cannot be predicted. Hence, some institutions never change, whereas some institutions change slowly. However, modernization does not intend that the Arab region develop in similar ways to Western states. Although modernization might take place, its pace and form might differ significantly from the West. Hence, little can be done to predict and foster the process of informal institutional change and modernization in the MENA region. The only successful instrument might be economic development itself. However, economic growth is at least partly inhibited by the institutional environment.

Concerning formal institutions, however, more concrete statements are possible. The MENA region is characterized by bad governance. The formal institutional factors that are growth supporting are generally missing. Hence, property rights are poorly secured, the judiciaries are not independent, and no Western-style rule of law exists in that the governments are authoritarian, bureaucracies are too large and inefficient, political participation is restricted, and political freedoms and civil liberties are not sufficiently implemented. These political and legal deficiencies impact on the implementation of economic institutions. Hence, the dominant public sector inhibits the development of a sound private sector, financial sectors and banking systems are underdeveloped, and business regulations and restrictions on foreign trade are manifold and inefficient. Red tape and corruption pervade the political, legal, and economic sectors. However, oil-richness, rents, and foreign aid enable the perpetuation of bad governance and inefficient states.

Why did institutions in the MENA region develop in this way? Why did they not develop similar, for example, to Western European institutions? Institutional development is path-dependent because it depends on historical accidents, which appear at random and shape a society or a region's development significantly. Therefore, institutions are non-ergodic. To understand their shapes we must possess knowledge about their pasts. Historical accidents, however, can cause a deviation from the hitherto existing development path. The new path might yield immediate or later changes, which might not have occurred if the society had remained on the former path. Whether the former or the current path would have led to more efficient outcomes in the long run is unknown. Path-dependent changes cannot be reversed, and it cannot be detected whether an alternative path should have been preferred. These considerations are 'off the path of play' anyway and do not make sense. The particular path cannot be consciously chosen since historical accidents happen at random, without conscious human assistance. Random events and reverse causalities between institutions themselves and other factors render the valuation of a certain path or its alternatives impossible. Hence, to examine why institutions developed in a certain way, we have to consult a society or a region's history. A logical, efficiency-based theoretical explanation is not possible. Institutions are path-dependent and thereby their development depends on random events and cannot be theoretically explained.

The Arab region's history has to be consulted to reconstruct its institutional development. However, historical accidents are manifold and not every single one of them can be identified. Actually, historical accidents happen all the time, permanently. A region's development path is explained by its whole history, including every single detail, and not by a few obvious events. Furthermore, past and current institutions were and are influenced by a myriad factors, many of which will remain unknown. Therefore, Arab institutional development cannot be presented as a whole. Nevertheless, a few events that had severe impacts on further institutional development are now going to be depicted.

However, to really explain the current institutional status quo of the MENA region one should consult a book on the entire Arab history. This is not possible within the current study and it is also not its objective. The next chapter's objective is to focus on the starting point of institutional differences. Hence, path dependence devotes attention to the earliest events. Differences at the very beginning of certain development paths can be responsible for a permanent separation and unequal evolutions. That is to say, the decisive events that led the MENA region on its irreversible and unique development path date back a long time. Of course, since then many other events have influenced the region's institutions and changed the direction of its development path. However, the current study emphasizes the fact that the Western and the Arab paths were never unique but differed right from their respective starting points. This work concentrates on the early events that indicate why developments in both regions could never be the same. It emphasizes the period between the seventh and 15th centuries. Of course, determining events occurred after the 15th century, but the institutional lock-in and the irreversible separation happened much earlier.

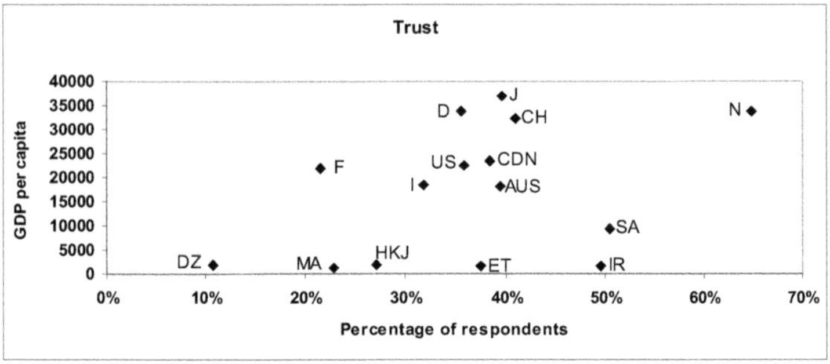

Figure 4.34: trust in MENA and advanced economies. Source: own illustration. Data accessed 27 October, 2009, [online] from WVS and WDI.

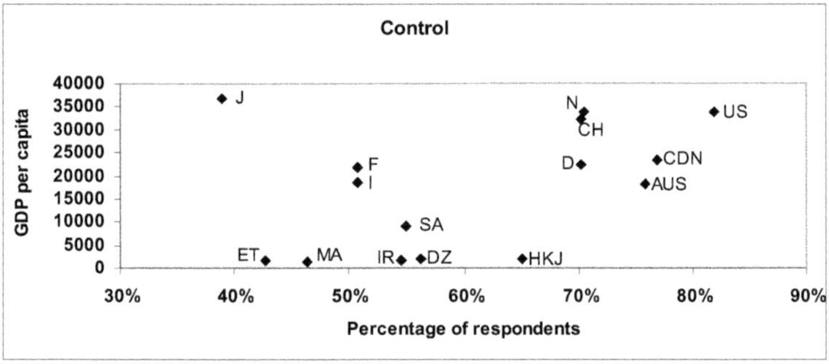

Figure 4.35: control in MENA and advanced economies. Source: own illustration. Data accessed 27 October, 2009, [online] from WVS and WDI.

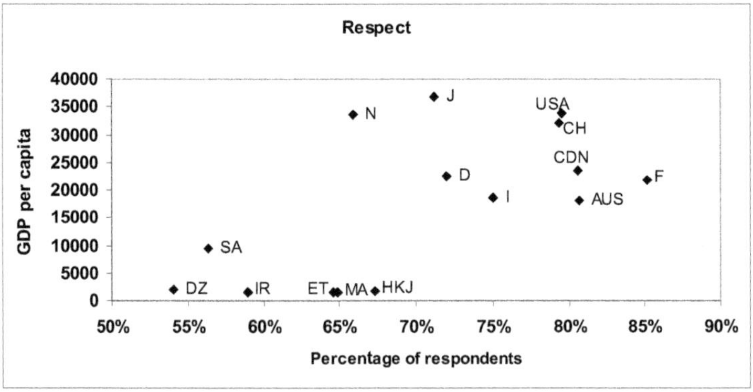

Figure 4.36: respect in MENA and advanced economies. Source: own illustration. Data accessed 27 October, 2009, [online] from WVS and WDI.

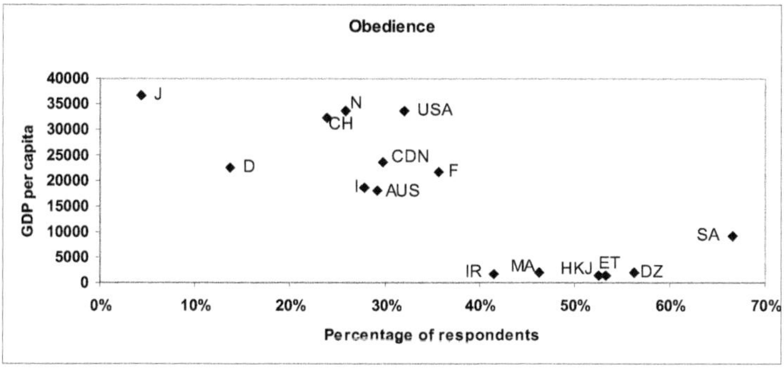

Figure 4.37: obedience in MENA and advanced economies. Source: own illustration. Data accessed 27 October, 2009, [online] from WVS and WDI.

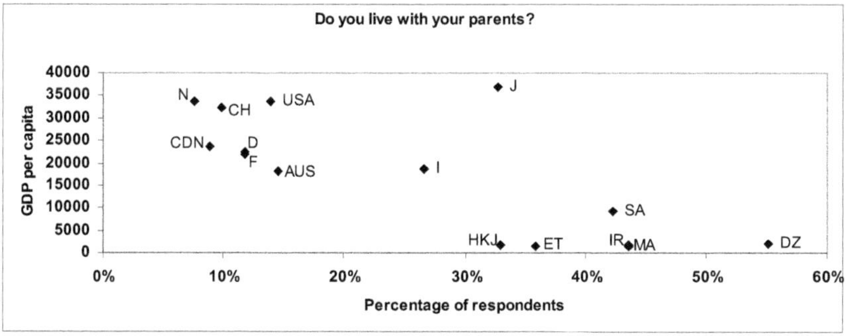

Figure 4.38: live with parents, MENA and advanced economies. Source: own illustration. Data accessed 27 October, 2009, [online] from WVS and WDI.

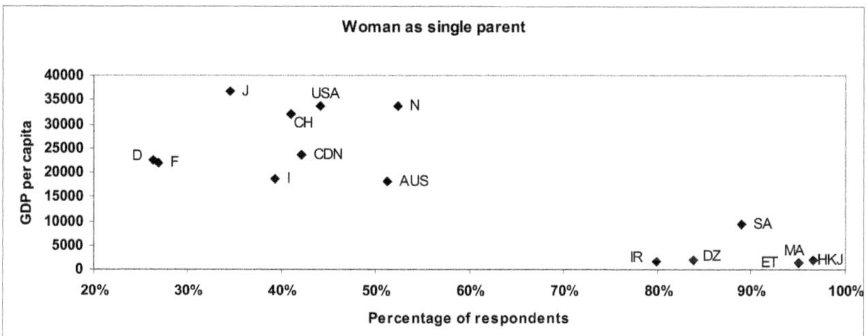

Figure 4.39: women as single parents, MENA and advanced economies. Source: own illustration. Data accessed 27 October, 2009, [online] from WVS and WDI.

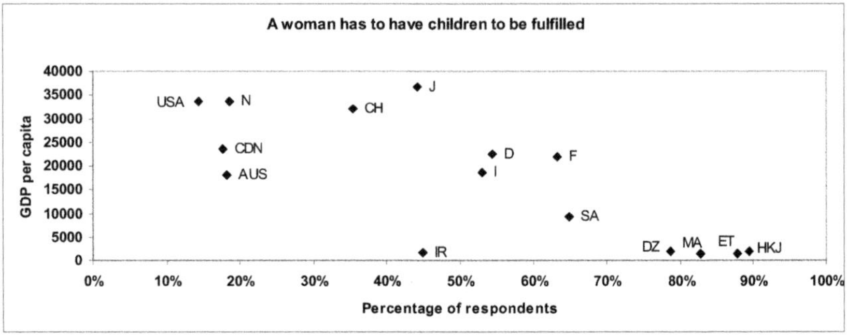

Figure 4.40: women have to have children, MENA and advanced economies. Source: own illustration. Data accessed 27 October, 2009, [online] from WVS and WDI.

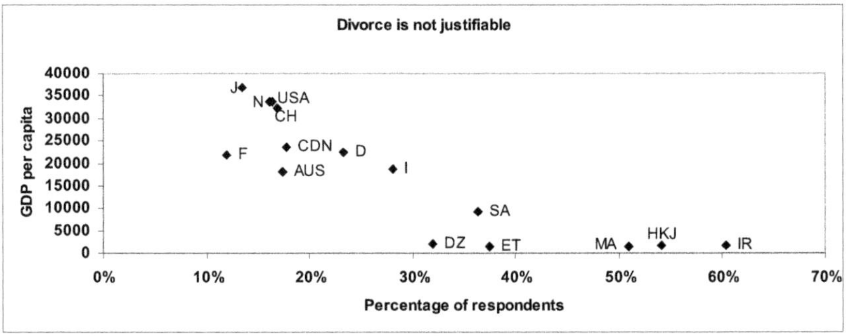

Figure 4.41: divorce not justifiable, MENA and advanced economies. Source: own illustration. Data accessed 27 October, 2009, [online] from WVS and WDI.

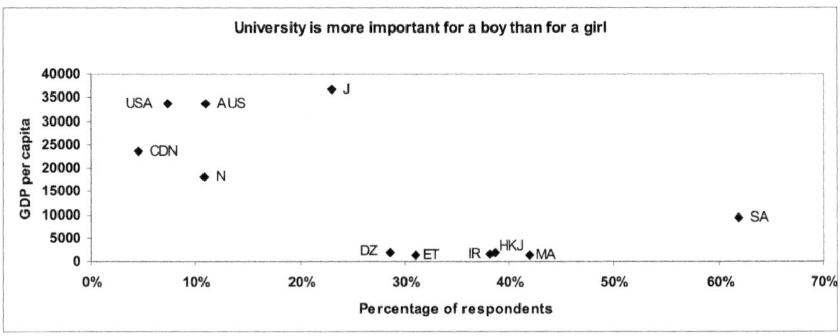

Figure 4.42: university important, MENA and advanced economies. Source: own illustration. Data accessed 27 October, 2009, [online] from WVS and WDI.

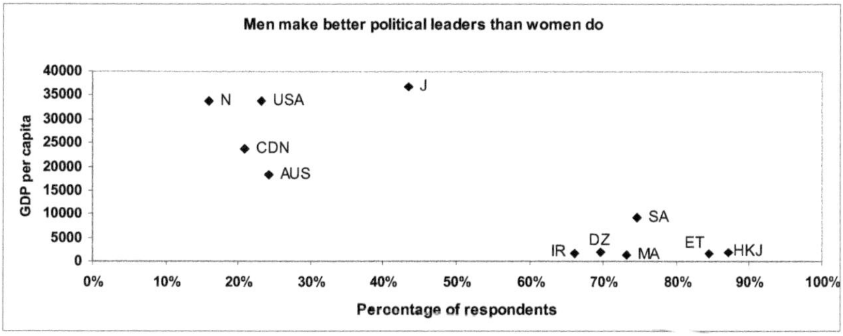

Figure 4.43: men better politicians, MENA and advanced economies. Source: own illustration. Data accessed 27 October, 2009, [online] from WVS and WDI.

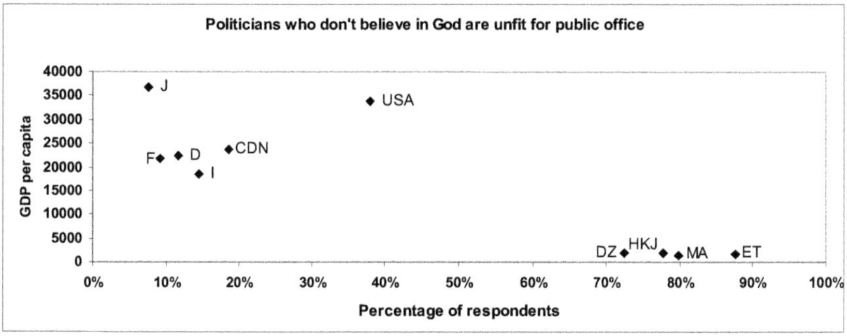

Figure 4.44: politicians' beliefs in God, MENA and advanced economies. Source: own illustration. Data accessed 27 October, 2009, [online] from WVS and WDI.

5. Differences in early institutional development

5.1 Introduction

As we have seen, the institutional environments in the MENA region differ widely from those in Western Europe. Since institutional quality significantly impacts economic development, it is not surprising that we observe divergent economic performances. However, since Western European institutional structures seem to be more conducive to economic growth, why did institutions not emerge equally in the Arab region? Different starting points, historical accidents, cultural developments, and path dependence turn a society and its institutions into what they are. Hence, to understand the state of MENA's institutions, looking at the history of the region is unavoidable. Of course, historical explanations cannot directly help improve MENA's current economic situation. However, a historical investigation into the origins of the differences in institutional developments between the Arab region and Western Europe might induce a better understanding of the MENA region per se. This would in turn improve the understanding of the institutional structure and, hence, more useful approaches for exogenous institutional change can be expected. In general, it might be possible to judge whether exogenous institutional change could be helpful at all. Furthermore, a better historical understanding helps detect growth-inhibiting institutional structures in detail. Hence, exogenous interference might be successful, since the inefficiency might be placed at a less obvious and unexpected point in the institutional system, which can only be detected via a profound historical knowledge of the respective region.

To examine the Arab institutional development right from its state of emergence, with respect to institutional consequences for the region's long-term economic development path, Western European institutional history must also be observed otherwise the differences would not become obvious. Nevertheless, this section does not emphasize Western Europe's development. Western European history is exhibited when necessary for a comparison with the Arab region. But a description of Western institutional development is not provided in detail. The MENA region is the focus and events in Western Europe are depicted and analyzed regarding their institutional relevance if necessary. This is even more the case since we must not only ask why regions such as MENA lagged behind in their economic development, but also why Europe developed so differently.

At a certain point in time, the Arab region was the most advanced region in the world and by far outperformed Western Europe. Between the ninth and 15th centuries the Arab region was far superior in scientific, intellectual, and economic matters. This makes it the more surprising that fortune became completely reversed. One could have expected that the Arabs benefitted from their advances and that what happened in Europe from the 16th and 17th centuries onwards should have happened in the MENA region several centuries before. On the contrary, the Arab countries underwent a period of scientific, intellectual, and economic decline. They were overhauled by Western Europe and have been unable to re-attain their glorious times of around the turn of the first millennium.

Since history and path dependence are crucial for institutional development, the turning point in Arab history is an interesting object of study. The institutional environment was supportive of societal and economic progress until a certain point in time. Afterwards, decline, at least in relation to Western Europe, and stagnation characterized the region for centuries. Compared with Western industrialized states, the divergence in living standards has lasted until today. Hence, certain key events must have altered the institutional system. Since institutions are inertial and complementary, the reversal might have initiated the institutional modifications and developments that have endured until today. Further institutional alterations and developments built on the changes that must have occurred. Therefore, this part of the study concentrates on certain historical events that strongly modified the institutional structure. Since emphasis is on the turning point, the consulted events occurred a long time ago. It will be examined why Arabic supremacy came to an end. Therefore, history after 1500 will be regarded to a lesser extent, although the historical events of the past 500 years have still influenced Arabic institutions. However, the starting point of institutional divergence between the MENA region and Western Europe will be examined.

This also means that certain developments in Western Europe shaped the prevalent institutional environment in a way that supported the Industrial Revolution and the unique growth performance observed since. Several authors trace Western Europe's unique development path, which cumulated in the Industrial Revolution and the emergence of sustained economic growth, back to events taking place hundreds and even thousands of years ago. Accordingly, the Industrial Revolution was based on a particular worldview that emphasized Newtonian mechanics and infiltrated Western societies in the 18th and 19th centuries.[66] In turn, the development of Newtonian mechanics required the emergence of modern sciences in the 16th and 17th centuries, which, again, depended on the acceptance of naturalism and, therefore, of human reason and rationality during the Middle Ages. The comeback of Greek philosophy since the 12th and 13th centuries, and thereby a natural philosophy based on natural laws and reason, permitted the emergence of a social value system that supported the detection of nature as an autonomous entity. Of course, naturalism faced several challenges

[66] See, for example, Grant (1996); Huff (2003); Jacob (1997); Lipsey, Carlaw & Bekar (2005).

in Europe as it did in other societies. However, historical accidents made the unique development possible. Therefore, Western Europe's political pluralism was a decisive development factor. The many countries with their changing borders and powerful city states, as well as ecclesiastical and terrestrial power struggles, made the overall oppression of naturalism impossible. The acceptance or rejection of naturalism often depended on political strategies; hence, rulers formed alliances and supported or rejected the natural worldview.

Western European societies were, to varying degrees, infused with a value system and a worldview based on naturalism. This allowed the mechanical innovations that were necessary for the Industrial Revolution and thereby sustained economic growth. Modern sciences afforded the knowledge as well as, even more importantly, the mental attitude necessary for the discovery of nature and the universe. It is exactly this relationship between worldview and sciences and technology that differed in other parts of the world. The story of Western Europe's economic success can inter alia be ascribed to its handling of natural philosophy and human reason and, in the end, with the emergence of modern sciences. The acceptance of a naturalistic worldview happened accidentally. Western Europeans did not consciously decide to accept naturalism because they knew this would lead to a unique process of economic growth centuries later. Hence, Western Europe's whole scientific and economic history can be traced back to accidental events that pushed the region onto a certain development path. Further historical accidents were necessary for Western Europe to end up in the Industrial Revolution. The Arab region, or China, for example, accidentally took other paths and ended up in different situations.

First, the build-up of the state and the early relationship between state and religion was a decisive factor for the different developments in the Arab region and Western Europe. Then, as already indicated, the varying worldviews based on the acceptance of naturalism or Islamic occasionalism, respectively were formed. It might seem abstract from a modern educated economist's perspective that a society's worldview is described as a significant factor for economic development. Nevertheless, worldview and metaphysical beliefs have been a central part of economic thought. Only in recent decades has the enthusiasm regarding these philosophically touched subjects as part of economic theory been lost. In any case, they did not lose their significance for economic matters.

The particular system of law also plays a decisive role in shaping societies. In addition, the emergence of corporate bodies in the West had a crucial impact on economic and societal progress, which was missing in the MENA region. The education systems and the degree of independence of the universities differed between the regions. Western Europe's political pluralism, the Arab *waqf* system, and Arab hereditary law as well as further historical differences were significant factors that influenced the directions of the development paths.

5.2 The emergence of state and religion

Although differences in religious thought are not emphasized in this work, the formative influence of religion cannot be denied in both Western Europe and the Arab world. Western Europe is shaped by Christendom. Its history is governed by events that can be ascribed to religious matters in one way or another. However, the differences in the emergence of the religion and the state, as well as the relationship between religion and state-run structures are conspicuous in both regions (Lewis, 2002).

After emerging in Judea Christianity spread westward, overcoming many cultural and societal borders. However, compared with Islam, Christianity spread slowly. It took nearly 400 years until Christendom became an official state religion. Christianity had to compete with the culturally and intellectually advanced societies of the Roman Empire. On its way westward, it was forced to adjust to the surrounding world and was affected by external influences. In addition, early Christians were not endued with military forces. Hence, they could not conquer the Roman Empire and impose their rules and structures on it. Christians had to diffuse their beliefs by conversion and, at least for some time, against the power of the state (Grant, 1996, p. 182; Lipsey, Carlaw & Bekar, 2005, p. 225). Furthermore, conversion had to take place within the prevalent governmental and societal structures. That is to say, Christianity was born into the pre-existing structures of the Roman Empire. Therefore, formal institutions such as the judiciary, political system, and commercial structures already existed before the emergence of the religion. Thus, Christianity had to accept the pre-existing structure of institutions. Since its adherents had lived within these structures before becoming Christians, they did not refuse all of the prevalent institutions. Of course, Christians tried to reform institutions according to their vision. But right from the start, Christianity developed within an existing and functioning state. Its adherents were influenced by the structures and institutions of the Roman Empire and did not abandon all of those structures. They rather diffused their beliefs within the structures of the state and retained the system where possible following their conviction. In the end, Christianity became the state religion.

Although attempts were made to establish ecclesiastical supremacy, the target was not to establish a theocracy. The dominance of church and state might have changed several times; however, they have always been regarded as two independent entities.[67]

[67] Christendom's secular tradition and the acceptance of a terrestrial power is confirmed in several passages in the Bible, the most popular being Matthew 22.21: *"Render therefore unto Cesar the things which are Cesar's; and unto God the things which are God's".*

Therefore, Christianity has a kind of secular tradition. Since the time of its emergence, Christianity has never been equal to the state. Despite tendencies to unite state and religion as one entity, Christians are used to being subordinated to both a terrestrial and an ecclesiastical power. That is to say, since its emergence, Christianity practically had to accept two kinds of jurisdiction: a terrestrial and an ecclesiastical one (Grant, 1996, p. 7ff.). The fact that Christianity met different cultures and societies on its way westwards, and that it grew up in the already developed structures of a state, led to its pluralistic tradition, which became important for its further development as will be seen.

Events were different in the Arab region. Islam emerged within a stateless environment. Muhammad established a state on the Arab peninsula where there had been none before. Prior to the Arab state, social structures had been solely ruled by bloodline, clanship, and familial and tribal affiliation. Of course, social affiliation remained important. But, decisively, no general state-run structures, no formal institutions, no legislature, no overall legitimate power, and no citizenship subsisted. The first structures of a state were founded simultaneously with the emergence of Islam. During the time of revelation (610–632), Muhammad formed the religious community and simultaneously created the first state structures. Hence, the Arab state originated in religious revelation. Religious doctrines and then prevalent social norms and structures were the basis for the build-up of the Arab state. Therefore, religion and state were equivalent right from the start. No difference between a terrestrial and an ecclesiastical side existed. State and religion were one entity. Islam never had to adjust to any kind of pre-existing institutions, apart from the customs at that time, which, of course, entered the Scripture. Islam by itself created the institutions. That is to say, only one instance existed, which explains the theocratic tradition of the Arab region (Lewis, 2002).

During Muhammad's lifetime (570–632) the first structures of a state were created. These comprised a kind of judiciary – the sharia was written down later – the emergence of a bureaucracy, and a system of taxation (Halm, 2006, p. 26). After Muhammad's death, almost the entire Arab peninsula belonged to the new Arab state. The locals converted to Islam and, by that, subordinated themselves to the religious and statist doctrines.

In the following centuries, the expansion of the Arab Empire continued and reached its peak in the second half of the ninth century. At that time, the Empire stretched from the Pyrenees to Central Asia and comprised nine to 10 million km^2 and between 35 and 40 million people (around the 10th century) (Issawi, 1995, p. 39). Even before the emergence of the Arab Empire, the MENA region's geographic location made it a main trade centre. All goods traded between Western Europe, Byzantium, India, and China had to cross the Middle East, North Africa, or the Arab peninsula (Issawi, 1995, Ch. 2, p. 31–55).

The conquests of the Arabs, however, occurred within a relatively short period of time and stretched over a large area. Therefore, the Empire suddenly included many different social groups and cultures. The conquered regions were not forced to convert to Islam. Instead, the inhabitants received the status of protégés and were relatively free to pursue their own religious and cultural traditions. The protégés were guaranteed protection of body and life, of property and religious freedom. Service in return was a poll tax the non-Muslims had to pay. This tax was an important source of income for the Empire and its military forces. However, the Arabs were not interested in the religious and cultural affairs of their protégés.

Religious freedom and the acceptance of other cultures and traditions within the Arab Empire meant that Muslims were not forced to critically assess the alien as well as their own cultural and religious doctrines. Critically assessing a strange subject usually leads to a critical view on your own. Since medieval Arab religious leaders were not interested in the alien religions and traditions within their Empire, they did not critically deal with the foreign or their own religious and social doctrines.

The disinterest incorporated the worldviews and the work of foreign scientists that, since the beginning of the ninth century, travelled to the Arab scientific centers such as Baghdad, Damascus, and later Cordoba. Non-Muslim scientists and philosophers, whether from within or from outside the Empire, were allowed to practice their religions and follow their own convictions. Furthermore, Islamic religious leaders were not even interested in the alien religions and worldviews. According to Lipsey, Carlaw and Bekar (2005), this ignorance with regard to non-Muslims hindered Islamic religious leaders from becoming natural philosophers compared with Christian clerics. "Also, since no attempt was made to persuade a sophisticated public to convert, the religion's leaders did not need to engage them in intellectual debate on their own terms. Thus, although many of the conquered areas contained highly sophisticated societies with many scholars who were well versed in all branches of philosophy, including natural philosophy, the religious leaders themselves did not develop a serious knowledge of philosophy" (Lipsey, Carlaw & Bekar, 2005, p. 269). Grant (1996) also considers the fact that Islamic theologians (at least those that came after the Mutazilites, an early rational theological school) and religious leaders were not natural philosophers, which could have been decisive for the decline of Arab sciences after the 15th century.

In Western Europe, prospective theologians were required to have a master of arts and, hence, be educated in natural philosophy (Grant, 1996, p. 174f.). Christian theologians, even the conservatives, utilized natural philosophy, although it might have been considered suspect in parts. However, in Islam natural philosophy was always forced onto the defensive. It was not officially taught at the *madrasas* or universities, but privately at the scholar's home. Religious leaders and Islamic theologians of the 11th century and later were not educated in natural philosophy. The philosophers and scientists, on the contrary, were influenced and embedded by orthodox Islamic thought since they also had to fulfill their public and religious duties.

Regarding the emergence of state and religion, two points must be recorded. First, the foundation of the state and religion and the interrelationship between them differ greatly between Western Europe and the MENA region. Right from the start, both regions were situated on different development paths. That is to say, both regions fall back on different starting points and, hence, the different development paths the regions took are a logical result. We cannot use the same standards to judge the developments in the two regions since the bases differ. Nobody can judge medieval Muslims for their theocratic traditions or for their recognition of sharia as the only valid law. Furthermore, if religious structures are the foundations of the state, it is easier for religious conservatives to exert influence and oppress opposing views.

5.3 The acceptance of Islamic occasionalism and the role of foreign sciences

It might seem strange that a certain worldview should have a significant impact on a region's economic development. 'Worldview' itself is not a typical economical variable and educated mainstream economists might find it difficult to establish a connection between a former value system and contemporary growth. This might be all the more the case since the observed period dates back almost a millennium. In any case, the distinct origins on which both societies were built will be elucidated and their significance for economic progress will become obvious.

The crucial differences are in the realm of metaphysics and relate to the idea of man and nature. The Christian belief states that God endowed man with reason and free will. God created the world and, therefore, everything that is created has a cause, even the world and God. Nature was created by God as an independent, autonomous entity and, therefore, nature can exist independently without God intervening. This is the case since natural laws exist that follow from causality. Occurrences without a cause are called miracles. But it is not God who lets the Earth circulate around the sun or who is responsible for rainfall or droughts. He does not make plants grow, the sun shine, and so on. These are things nature does by itself based on natural laws and, hence, on causality. God wanted man to be capable of understanding and, therefore, examining the natural world. Man should be reasonable and able to judge his actions and, hence, should be able to assess the trueness of moral values. Man can consider and decide independently which morals and values are right and which are wrong. Furthermore, man is allowed and capable to examine the world, God, and the Scripture, which, therefore, is open to interpretation (Grant, 1996; Huff, 2003, p. 89–117; Lipsey, Carlaw & Bekar, 2005, p. 232–235).

The orthodox Islamic theory, on the contrary, states that God is above or without reason. God and everything concerning His existence is situated in a sphere or dimension that man is incapable of understanding. Therefore, man cannot know which values are right and, hence, he is not endowed with reason and free will. Even the interpretations of the terms 'reason' and 'free will' are manmade and not God-made or God-given. God is the only creator. Man does not know which values are right and which are wrong, since he cannot judge whether something is logical, rational, and reasonable. He cannot know because he is incapable of understanding. Therefore, the only thing man can do is obey. Because man has no reason and cannot understand, God gave him the revelation, the Quran, which was not created but is perpetual. Everything man needs to know is written down in the Scripture. He shall not consider by himself. All he has to do is follow the rules. The Quran is not meant to be full of bans but instead is a guide to help man live his life in a way that leads to salvation. This guidance is not open to interpretation, since man is not able to interpret. The Quran is given once and for all by God; at the time of the revelation it was perfect, complete, and unchangeable. Hence, the Quran was given to man in a final version.

The orthodox Islamic doctrine rejects causality since God is the only cause. The Earth, for example, circulates around the sun because God wants it to. If He wanted to, He could stop the Earth circulating immediately. If a person is thirsty, drinks some water, and is no longer thirsty, this is not because of the water he drank. Drinking the water is not the reason for not being thirsty anymore. It is just the way God wants it to be in this moment. Hence, causality and, therefore, natural laws do not exist, because God is the only creator. This doctrine is called Islamic occasionalism and was accepted at the disadvantage of naturalism, which asserted itself in Western Europe (El-Affendi, 1998; Fakhry, 1998; Hye, 2004; Sheikh, 1982).

However, modern science is based on causality and natural laws. Hence, the rejection of causality and rationality inhibited the necessary developments for the emergence of modern science, which, in turn, enabled the mechanistic worldview required for the Industrial Revolution.[68] Since Islamic occasionalism rejected causality, natural philosophy per se came to an end in the Arab region. Hence, the implementation of Islamic occasionalism and of orthodox Islam was

[68] See, for example, Grant (1996); Huff (2003); Jacob (1997); Lindberg (1992); Lipsey, Carlaw & Bekar (2005).

a watershed in Arabic scientific history. The emergence of modern sciences had become impossible.

The body of natural sciences can be traced back to the Greeks and the Hellenistic doctrine. In Europe, after the end of the Roman Empire, Greek learning was lost for hundreds of years and was brought back by the Arabs in Spain. Mainly in Cordoba, the works of the Greek philosophers and scholars were translated from Arabic into Latin and entered Middle Europe via the Pyrenees in the 12th and 13th centuries. The Arabs had earlier been influenced by Greek learning. Under the Abbasid Caliphate (750–1258), which brought the capital of the Arab Empire from Damascus to Baghdad, great scientific efforts were made and science flourished in many places, especially in Baghdad and, about two centuries later, in Cordoba. At the beginning of the ninth century, systematic translation efforts from Greek into Arabic were conducted and soon all important works were available in the new language of science: Arabic.[69] From the ninth century until the end of the 15th century, the Arab region had the most advanced sciences worldwide. As Huff writes, "Considered altogether, in mathematics, astronomy, optics, physics and medicine, Arabic science was the most advanced in the world" (Huff, 2003, p. 52). Arab mathematicians in the 11th and 12th centuries achieved mathematical innovations that were not accomplished by Europeans until the 15th and 16th centuries (Huff, 2003, p. 51). Scholars from all over the world met in Baghdad, where they brought their knowledge together and created new ideas. This means that it were not necessarily Arabs who forced scientific thought and research. Iranians, Christians, Jews, and people from other parts of the world were involved. Greek science and the thoughts of rationality and reason affected the work and the worldview of the philosophers, scientists and, therefore, urban society in general, as it did in Western Europe hundreds of years later.

Between the 12th and 14th centuries, many popular Arab astronomers tried to overcome and reform the Ptolemaic planetary system or geocentric model, in which the Earth is seen as the centre of the universe with all other planets, including the sun, circulating around it. In Western Europe, this evolution took place in the 16th and 17th centuries. The Arab astronomer Ibn al-Shatir (d. 1375) developed planetary systems that were identical to those of Copernicus (1473–1543) except for some parameters (Huff, 2003, p. 55ff.). Mathematically these models were equivalent to later European models. But, for some reason, the Arabs did not take the last step to the heliocentric worldview, the starting point for modern science. As Huff writes: "To the degree that the planetary models of Ibn al-Shatir and those of Copernicus are virtually identical with only minor differences in some parameters, the problem was not one of mathematical

[69] Most Greek works were already available in Aramaic and just had to be translated further into Arabic by Aramaic-speaking Christians in the Fertile Crescent (Halm, 2006, p. 43).

modelling, but one of conceptual or metaphysical innovation or both" (Huff, 2003, p. 61).

Hence, early Islamic philosophers and scholars were not reluctant to Greek learning. On the contrary, Greek philosophy had a significant influence on medieval Arabic sciences and even on Islamic theology. However, science in early Islam consisted of the mathematical sciences, (natural) philosophy, theology (*kalam*), and Islamic law (*fiqh*). Mathematical sciences "primarily comprised the quadrivium of late antiquity: namely, arithmetic (...), geometry, astronomy and musical theory, and their applications in fields such as optics and mechanics" (Sabra, 1994, p. 1f.). Philosophy was closely related to science and theology. It "always explicitly or implicitly signified a body of doctrine and a style of thought that was dominated by a Neoplatonized Aristotelianism carried over from Aristotle's late Greek commentators" (Sabra, 1994, p. 3). Hence, Greek ideas were well received in Islamic philosophy between the 9th and 14th centuries. Greek philosophy was further developed in Arab scientific centers, and many popular philosophers at that time were Arabs or foreign scholars carrying out research in popular Arab cities (Huff, 2003, p. 68). Nevertheless, in medieval Islam philosophy was called the foreign science. It had already existed before Islam came into the world and was imported into Arabic culture from the Greeks. Although the Arabs were the leading scientists and philosophers for several centuries, their subject was considered foreign, since it had not emerged within Arabic culture and society (Huff, 2003; Sabra, 1994). Therefore, natural sciences and philosophy were the least respected sciences. The efforts of scholars and philosophers were appreciated, for example, regarding their medical services. However, most of them held an official job such as physician, teacher, or court-appointed official. Their profession as a natural scientist or free-thinker was, in general, not popular. Especially after the Islamic doctrine was almost fully developed after the 11th century, the work of natural scientists and philosophers was regarded as disrespectful to Islam and was dismissed as blasphemous.

However, Islamic theology or *kalam* depicts a specific form of theology based on reason and rationality (Huff, 2003, p. 47ff.; Sabra, 1994). According to Sabra (1994, p. 11), "kalam was an argumentative approach to religion which sought, through discussion and discursive thought, to interpret and transform the content of the Islamic revelation into a rationally-based doctrine." The theologians were called *mutakallinum* in Arabic. The fact that reason and rationality were discussed within the theological context already indicates the controversy regarding the traditional orthodox Islamic doctrine.

The traditional view held that man did not possess reason and conscience, since he was not able to understand. Accordingly, God is the only creator, causality does not exist, life is predetermined, and, since man can neither conceive God, nor the Scripture or human life per se, he must obey and take the Quran literally. To study (not to interpret!) the Quran and the sunna was the subject of Islamic law or *fiqh*, which, therefore, was the most reputable science. Theology and philosophy were less accepted since both subjects tried to examine God and nature. However, such an approach was blasphemous, since God and nature did not need to be examined. Everything necessary to human life was given by the Quran. The Quran was perfect and complete. It should not be interpreted, changed, or adjusted. Hence, to deal with theology or philosophy was just not necessary or even forbidden from a religious point of view. It was more honorable to study the Quran, without intending to interpret it. Hence, the *fuqaha*, or jurisconsults, were not allowed to use their reason, conscience, and intellect to create statutes. Everything concerning human behavior, all rules and required punishments, were written down once and for all in the Quran. Man was not allowed to interpret, change, or enlarge these documents. What was written down had to be taken literally.

Several theological schools, rational and orthodox, emerged since the early beginnings of Islam. *Kalam*, which means 'speech', 'word', or 'discussion', however, became associated with the school of the Mutazila. The Mutazilites held that reason was the basic truth of everything, even religion. Hence, their system of theology was purely rational (Sheikh, 1982, p. 14). The Mutazilites were persuaded by the creation of the Quran, man's free will, and indicated the grave sinner as being neither a Muslim nor a nonbeliever, but an intermediate person (El-Affendi, 1998). The biggest controversy compared with orthodox theology and, hence, *fiqh* involved the creation of the Quran. Although the Mutazila insisted on the creation of the Quran, the traditionalists held the view that the Quran was perpetual. Furthermore, the Mutazila conceded reason, conscience, and free will to man. Hence, human life was not predetermined. Man was able to understand and interpret the created Scripture. He could differentiate between good and evil and, hence, make moral judgments. They allowed man intellectual activity and developed a remarkable theory of knowledge in Islamic intellectual history (Sabra, 1994). The Mutazilites were able to further develop and foster their ideas of reason and rationality through the influence of Greek philosophy and were politically supported by the caliphs at the time. For its adherents religion meant no more than superstition (Huff, 2003; Lipsey, Carlaw & Bekar, 2005). However, under the Mutazilite predominance, opponents of their view could be punished and imprisoned.

The Mutazilite school dominated Islamic theological thought for 100–150 years. Things began to change under the rule of Caliph Ja'afar al-Mutawakkil (847–861). The caliph himself was not an adherent of the Mutazilite school. Instead, under his rule the Asharite school (al-Ashari, d. 935) gained momentum. The Asharites did not totally reject rationalism. Nevertheless, the Asharite school was persuaded by the perpetuity of the Quran; hence, according to them, the Quran was not created but existed in eternity. Furthermore, the Asharites differed from the Mutazilites regarding man's free will and reason. Accordingly, God is the only creator and every action is created by Him. For example, if one wants to write something on a piece of paper, "God creates in his mind the will to write and at the same time He grants him the power to write" (Sheikh, 1982, p. 19). Hence, the Asharites take a path in between free will and complete determinism, since God creates the will to write, but does not accomplish the action by Himself (Sheikh, 1982, pp. 15–20). Further differences between Mutazilites and Asharites existed, for example, regarding God's attributes, beatific vision, and the legitimacy of political power (Sheikh, 1982, p. 14f.).

However, al-Ashari (873–935) can be described as the finisher of the idea of Islamic occasionalism, which was modified and further distributed by al-Ghazzali (1058–1111) and established itself as a main doctrine in Islamic theology (Halm, 2006, p. 37; Sabra, 1994, p. 26). Hence, although rationalism and reason played a decisive role in Islamic theology, the orthodox Islamic doctrines could at least prevail.

The discipline of *kalam*, however, was not able to resist the orthodox tendencies. From the 11th century onwards, *kalam* declined rapidly. This was because of the pro-traditionalist tendencies within *kalam* itself, which broke with its original basis of rationality and reason; but the decline was also rooted in *kalam's* failure to develop a complete philosophical system (El-Affendi, 1998). The dialectic theologians (*mutakallinum*) who succeeded the Mutazilites –the Asharites – at least rejected causality and natural law and accepted Islamic occasionalism. For them, God was the only creator. They could not tolerate the idea of the creation of the Quran and of man being able to interpret the Scripture. Hence, the Quran was never subjected to the kind of criticism to which the Bible was exposed in the West. *Kalam* became mingled with Islamic philosophy and, therefore, was defeated by orthodox Islam, as were natural philosophy and sciences per se.

Two theses exist to try to explain the decline of natural sciences in medieval Islam, the discipline for which medieval Arabs were so well known. The marginality thesis states that natural sciences never played more than a marginal role in Arab society (Huff, 2003). The so-called foreign sciences never belonged to the body of Islamic society and culture. Therefore, the marginality thesis affirms that natural sciences finally played a minor role, even in the lives of Arabic scientists. Huff explains that "people are always located in multiple roles and statuses. Consequently, the attitudes, interests, and capacities of one situation are often extended to another. This means that all social organizations and institutions are interdependent" (Huff, 2003, p. 64). Huff states that Arab natural scientists and philosophers were not merely scientists, but also participated in further societal spheres. Therefore, they became influenced by orthodox Islam, and after generations of scholars had grown up in an Islamic orthodox environment they at least accepted the orthodox doctrines. At least the scholars of the 13th and later centuries, despite their professions, accepted orthodox positions on the most central issues. As an example, Huff cites the famous Arab astronomer Ibn al-Shatir of the 14th century. Ibn al-Shatir's profession was not only astronomy; he was also the timekeeper of a mosque in Damascus. Hence, on one hand, he was a strictly religious official and, on the other, he was a scientist. Furthermore, Averroes (Ibn Rushd, d. 1198), although a scientist (natural philosopher), worked as a *qadi*, that is, a judge specialized in religious law (Huff, 2003, p. 64f.).

Sabra (1994), however, rejects the marginality thesis, arguing that natural sciences did not play a marginal but a grave role in medieval Islamic society. Therefore, the term "naturalization" is central, which "refers to the domesticating of the foreign and ancient sciences, thereby incorporating them into an indigenous cultural and philosophical system" (Huff, 2003, p. 65f.). It depicts the full acceptance of the foreign sciences in every dimension of society. When naturalized, the foreign sciences are a part of Arab institutions and Arab culture. According to Sabra (1994), this is what happened to sciences and natural philosophy in the Arab region. Hence, in the course of naturalization natural sciences should have become institutionalized and thereby gained autonomy and independence. However, although natural sciences and philosophy did become institutionalized, they never obtained an autonomous space. Instead they were completely interfused with Islamic philosophy and theology and, therefore, lost their independence. Hence, the critical doctrines that did not fit with orthodox Islam could be deleted over time. From Sabra's point of view, the penetration and mixture of natural sciences and orthodox Islam was the crux. The inconsistency of both views forced one to make large compromises. Therefore, natural philosophy more and more adapted to the orthodox Islamic doctrine and was lost on the way.

Western Europe, however, experienced a renaissance in the 12th and 13th centuries that was grounded in the legal revolution. This intellectual transition can be traced back to the influence of Plato's Timaeus. Of course, Plato was also known by the Arabs; however, his effect differed widely between both civilizations. Decisively, the European Platonism of the 12th century led to the idea of the atomic world and to the intention of examining everything to find a cause and effect (Huff, 2003, p. 100). The new Aristotelian translations that arrived in Western Europe in the 12th and 13th centuries caused severe alterations to the Platonist view, but it had laid the groundwork for the Western European idea of the physical nature of the world.[70]

[70] Of course, Western Europe's rationalism also faced severe counterattacks by the conservative forces of the church and society, especially in the second half of the 13th century. However, European naturalism succeeded because the Christian church did not condemn Greek philosophy in general. Instead, it tried to connect religious and rationalist ideas where it seemed to fit and, therefore, adopted naturalistic views. Furthermore, European pluralism and

In Western Europe, science in the Middle Ages was split up into medicine, exact sciences (mathematics, astronomy, statistics, optics), and natural philosophy. What Aristotle called physics is approximately similar to what is understood by natural philosophy or natural science. Hence, natural philosophy dealt with "the study of the first causes of nature, change and motion in general, the motion of celestial bodies, the motions of transformation of the elements, generation and corruption, the phenomena in the upper region of the atmosphere right below the lunar sphere, and the study of animals and plants" (Grant, 1996, p. 136). However, during medieval times and even later, these topics were not examined from a purely naturalistic point of view, but rather from a theological and philosophical one.

The transitions between the sciences were smooth; mathematics, for example, was sometimes included in natural philosophy. Philosophers used mathematical tools and both sciences examined the same bodies in different aspects. However, natural philosophy or natural science was not similar to modern science or to what is currently understood as natural science. Medieval science included mathematical, physical, and chemical tools as well as philosophy and theology. The emergence of modern sciences in the 16th and 17th centuries added a mechanical component and, hence, by 1850, natural philosophy was divided into "mechanics, hydrostatics, hydrodynamics, hydraulics, pneumatics, acoustics, optics, astronomy, electricity, galvanism, magnetism, and chromatics" (Grant, 1996, p. 193, referring to Guralnik, 1975, p. 61). Even the already mechanical sciences of the 18th century must be understood as "dark thread entwined in a tapestry of many colors, a whole cloth made up of religious and secular values crisscrossed with scientific learning. [...] We separate science from religion, science from technology, theories from practice. They did not" (Jacob, 1997, p. 104). Hence, it is important to differentiate between medieval natural philosophy and medieval natural sciences; modern sciences; and contemporary natural sciences.

In any case, the rationalist and mechanical worldview established in Western Europe from the 16th century onwards caused the emergence of modern sciences, which enabled the required technological progress and the particular state of mind to create the necessary kind of knowledge. Huff (2003) explains that "the modern scientific worldview is a unique metaphysical structure. This means

---

the establishment of the university as a corporate body made a general rejection impossible (Lipsey, Carlaw & Bekar 2005, p. 234). However, it should not be concealed that the success of naturalism in Western Europe and, therefore, the implementation of a mechanistic worldview were also down to luck. Several historical accidents, most of them too negligible to attract attention, might have played a significant role. Nevertheless, the acceptance of naturalism and especially of modern sciences varied between countries in Europe. Southern Europe, for example, fell far behind Northern Europe regarding progress in modern sciences (Lipsey, Carlaw & Bekar 2005, p. 237).

that the modern scientific worldview rests on certain assumptions about the regularity and lawfulness of the natural world and the presumption that man is capable of grasping that underlying structure" (p. 67). Hence, it was the atomic, rationalist, and later mechanical worldview that permitted Western Europe's unique development path, which resulted in the Industrial Revolution and sustained economic growth. Orthodox Islamic theologians rejected the regularities and the laws of nature as well as the assumption that man is able to understand the world and its sense inherently. Hence, the worldview necessary for the development of modern sciences and the one predominant in medieval Islam could not be combined. Differences in the fundamental issues were too large.

Of course, *kalam*, natural philosophy, and medieval sciences per se did not disappear straight away in the Arab world. The attitude regarding rationalism and Greek philosophy was not universal in the whole Empire. Since Islam has no central authority and, therefore, has no organized structure like the Christian church, it was not possible to generally dictate certain orthodox doctrines. Hence, discussions concerning naturalism and philosophy continued. Nevertheless, by the end of the 14th century orthodox Islam at last established itself as the only doctrine. Although rational ideas kept on circulating within particular groups, a general denial of natural philosophy had at least been implemented.

Both the diffusion of rationalism since the eighth century and the spread of Islamic occasionalism since the 11th century were supported by the fact that Islam was a religion of the cities. Islam emerged in a vital and popular commercial town, Mecca, and further developed in another city, Medina. Its different schools and forms always emerged in cities, such as Basra, Kufa, Damascus, Baghdad, Buchara, and Samarkand (Huff, 2003, p. 18). The nomads in the deserts converted to Islam, mainly for economic reasons, but kept their own customs and traditions. However, the vital trade routes and the scientific exchange between the intellectual Arab centers made possible the fast diffusion of new ideas and doctrines. Hence, Greek philosophical thought and conservative Islamic doctrines were diffused apace among and within the cities.

5.4 Law

The unique development and application of Islamic law demonstrates the significance of the system of law for society in general. The Islamic law, the sharia, is directly grounded in God's word. It is based on the Quran and the sunna (the traditions of the Prophet). Thus, it is a religious law that is given to mankind directly from God. Most importantly, it was given to mankind in an already complete, perfect, and unchangeable state (Huff, 2003, p. 91). Trying to add, adjust, or change the law was blasphemous. Therefore, the continual development and adjustment of law that occurred in Western Europe was inconceivable in the Arab world.

The Quran was written down first by Caliph 'Uthmân (644–656), who compiled a complete collection of the records of the revelation (Halm, 2006, p. 13f.). However, a second source of Islamic law, which Halm (2006, p. 41) describes as being even more important than the Quran for a Muslim's everyday life, is the hadîth – that is, Muhammad's direct quotations and records. Using the hadîth, Muslims try to get to know and record the customs and traditions of the Prophet and his associates, that is, the sunna. The Quran and hadîth build the principles of the sharia, which is Arabic for path or street. The sharia comprises all areas of life and is thought to help realize the unity of belief and an individual's actions and, hence, attain salvation (Fischer, 1992, p. 26). This already demonstrates the crucial difference compared with Western law. The sharia is not a Western-style collection of laws. Instead, it is a guide that incorporates all human affairs in everyday life and, by obeying this guidance, a Muslim is situated on the right path to salvation. Since the Quran and the hadîth regulate an individual's everyday life in detail, and describe how a Muslim should conduct their public and private affairs, the whole Arab region is characterized by a unique lifestyle, even though Arabic customs and traditions vary by region (Fischer, 1992, p. 27).

Islamic law is based on four sources: the Quran, the sunna (and hence, the hadîth), analogical reasoning (*qiyas*), and the consensus of the Islamic community (*ijma'*) (Huff, 2003, p. 92; Halm, 2006, p. 45).[71] Since the revelation was given once and for all, and since it was already complete, no adjustments or additions were allowed. However, the Quran and the sunna do not contain a comprehensive legal code. On the contrary, they contain "a collection of piecemeal rulings on particular issues scattered over a wide variety of different topics; far from representing a substantial corpus juris, [...] [the legal material] hardly comprises the bare skeleton of a legal system" (Huff, 2003, p. 92). Therefore, Islamic jurists continually had to deal with new situations that were not appropriately written down in the Quran or the hadîth. Thus, an intellectual struggle (*ijtihad*) was indispensable to understand the sharia and deal with the problems that confronted the judges (*qadis*) and jurists. Since the Quran and the hadîth were complete and unchangeable, an intellectual struggle was only possible in the form of conclusion by analogy. Hence, it was examined whether the case in question was in accordance with a situation described in the Quran or the hadîth. If this was not the case, the situation with the nearest similarity had to be con-

[71] The method of consensus (*ijma'*) might not seem to fit into the theory since agreeing on something incorporates different opinions that exist before the consensus is found. However, personal reasoning and opinion was ruled out in Islamic legal thought. The argumentation concerning this seeming conflict is that God would not allow the whole Islamic community (*umma*) to make a mistake. Hence, a scholarly consensus on Islamic legal issues cannot be wrong, since God would avoid an error made by the *umma*.

sulted. Therefore, Islamic legal theory was based on strict analogy (*qiyas*) and the avoidance of personal opinion and personal discretion. The theory of Muhammad ibn Idrîs al-Shafi'i (767–820), who is known as the founder of Islamic legal theory, reduced *ijtihad* to *qiyas* and thereby reason had to be completely subordinated to divine law (Huff, 2003, p. 92f.). The fact that no adjustments, modifications, and additions were possible led to the static character of Islamic law. Although Roman law was known to the medieval Muslims, they never considered it an additional source of legal principles, since God's revelation was complete already. Furthermore, the ruler of the Muslim community was the law enforcer. Since human life in general was not differentiated in secular and sacred spheres, the ruler was the divine and the earthly head of state. According to Huff (2003, p. 94), this explains why "legal personalities and institutions such as corporations do not exist, why the idea of personal liability and the concept of negligence are unknown to Islamic law, why the rules of evidence are hardly developed at all, and why Islamic penal law, as well as Islamic codes of public administration, are completely inadequate for a modern state". This is also why modernizing Arab states in the 20th century had to adopt Western legal codes and retained the principles of the sharia merely regarding family affairs and inheritance law.

The sharia is based on the Quran and the sunna since these sources incorporate the Prophet's volitions and actions. However, it is not a finished code of law that is written out and available in book form. On the contrary, the construction and handling of the sharia depend on regional legal customs and on the results achieved through consensus and analogy in the particular region or in the particular case. Furthermore, Islamic law is not uniform, but differentiated into four major schools: the Shafi'i, the Hanafi, the Hanbali, and the Maliki (Halm, 2006, p. 43ff.; Huff, 2003, p. 96). Additionally, the differentiation between Sunnites and Shiites is important since Shiites exhibit their own sunna, which results in different constructions of the sharia (Halm, 2006, p. 75).

However, this is not meant to say that the sharia is a uniform code of law applied in the same way in the whole of the Islamic world. On the contrary, Islamic law can vary greatly depending on the particular region and school. The crucial difference to Western Europe is the totally different character of law, which pervades all Islamic schools of law and all regional customs. First, Islamic law is not just a legal code, but a guide that leads to salvation. Separation in sacred and secular does not exist. Second, Islamic law was given to mankind in an already complete, perfect, and unchangeable state. Therefore, no legal principles can be changed or added.

Together with the development of modern sciences, the modifications made in the system of law in the 12th and 13th centuries were probably the most important factor necessary to initiate the unique development that took place in Western Europe. Compared with Islamic law, the development paths varied greatly right from the start. Western European law is composed of several sources. Legal principles taken from the Old and the New Testament, customary law, Hellenistic sources, and Roman law were known, discussed, and applied or combined. Furthermore, Germanic tribes had already disposed of a kind of jurisprudence by codifying their customs, which left a mark on the respective Western regions of the Roman Empire (Lipsey, Carlaw & Bekar, 2005, p. 227). Hence, from its origins Christianity had to respect a secular law; it emerged within the legal code of the Roman Empire and adapted to it. The conflict between the sacred and the secular can be traced back to Christ's lifetime and since then has shaped the development of the ecclesiastical and the terrestrial sphere. The main difference with the Islamic world is that there has been a conflict in Western Europe.

However, the major changes were introduced during the legal revolution of the 12th and 13th centuries. Within the papal revolution (ca. 1072–1122) the Christian church cut itself off from worldly powers, especially regarding the appointment of the clergy. Prior to that, terrestrial rulers labeled themselves as the sources of law and the custodians of the religious realm (Huff, 2003, p. 120). The re-created canon law constrained the secular authorities and established a separate and autonomous system of law, which amounted to a radical and revolutionary transformation, depicting the church as the first corporate body. Besides the principles of church law and customary law, canon law was deeply rooted in Roman principles; therefore, the church was also the bearer of Roman law. With the introduction of canon law, the church separated from the secular rulers and began to govern its own affairs. It established its own jurisdiction and the first separation between the degrees of jurisdiction was made.

However, the pure separation between the ecclesiastical and the terrestrial sphere was not the only innovation of the Western European legal revolution. The justification of the separation was based on reason and logic. It tried to establish a harmony among divine, secular, and natural law, which could be deduced from logic. The Benedictine monk Gratian and others worked on the establishment of a legal hierarchy, which ended up in the subordination of secular and ecclesiastical law, and the superiority of natural law. A standard was established, by which ecclesiastical and terrestrial law, and thereby worldly and religious authorities, could be judged regarding their fittingness of natural law (Huff, 2003, p. 126). Hence, the principle of reason was superior to worldly and religious authority, and even to the Scripture. This amounted to an intellectual revolution not possible in the Islamic world. It became officially recognized that man had the intellectual capabilities to discover the world, to add new principles, and, hence, that man possessed reason and conscience.

The most important innovation of the legal revolution was the establishment of the corporation, and, therefore, of different degrees of jurisdiction. The implementation of the concept of the corporation could be traced back to the application of reason and logic to the concept of law. However, canon law broke the first ground for the idea of the corporation. Economic, educational, professional, and communal corporations followed. A corporation, however, required a legitimate representation. Hence, the idea of the corporation not only led to the establishment of the principle of different degrees of jurisdiction, but also to the system of elected representatives; usually one person who was elected by majority vote and represented the corporate body in court or opposite the terrestrial rulers. According to Huff (2003, p. 135), the idea of group representation was the beginning of the constitutional government. Cities and municipalities adopted the idea of the corporation, implemented their own jurisdictions, and partly became represented in parliaments by elected officials. This was the case, for example, in England in the 13th century.

The Western European legal revolution of the 12th and 13th century and the emergence of the concept of the corporate body created new social actors, influenced the distribution of power, implemented reason and logic into the legal system, established different degrees of jurisdiction, and, at least, innovated the institutional system and the principles of society.

Of course, the new ideas and concepts were not immediately implemented. On the contrary, political revolutions and uprisings as well as oppression and abolition continued for centuries. In many states, the political structures to bring worldly rulers to justice did not exist. The introduction of the concepts of reason and rationality into the body of law, and the embodiment of the corporation and of autonomous jurisdictions, continued and it took several centuries until the principles were installed. Furthermore, developments varied between countries and were influenced by differing historical accidents. Nevertheless, the basic principles of jurisdiction, reason, pluralism, constitutional government, and the rule of law were laid.

These developments could never happen in medieval Islam. The rejection of human reason, the different principles of law, and the unchangeability of Islamic law inhibited a legal revolution. The Islamic legal system remained nearly unchanged until the 19th century, when European influence in the region necessitated new legal forms. European legal codes often had to be adopted as a whole since a mixture or adjustment was not possible. Therefore, in many Arab states only family and inheritance law remained in the hands of the sharia.

5.5 Corporate institutions

The emergence of corporate bodies in Western Europe had three important implications. First, it offered a way to treat a group of individuals as a unit and, therefore, as a single legal entity. Hence, even if the corporation was accused, no private individual was affected. For example, individuals could not be prosecuted for a debt owed by the corporate body. Furthermore, a corporation did not end with the death of its members. Instead, it lived on, although its members might have changed (Tierney, 1982). Second, the creation of this abstract entity necessitated the establishment of different degrees of jurisdiction. Not only terrestrial and ecclesiastical jurisdiction had to be differentiated, but also the civil code and corporate law. Third, the corporate body created a free and independent space for scholars, merchants, craftsmen, and so on that allowed them a free exchange of ideas and opinions. Within this space, the members did not have to fear oppression or personal accusation.

The concept of the corporate body was not known in the Arab region because of the relationship between the state and religion. In the West, the emergence of corporate bodies can be traced back to its secular tradition and the separation between certain spheres. In the MENA region with its theocratic tradition, these separations were unknown. Individuals rather than corporations were accused and punished. Furthermore, the implementation of different degrees of jurisdiction was not necessary. It was not possible to differentiate between jurisdictions since Islamic law was neither changeable nor interpretable. Therefore, individuals could not syndicate within an independent corporation.

The absence of corporate bodies in the MENA region and their implementation in Western Europe had far-reaching consequences. Of capital importance was the establishment of corporations for Western universities. The possibility of aligning with other scholars as an independent, corporate group that imposed its own rules upon itself and constituted a legal entity increased scientific autonomy. Furthermore, universities were connected and thereby scientific subjects that were forbidden in one place could be further examined elsewhere. Networks and the legal statuses of universities made oppression much more difficult. In the Arab region, a university was just a sum of individuals. No general curriculums or standards existed. The subjects taught had to be in accordance with the founders' wishes and with Islamic doctrines. Therefore, the oppression of unwanted subjects and scientific efforts was easily accomplished.

However, the absence of corporate bodies did not only affect the academic environment. Specific features of Islamic contract law, the Islamic inheritance system, and the absence of corporate law inhibited the establishment of double-entry bookkeeping and other organizational innovations in the Arab region. Firms were usually small, since partnerships to pool labor and money involved only two partners customarily (Kuran, 2003; Kuran, 2004a,b). Around 1000, Arab and Western European contract law was almost similar but the latter further developed and was modernized continually. Arab contract law, on the contrary, stagnated because of the inheritance system. Islamic hereditary law inhibited the accumulation of capital over several generations. Accordingly, parents were not able to favor one child or a relative and bequest their wealth en bloc.

Instead, two-thirds had to be left to the children and other relatives, and females received half the share of males (Kuran, 2004a,b). Hence, the owner of an asset was not allowed to freely decide their heir, and the estate was usually allocated between the several heirs since many wives and all children had to be considered. Therefore, the allocated parts of the capital stock were relatively small and firms were closed after the death of the owner. That is to say, large Western-style enterprises that persisted for several generations could not emerge in the Arab region. Around 1000, in the MENA region and in Western Europe, a commercial partnership ended with the death of one of the partners if he died before the official end of the contract. However, according to Islamic heritage law, the capital of the partnership was bequeathed to the remaining partners and the heirs of the deceased. Therefore, the contract partners usually received a relatively small portion of the capital. The inheritance system kept the quantity of commercial partners low. Fewer business partners and smaller firm sizes made the organizational innovations that were characteristic in Western Europe redundant (Kuran, 2003). In Western Europe, from the end of the medieval period onwards, the size of enterprises and number of business partners and employees required new forms of production, organization, communication, and funding. Banks and stock markets emerged, contract and corporate law were adapted, and new accounting techniques and management practices were developed. These developments did not take place in the MENA region since no need existed. The small firm sizes, their short lifespan, the restricted and short commercial partnerships, and the absence of corporate law made double-entry bookkeeping and other Western-style commercial innovations unnecessary. Credit, for example, was granted by private individuals and not by banks. Hence, while the West further developed its banking system, no similar development was observable in the MENA region. The same applies for stock markets. The mentioned contractual peculiarities, small firm sizes, and lending between private individuals inhibited the development of stock markets since they were not needed within this system (Grant, 1996; Huff, 2003; Lipsey, Carlaw & Bekar, 2005; Kuran, 2003; Kuran, 2004a,b; Kuran, 2008).

5.6 Education

The medieval education systems of the MENA region and Western Europe differed strongly. A decisive factor in Arab education was the establishment of the *madrasa*. The *madrasa* developed as the most important institution of higher learning in the Arab region. However, since the *madrasas* were founded as charitable trusts, that is to say as *waqfs*, they were subject to the law of *waqf*. Therefore, *madrasas* were only allowed to teach and work within the realm of

Islamic teachings and statements. Natural philosophy, natural sciences, and even theology were not the main subjects, and further lost importance during the emergence of orthodox Islam since they were not thought to be in accordance with Islam. The *madrasas* were schools of law (*fiqh*). Hence, the subjects dealt with Islam per se. Despite the great Arab efforts in natural philosophy and mathematical sciences, the education on these subjects reduced with the emergence of the *madrasas*. At the same time, the *madrasas* forced the distribution of the doctrines of Islamic occasionalism onto society.

Furthermore, the Middle Eastern educational system was based on personal relationships between the master and his student. Prominent scientists and philosophers lived in different places, not connected with each other. Eventually, they did not teach their students at university, but at home. Students interested in a particular subject had to seek out their favorite scholar and were taught at his home. Because of a missing subordinate organization, curriculums for certain subjects were not available. Hence, every teacher was responsible for his subjects and set his priorities accordingly. Degrees, however, were not given to students after passing comparable examinations. Instead, the teachers had to decide when a student had finished his studies successfully. "When in the eyes of the professor students had mastered the subjects taught in the *madrasa* – [...] – they were given an ijaza, an authorization to teach these matters to others [...] It should be stressed that this sort of education was highly personalistic; [...] neither the state, the sultan, nor the caliph had any influence over the recognition of educational competence" (Huff, 2003, p. 78). This also meant that students' efforts were not comparable since they were not rated on a general level. Students travelled around, accumulating ijazas from different scholars in different places.

The structures of the Middle Eastern educational system can be traced back to the missing corporate bodies. Corporate bodies were not known per se and thereby no corresponding judicial basis existed. This meant that Arab medieval universities were not independent spaces of science and research and were not connected with each other. Knowledge was not systematically discovered and distributed. Every university acted on its own and depended on the goodwill of its particular local ruler. No general organization or network connecting the Arab universities existed. This facilitated the influence and infiltration of conservative ideas. Freedom of education and research could not be generally enforced.

Furthermore, ordinary citizens were seen as unable to understand and discuss philosophical matters. There existed a "sharp division between the knowers and the novices" (Huff, 2003, p. 82). "Such devices run against the grain of the scientific ethos, [...] This Averroist view, according to which one must use one form of expression for the masses and another for the cognoscenti, was later condemned by the Christian Church as the doctrine of two truths" (Huff, 2003, p. 83). The personal and subjective character of the Arab educational system and its missing independence from societal and ideological matters inhibited objectivity and the development of a universal, naturalistic norm.

In Western Europe, the universities that emerged from the beginning of the 13th century in Bologna, Paris, and Oxford benefitted the most from the simultaneous emergence of the concept of the corporate body. These European universities were independent entities governed by their own internal rule systems. This made the universities a powerful force; for example, they were allowed to depart from the cities in which they were located if the universities' rights were violated (Grant, 2008, p. 36). Furthermore, professors and students attained special rights when they travelled (Grant, 2008, p. 36). Professors taught their students in classes and general curriculums and degrees were established to create comparability between graduates and universities. In Western Europe, universities were the propagators of naturalistic teachings. Although the church occasionally opposed the naturalistic view – especially in Paris, which ended up in the condemnation of 1277 – the autonomy of universities and political pluralism made general oppression impossible.

5.7 The *waqf*

The *waqf* was a social trust that developed because the medieval Arab states were not interested in the provision of social services and public goods. Therefore, education, orphanages, sanitation, mosques, water supply, soup kitchens, and so on were provided through *waqfs*. Nearly all social services and public goods in Arab cities were supplied by thousands of *waqfs*. A *waqf* was established by "turning immovable private property into an endowment to support any social service permissible under Islamic law" (Kuran, 2004a, p. 75). Hence, by providing some kind of social services or public goods, a wealthy individual could turn his assets into a *waqf*. A *waqf* was thought to persist in its original form in perpetuity. That is to say, the founder assigned which social good should be provided by the *waqf* and how the trust was to be run. Afterwards, the trust and its mission could never be changed. Even when the founder died, the *waqf* had to be run according to his wishes and, of course, according to Islamic doctrines. However, the founder of a *waqf* was bestowed with several privileges. He could appoint himself as manager and trustee. Therefore, the founder was allowed to pay himself a considerable salary and employ family members. Furthermore, the founder could circumvent Islamic inheritance law by appointing one child as his successor. Hence, the founder was able to avoid the fragmentation of his capital and favor one child or relative. In addition, a *waqf* could not be taxed and was safe from expropriation. Hence, the foundation of a *waqf* was a way for landowners to protect their properties from statist despotism (Kuran, 2003; Kuran, 2004a,b; Shatzmiller, 2001).

However, the main problem with the *waqf* system was that it was unchangeable in perpetuity. Hence, a modernization or an adaption to changing circumstances was not possible. This was less of a problem during medieval times. However, in the 18th and 19th centuries, when economic growth in parts of Western Europe started to take off, the rigidity of the *waqf* system was a severe issue. Most of the services provided by *waqfs* were supplied by corporations in Western Europe, for example, universities, municipalities, or churches. However, these institutions were able to adapt vastly and reallocate capital according to the particular requirements. In the MENA region, capital was fixed and could not be reallocated or reinvented when it was necessary to keep pace with modernization and economic growth in the West. Not all *waqfs* remained fixed and rigid, but to circumvent the severe rules a *waqf*'s manager had to be prepared to agree on certain backhand solutions. That is to say, he had to bribe the respective person in charge. These methods fostered corruption and other illegal procedures, which still pose a severe problem for the MENA region today (Kuran, 2004a,b). However, in the 19th century Arab municipalities began to take over the *waqfs*' missions. Nevertheless, fast adaption was not possible since traditional task sharing had existed for hundreds of years.

Furthermore, the *waqf* system had an indirect but decisive effect on society in general, since it inhibited the emergence of a civil society. On the one hand, a *waqf* provided some kind of associational freedom. On the other hand, it hindered the development of self-governed entities such as corporations and municipalities. These kinds of self-contained corporate bodies were responsible for operating economically to avoid coming into conflict with the law and to establish their own rules. A similar kind of self-governance was missing in the MENA region (Kuran, 2004a,b; Kuran, 2008; Shatzmiller, 2001).

5.8 Foreign rule and historical accidents

An important reason why Western Europe stepped into modern science despite conservative religious forces was the multitude of independent nation states and cities. The suppression of natural science might have been possible in some regional parts of a country or even a whole state. But in the neighboring countries other powers were at work and a unique ban was thereby impossible. When something was forbidden in one country it flourished in another. Different heads of state had different opinions on natural sciences. Some supported it, others fought against it. Some acted in a tactical manner because they wanted to support or harm the church or other rulers. Additionally, universities were connected and organized and this made suppression difficult. To suppress the whole corporate body in every country was impossible. So at last science could gain acceptance.

The Arab Empire, however, was not a united state. On the contrary, the power of the caliphate soon deteriorated. By the beginning of the Abbasid caliphate, which existed between 750 and 1258, the political power started to fall into the hands of provincial governors. Since the caliph was obliged to equip the governors with the required military, it became practice to appoint military commanders as provincial governors, who de facto acted independent of the caliph and his court (Lewis, 1970, p. 103).

Furthermore, it became difficult to control the peripheral areas over time. Before the turn of the millennium, independent states emerged in al-Andalus and Morocco, and de facto independent provinces arose in Egypt, Tunisia, Eastern Iran, and Central Asia. At the beginning of the 10th century, a second caliphate was established in Qairawan and, later, a third caliphate in Cordoba, meaning that at least three caliphs challenged for the legitimate succession to the Prophet (Halm, 2006, p. 37f.).

In 932, Baghdad fell under the protectorate of the Buwaihids, a Persian dynasty who degraded the caliphs to mere puppets (Lewis, 1970, p. 102). The Buwaihids were detached by the Seljuqs, a Turkish dynasty who conquered Persia and, later, Syria and Palestine, as well as large parts of Anatolia.

Another source of foreign rule were the Mamluks, originally Turkish slaves from Central Asia who had been used as soldiers by the Baghdad caliphate since the ninth century. Since slaves in Islam relished a certain legal status and could even be released, the freed Mamluks worked their ways up to high military positions and even became provincial governors. They held enough power to decide on the position of the caliph and, in 1250, established the Mamluk Sultanate, which incorporated Egypt, Syria, Palestine, and the holy sites (Halm, 2006, p. 56ff.).

In 1258, the Mongol conquest finally brought an end to the Baghdad caliphate. The Mongol invasion had dramatic consequences for Iraq, especially Baghdad, which did not recover until the 19th century. The irrigation systems, which were indispensable for the country, were destroyed and the civil government broke down. Furthermore, the Mongols established Persia as the centre of their newly conquered empire, degrading Iraq to a peripheral area, which no longer channeled the rich East–West trade. Centuries of decline and stagnation were the consequence (Lewis, 1970, p. 111).

The Middle Eastern region and Egypt suffered from the strategy of appointing provincial governors who transformed the economic structure from a monetary to a feudal economy. Before the emergence of Islam, the Arab economy was based on foreign and transit trade and was characterized by commercial and monetary structures. The introduction of provincial governors and other self-appointed patrons, who were endowed with a certain quantity of land and collected taxes in their sovereign territory, reversed the original economic structures. Fiscal policies were directed to increase the patron's or the ruling dynasty's wealth – the lifestyles at the courts were quite extravagant – and to satisfy the urban population. The centre, on the contrary, lacked organization and bureaucracies were bloated. A feudal economic structure based on subsistence agriculture was established (Lewis, 1970, p. 103ff.).

In Egypt, trade with Europe and the transit trade between Europe and the Far East were of great significance for the Mamluk sultanate's finances. At the beginning of the 15th century, however, the Mamluk state was hit by several blows, for example, Mongol troops captured Syria, the plague sprawl within the region, and Bedouin raids occurred, which led to a severe economic decline. The Mamluk rulers first decided to increase their revenues from trade by higher tariffs. Monopolies on trade, for example sugar and other commodities, were established so that the state could absorb the complete gains achieved. The strategy resulted in a complete collapse of the economy and a subsequent currency depreciation as well as severe taxation. In 1498, however, Vasco da Gama discovered a new sea route to India that was safer and cheaper than the one through Egypt. Trade, and thereby the government's revenues, declined and the end of the Mamluk state was heralded (Lewis, 1970, p. 111ff.).

By the end of the 15th century, Arab supremacy had ended. The scientific and intellectual decline was accompanied by the transformation into a society based on agricultural production and feudal structures. Mediterranean trade has become redirected to the Europeans. Arab trade routes were outflanked by new sea routes. For centuries, MENA's trade structure had been characterized by the import of primary products and the export of manufactured goods (as well as transit trade). However, between 1000 and 1500, this was reversed.

The lack of interest in Europeans on the part of the Arabs yielded a distorted picture of Western European progress. For centuries, the only field in which Arabs recognized Western superiority was the military. Intellectual, scientific, and technological progress as well as the economic development of Western Europe remained unnoticed by the Arabs for a long time. Only when European strength could no longer be ignored at the beginning of the 19th century did the Arabs realize the technological and economic progress made there. However, by that time, the MENA region lagged too far behind to catch up rapidly (Lewis, 1970, p. 119).

Since the objective of the current work is to demonstrate the origins of the divergent developments between the MENA region and Western Europe, the investigation ends here. However, the emergence of the Ottoman Empire and, later, the appearance of European colonial powers, the impact of the two World Wars, the foundations of independent Arab nation states, and, of course, of the state of Israel depict further historical incidences that have impacted economic development. Nevertheless, the origins for the divergent development paths – which were different right from the start – lay much further back in time.

After the acceptance of Islamic occasionalism and the rejection of naturalism, the Arab region could not pursue a development path similar to that of Western Europe. The metaphysical and societal orientation pointed towards a totally different direction. Furthermore, certain accidents, such as the build-up of state and religion and the theocratic tradition of the Arab state, reinforced this direction. Several authors assert Arab development to its disability to enforce modern sciences (Grant, 1996; Huff, 2003; Jacob, 1997; Kuran, 2004b; Lewis, 2002; Lipsey, Carlaw and Bekar, 2005). However, here it is argued that modern sciences could not emerge in the Arab region since the institutional structure evolved in a different way and, hence, induced different results compared with Western Europe. The Arab understanding of man, society, state, and religion per se was different. Hence, the fundamental institutions – that is, worldview, the idea of man, the value system, morals, norms, attitudes, and so on – differed between regions. All constitutive institutions, for example, the understanding of the state, the political system, the legal system, and, the economic structures, must then differ. Institutional differences can best be seen in the theocratic tradition of the MENA region, its legal system, and in the absence of corporate bodies, since these institutions can be clearly defined and are less liable to subjective matters such as culture and worldview. State, religion, and jurisdiction are enmeshed with each other since a separation in several independent spheres never occurred in MENA. Hence, the religious target to gain salvation is not independent of politics and jurisprudence. The rejection of naturalism and, hence, a further examination of nature, as well as the assumption that the Quran is complete, perfect, and unchangeable, led to an ossification of the institutional structures.

Western Europe, on the contrary, is characterized through its institutional dynamism. This does not mean that Western institutions are easily modified and less fixed in their culture. But the recognition of human reason and rationality and the superiority of reason above both worldly and religious power enabled the emergence of a dynamic institutional structure that is able to adjust and change. Institutional change is a complex process that can require a lot of time depending on the particular institution. But Western institutions were by definition allowed to change and adjust endogenously since an internal modification caused by alterations that can be asserted to human reason and rationality was possible. The incapability of man to understand God and, therefore, nature precluded the possibility of endogenous change of Arab institutions.

Historical accidents, however, also played a key role since random events in both regions had strong impacts. The development in Western Europe did not merely depend on institutional dynamism. For example, the fact that conservative forces were finally not able to oppress the naturalistic worldview from the 12th century onwards must be asserted to the secular tradition and political pluralism, but mere luck also played a role. Furthermore, historical events that might not even be known today or whose impact seemed to be only marginal at the time might have been crucial in reality. The many dependencies and decisive factors will never be known. However, the institutional structures in the MENA region and in Western Europe had always differed because of developments and historical accidents that occurred hundreds or even thousands of years ago. When two regions whose institutional foundations differ and whose institutional structures vary are compared, the levels of economic development will also differ.

This observation might not directly help promote growth in Arab countries, but it deepens the understanding of the differences between the institutional structures in the MENA region and those in the Western industrialized world. Since institutions are persistent, a deeper understanding of the reasons for institutional differences between regions is all the more important for the analysis of economic development.

5.9 Prohibition of interest

A popular Islamic peculiarity omitted from this study is the prohibition of interest. However, the interest ban has not been further examined since it is not considered to have played a decisive role in early institutional development. During medieval times, the prohibition of interest was also effective in Christian regions. In any case, the end of the Christian interest ban can be related to events taking place since the 13th century and, therefore, with the emergence of the Italian city states inter alia. The prohibition of interest in the Christian West did not become irrelevant before the 17th century (Schumann, 2007, p. 198f.). Hence, institutional developments played a role in the abolishment of the Christian interest ban, and the stagnation of Islam has probably been decisive for its maintenance in the Arab region. The Islamic prohibition of interest might be a reason for lower investment in the region; nevertheless, it is not considered a decisive determinant of institution building and of the accidental events between the seventh and 15th centuries that sent the region on a specific development path. This path was the beginning of economic backwardness and stagnation. The maintenance of the interest ban can rather be seen as a result of the institutional lock-in and the historical events. Hence, its perpetuation is a result of the development path, as is the region's economic performance in general.

The Islamic prohibition of interest, or rather *riba,* has its roots in the Quran. Therefore, it is difficult to debate and, according to conservative Islamic thinkers, cannot be changed. However, the discussion about which kind of business the interest ban refers to is ongoing. The ban does not forbid all forms of interest; for example, it does not necessarily prohibit interest resulting from an increase in value through investment or from the profits of a business transaction. *Riba* describes interest from a loan or rather the interest that becomes due when "money is made from money" (Tripp, 2006, p. 126). It is assumed that the original ban meant to prohibit the pre-Arabic custom of doubling the borrowed amount in case it was not repaid on time (Schumann, 2005, p. 497; Schumann, 2007, p. 186; Tripp, 2006, p. 127f.). Hence, the interest ban must be regarded in a historical context. It originates in the avoidance of injustice, since in seventh century Arabia most credits corresponded to consumer credits and less to commercial credits. Therefore, the necessity to borrow resulted from natural disasters such as droughts and the resulting crop shortfalls or from the death of the head of the family (Tripp, 2006, p. 128). That is to say, the borrower was in a worse economic situation than the lender and, therefore, to charge interest was considered exploitation. Furthermore, interest from money loans incorporated no effort by the lender and was, therefore, regarded as unjust. A fixed interest rate was also prohibited because it applied an unequal distribution of risk.

The objective was to install justice by avoiding usury; therefore, consumer credits should not be charged interest and commercial credits were not popular during the time of the revelation. Influential conservative thinkers even nowadays consider the interest ban to be valid for all kinds of interest (Tripp, 2006, p. 131). The prohibition of *riba* was the initial point of Islamic banking and also plays an important role in Islamic economics, neither of which, however, form part of this dissertation project.

6. Conclusion: connection between the general institutional analysis and the case study on the MENA region

This study has examined whether formal and informal institutions separately influence economic growth and whether the economic performance of the MENA region can be traced back to its institutions. It further questioned why Arab institutions developed in this special way and not as, for example, Western European institutions. Since the illustration of the whole institutional development path went beyond the scope of the study, emphasis has been placed on how early institutional development was responsible for varying development paths as well as formal and informal institutions. Not only political, legal, and economic systems have been considered, but also cultural components such as value systems, worldviews, and the resulting morals and norms. These informal institutions determine the form of societal organization, which has a direct impact on economic development.

During the analysis it was demonstrated that institutions significantly impact on economic development. If institutions differ between regions the economic performances must also differ. However, the analysis partly supports a kind of cultural determinism. This would indicate that Arab countries are in a hopeless state or an institutional trap. The hypothesis of cultural determinism was partly affirmed through the equilibrium view of institutions. This view leaves no space for institutional change and adaption besides an exogenous shock.

However, the current study does not only depict the equilibrium view. Theories of institutional change, incorporating institutional transplantation, are also discussed. Since the equilibrium view depicts a model or a theory, it might not reflect the real world. It can be used to theoretically demonstrate and explain the persistence of institutions resulting from equilibrium strategies. Since institutional persistence inter alia depends on deadlocked behavioral rules, the application of the theory is justified. Traditional value systems, which determine the behaviors of societies, cannot be easily changed because informal institutions are mental constructs that provide individuals with mental stability and self-identification. To understand the rigid character of value systems, these can be described as institutions resulting in equilibrium strategies that cannot be changed.

However, the equilibrium view has its drawbacks. It omits further possibilities of endogenous institutional change, even though Aoki's (2001) model includes the possibility of action profiles influencing the institutional environment. Accordingly, institutions are exogenous to a single agent, but are endogenous regarding the set of technologically possible action profiles or rather society per se. Hence, institutions are shaped by society, often unconsciously, but are exogenous constraints to the single individual.

Even the equilibrium view, and classical game theory in general, must be described as an inadequate instrument to examine institutions in their entirety. Institutional dynamics cannot be examined using these tools. In any case, institutional dynamics are not the main issue in institutional analysis, since institutional persistence is the bigger problem to first understand before considering solutions for institutional change. Game theory and the equilibrium view emanate from rational agents and predetermined strategies. History plays no role and behavior is future-oriented. Furthermore, the equilibrium view contradicts some of the statements made in the first part of this study. It was emphasized that institutions are influenced by innumerable factors with a society's history playing a decisive role. In addition, several drawback mechanisms between institutions and the level of economic development must be considered. However, it was also stated that the application of every theory can be justifiable; the user, however, must clearly describe his intentions and must be aware of the fact that the theory does not depict a world formula, but solely describes one channel that could be useful for understanding the bigger picture.

To use Greif's (2006) words, who also uses game-theoretic tools to analyze institutions, "Institutions are not game-theoretic equilibria, games are not the basic unit of institutional analysis and game theory does not provide us with a theory of institutions. Indeed, the key to advancing institutional analysis by using game theory is precisely to recognize the difference between game-theoretic equilibrium analysis and institutional analysis" (p. 19).

Using the equilibrium view, the issue of institutional persistence and thereby unchanging value systems and codes of conduct is depicted. Using Greif's (1994) model, it is further demonstrated that different belief systems result in different forms of societal organization. Since belief systems and the consequent behavior depict optimal strategies for society, its history, and further prerequisites, these systems are rigid and can be compared with institutional equilibria to demonstrate the influence rigid value systems have on societal organization and economic development. It does not intend to define every society as an equilibrium state and every individual as a rational, purely future-oriented agent.

According to the analysis, different value systems result in different forms of societal organization and, therefore, varying economic outcomes. It has been demonstrated that equilibrium wages vary between societies and that levels of social mobility and specialization depend on the form of societal organization. Accordingly, limited morality, which describes a collectivist, traditionalist society, leads to lower wages and a horizontal social structure, whereas generalized morality, which is defined an individualistic, modern society, results in higher wages and a vertical social structure. Both outcomes are optimal for the present conditions. Hence, a society with relatively lower living standards and growth rates cannot be described as inefficient per se. Every societal and economic outcome is a result of the society's history and its institutional environment (of course, geography plays a role but this factor is not included in this study).

If history and institutions determine everything and cannot be changed, then nothing can be done regarding the low living standards of less developed societies. According to the preceding analysis of this study, this is partly true. But institutional change is still possible and the feedback mechanism running from economic development to institutions should not be underestimated. Exogenous institutional change in the form of institutional transplantation can work. However, there can be no general solution or set of institutions that lead to economic growth in every society. Instead, every case must be individually considered. The transplanted institutions must fit the – often informal – institutional basis. However, this implies that the institutions of property rights, the rule of law, political participation, and market liberalization cannot be implemented immediately because they do not match the prevalent institutional environment. Even if it sounds strange to Western economists, free markets and the corresponding political, civil, and legal rights might not lead to immediate growth in every society.

Increasing living standards influence peoples' preferences. Material security alters utility functions and shifts the purpose of life from survival to self-realization. Hence, economic development induces institutional change. Values and attitudes change with higher incomes, although the basic identifying informal institutions might persist. But this does not imply that as time goes by every population will develop into a Western-style, individualistic society. Instead, differing institutional environments and forms of societal organization will prevail, implying varying economic performances. Underdevelopment should, therefore, not be accepted as an unchangeable matter of fact. Of course, living standards in poor economies must be increased. But how this can be achieved must be considered in every case anew, and it should be understood that societies do differ and do realize different outcomes, whether economically, politically, legally, or morally, and that some of these differences will always persist.

The enduring character of cultural differences was shown by regression analysis, which indicated that religious affiliation still influences the nature of institutions even though the currently affected parts of the population might not be practicing believers. Religious affiliation measured via the percentage of a population belonging to a certain religion indicates the underlying religious influence that is not consciously felt and implemented by the individual. That is to say, a certain religious moral prevalent in a particular region might no longer be consciously implemented by the population. But the values and morals resulting from the religion have become a part of the culture and of the general value system. Hence, people are still influenced by early religious values and morals, even if they describe themselves as non-religious since the prevalent culture and society was shaped by a certain belief.

This is demonstrated by the fact that countries with majority Muslim populations have significantly different formal and informal institutions compared with countries with majority Protestant populations. Because of data availability and the necessity to match several data sets, only two religious directions could be incorporated. However, since the present work emphasizes institutions in the Arab region the approach is adequate.

Accordingly, countries with mainly Muslim populations realize informal institutions that intend a form of generalized morality, and formal institutions that do not assure secure property rights, a constrained executive, and an independent judiciary. Countries with a majority of Protestant citizens implement informal institutions that can be equated with generalized morality. In addition, the formal institutional index indicates secure property rights, a constrained executive, and the implementation of an independent judiciary. Hence, Islam and Protestantism seem to result in partly different institutions. Furthermore, it was demonstrated via the regression analysis that informal and formal institutions have a significant impact on the level of per capita income.

The theoretical and empirical findings permit several conclusions regarding the MENA region. Institutions in Muslim countries differ to institutions in Protestant countries. Furthermore, institutions influence per capita income. Hence, the varying institutions of mainly Muslim and mainly Protestant countries result in different economic outcomes. This is further exemplified by the descriptive empirical analysis of the MENA region. Nearly all indicators show significant differences between institutions in the MENA region and the Western advanced economies (as a matter of interest, Japan is included as an advanced economy although it neither belongs to MENA nor to the Western hemisphere). According to the first part of the study, the institutions implemented in the MENA countries do not correspond to the institutions that were described as being neoclassically growth supportive. For example, insecure property rights do not allow optimal individual utility maximization. The same holds for a missing independent judiciary. Furthermore, autocratic governments are predominant in MENA and civil liberties and political rights are not ensured. These institutions inhibit individual utility maximization and restrain incentives to invest.

Regarding informal institutions, the evaluation of WVS data indicated a societal structure of limited morality in the MENA region. The results regarding *trust* and *control* are not that obvious; however, *respect* and *obedience* indicate a hierarchical society with an emphasis on collective and hierarchic structures. In addition, the analysis of further survey questions showed a traditional attitude regarding the roles of women, education, work, and family in general.

According to institutional theory, these patterns – whether informal or formal – are difficult to change. Consulting the equilibrium view of institutions to understand the issue of institutional persistence in the Arab region, only an exogenous shock could alter the equilibrium strategies determined by institutions. That is to say, the prevalent traditional and conservative value system that emphasizes the collective, attributes major importance to religion, disadvantages women regarding education and work, and supports hierarchic structures is persistent. The same holds for historically and culturally rooted formal institutions. The model indicated that change is not possible regarding the observed institution. However, apart from the equilibrium view model it was stated that in fact most institutions are dynamic entities. But marginal change can take hundreds of years to become obvious. This means that the institutional environment in the MENA region can and does change. However, a complete reversal is unlikely since the historical development path has pushed the region in a certain direction. Moderate modernization might take place but it will take time.

Regarding formal institutions, exogenous change is only partly promising. The successful implementation of exogenous institutions into MENA countries – for example, the rule of law, civil liberties, democracy, and market liberalization – depends on the distance to the prevalent institutional structure. Hence, the institutions might be abolished, they might be disregarded, or they might disturb the prevalent institutional structure and lead to destabilization; but they might also fit the prevalent institutions and lead to a general adjustment and thereby modernization, at least in the long run.

In most countries of the MENA region, the prevalent institutions lead to considerably lower per capita incomes and, therefore, living standards compared with highly developed Western states.[72] The historical analysis demonstrated why this is the case and showed that MENA institutions could only develop this way. Historical accidents and institutional and societal developments made other alternatives impossible. That is to say, the current institutional and economic situation of the MENA region is a logical consequence of its development path.

In particular, the historical analysis showed the importance of worldview and a certain belief system for societal and economic development, factors currently omitted from mainstream economic analysis. However, as stated in the

[72] However, some MENA countries realize high per capita incomes and growth rates, for example the UAE. At any rate, these are the RRLI countries and their richness can be traced back to special characteristics. All of the rich Arab countries are oil exporting countries, and thereby they owe their economic successes to resource richness and low indigenous populations. These countries are able to afford growth-inhibiting institutions since oil incomes compensate for the institutional environment. However, the descriptive statistical analysis of the MENA region shows that the oil states do not possess significantly different institutions to the non-oil countries of the MENA region. Still, the current work does not go into detail regarding the Arab countries with high per capita incomes. The objective of the study is not to examine how far the current structures of the MENA countries differ, but to demonstrate the unique institutional development and its implication on economic growth; omitting specialities resulting from resource endowment.

case study, Western European development depended on the acquisition and society-wide implementation of the naturalistic worldview. This was not an easy process and the Christian church battled naturalism and sciences. But, as shown, things were different to in the MENA region. The prevalent institutions and accidental events led to the Industrial Revolution, sustainable growth, and the development of a free civic society. The rejection of naturalism and the acceptance of Islamic occasionalism made a similar development in the MENA region impossible. Without being persuaded by cause and reason and thereby without natural laws, modern sciences and a physical worldview could not emerge. From an Islamic point of view, what happened was a logical conclusion. Assuming the Quran to be unchangeable and non-interpretable, and assuming God to be the only creator, natural laws indeed make no sense. However, for the same reason none of the two development paths, neither the Arab nor the Western European, can be described as better or worse.

Regarding the high population growth rates and low living standards, the MENA region will face even more economic problems in the future. Increasing economic growth rates in the past few years cannot hide this fact. However, studying institutions and institutional development in the MENA region helps explain why Arabic institutions developed by this means. Hence, we now know why the Arab region took this particular development path and we know why the economic performance is worse than other regions. However, what we cannot say is how the MENA countries should solve their problems. This is not possible since the analysis demonstrated that institutions, even if they are economically inefficient, can depict a kind of optimal state regarding the particular society and that exogenous institutional change is hardly possible. This is a depressing result for the MENA region and also for other less developed countries.

However, it was shown that institutions are dynamic and even the institutions of the MENA region can change over time. Furthermore, exogenous institutional change is possible. Hence, there is a chance for development economics and in- and outsiders that are interested in institutional change in the MENA countries. But the realization per se will be difficult. The transplanted institutions must fit the prevalent institutional environment. That is to say, they do not necessarily belong to Western-style political, legal, and economic institutions. However, Western organizations of any form will find it morally debatable and also theoretically senseless to exogenously install non-Western institutions in a foreign country. Indigenous forces might find it easier to induce change. They will also know better which institutions fit the cultural basis. However, IEX and IEN institutional change might still result in region-specific outcomes. Hence, the institutional environment and the corresponding economic performance might still not match Western and mainstream economic claims. Furthermore, indigenously introduced change, whether endogenous or exogenous, is not predictable. Actions fostering economic productivity and growth are desirable, since increasing living standards change preferences and thereby institutions. However, of all things the prevalent institutions in the MENA region hinder an increase in productivity and growth.

References

Abramovitz, M. (1986) Catching-up, Forging Ahead, and Falling Behind, *Journal of Economic History*, 46(2), pp. 385–406.

Acemoglu, D. (2009) *Introduction to Modern Economic Growth*, Princeton, Oxford, Princeton University Press.

Acemoglu, D. and Johnson, S. (2005) Unbundling Institutions, *Journal of Political Economy*, 113(5), pp. 949–995.

Acemoglu, D., Johnson, S. and Robinson, J. A. (2001) The Colonial Origins of Comparative Development: An Empirical Investigation, *American Economic Review*, 91(5), pp. 1369–1401.

Acemoglu, D., Johnson, S. and Robinson, J. A. (2002) Reversal of Fortune: Geography and Institutions in the Making of the Modern World Income Distribution, *The Quarterly Journal of Economics*, 117(4), pp. 1231–1294.

Acemoglu, D., Johnson, S. and Robinson, J. A. (2005) Institutions as Fundamental Causes of Long-Run Growth, in: Aghion, P. and Durlauf, S. N. (eds.) *Handbook of Economic Growth, Volume 1A*, Amsterdam, Elsevier B.V., pp. 385–472.

Acemoglu, D., Johnson, S., Robinson, J. A. and Yared, P. (2008) Income and Democracy, *American Economic Review*, 98(3), pp. 808–842.

Acemoglu, D. and Robinson, J. A. (2005) *Economic Origins of Dictatorship and Democracy*, Cambridge, Cambridge University Press.

Adelman, I. and Taft Morris, C. (1967) *Society, Politics, and Economic Development: A Quantitative Approach*, Baltimore, London, The John Hopkins Press.

Aidt, T. S. (2003) Economic Analysis of Corruption: A Survey, *The Economic Journal*, 113(491), pp. F632–F652.

Akerlof, G. A. and Kranton, R. E. (2000) Economics and Identity, *The Quarterly Journal of Economics*, 115(3), pp. 715–753.

Aoki, M. (2001) *Towards a Comparative Institutional Analysis*, Cambridge, MIT Press.

Asiedu, E. and Freeman, J. (2008) The Effect of Corruption on Investment Growth: Evidence from Firms in Latin America, Sub-Saharan Africa and Transition Countries, University of Kansas Working Paper Series in Theoretical and Applied Economics, Working Paper No. 200802.

Askari, H. (2006) Economic Failure in the Middle East, *BNL Quarterly Review*, 59(236), pp. 81–111.

Banfield, E. C. (1958) *The Moral Basis of a Backward Society*, New York, London, The Free Press.

Barro, R. J. (1999) Determinants of Democracy, *Journal of Political Economy*, Supplement, 107(6), pp. S158–S183.

Barro, R. J. and McCleary, R. M. (2003) Religion and Economic Growth Across Countries, *American Sociological Review*, 68(5), pp. 760–781.

Barro, R. J. and Sala-i-Martin, X. (1992) Convergence, *Journal of Political Economy*, 100(2), pp. 223–251.

Barro, R. J. and Sala-i-Martin, X. (2004) *Economic Growth*, Cambridge, London, MIT Press.

Baum, C. F. (2006) *An Introduction to Modern Econometrics Using Stata*, Texas, Stata Press Publication.

Baum, C. F., Schaffer, M. E. and Stillman, S. (2003) Instrumental Variables and GMM: Estimation and Testing, Working Paper No. 545, Boston College, Department of Economics.

Baumol, W. J. (1986) Productivity Growth, Convergence, and Welfare: What the Long-Run Data Show, American Economic Review, 76(5), pp. 1072–1085.

Becker, S. and Wößmann, L. (2009) Was Weber Wrong? A Human Capital Theory of Protestant Economic History, *Quarterly Journal of Economics*, 124(2), pp. 531–596.

Ben-David, D. (2000) Trade, Growth and Disparity Among Nations, *Trade, Income Disparity and Poverty*, World Trade Organization Special Study 5, Geneva, WTO Publications.

Besley, T. and Kudamatsu, M. (2008) Making Autocracy Work, in: Helpman, E. (ed.) *Institutions and Economic Performance*, Cambridge, MA and London, Harvard University Press, pp. 452–510.

Blum, U. and Dudley, L. (2001) Religion and economic growth: was Weber right? *Journal of Evolutionary Economics*, 11(2), pp. 207–230.

Bockstette, V., Chanda, A. and Putternam, L. (2002) States and Markets: The Advantage of an Early Start, *Journal of Economic Growth*, 7(4), pp. 347–369.

Boettke, P. J., Coyne, C. J. and Leeson, P. T. (2008) Institutional Stickiness and the New Development Economics, *American Journal of Economics and Sociology*, 67(2), pp. 331–358.

Caselli, F., Esquivel, G. and Lefort, F. (1996) Reopening the Convergence Debate: A New Look at Cross-Country Growth Empirics, *Journal of Economic Growth*, 1(3), pp. 363–389.

Coase, R. H. (1937) The Nature of the Firm, *Economica*, 4(16), pp. 386–405.

Coase, R. H. (1960) The Problem of Social Cost, *Journal of Law and Economics*, 3, pp. 1–44.

Cornelius, P. K. and Schwab, K. (eds.) (2003) *The Arab World Competitiveness Report 2002–2003*, New York, Oxford, Oxford University Press.

Creane, S., Goyal, R., Mobarak, A. M. and Sab, R. (2007) Measuring Financial Development in the Middle East and North Africa: A New Database, IMF Staff Papers, 53(3), pp. 479–512.

David, Paul A. (1994) Why Are Institutions the 'Carriers of History'?: Path Dependence and the Evolution of Conventions, Organizations and Institutions, *Structural Change and Economic Dynamics*, 5(2), pp. 205-220.

De Jong, Eelke (2009) *Culture and Economics: On Values, Economics and International Business*, London, Routledge.

De Jong, Eelke (2008) Religious Values and Economic Growth: A review and assessment of recent studies, NiCE Working Paper 08-111.

De La Fuente, A. (2002) Convergence Across Countries and Regions: Theory and Empirics, UFAE and IAE Working Papers, Working Paper No. 555.02.

De Soto, H. (2000) *The Mystery of Capital: Why Capitalism Triumphs in the West and Fails Everywhere Else*, New York, Basic Books.

Dolfsma, W. and Verburg, R. (2008) Structure, Agency and the Role of Values in Processes of Institutional Change, *Journal of Economic Issues*, 42(4), pp. 1031–1054.

Dollar, D. and Kraay, A. (2004) Trade, Growth, and Poverty, *The Economic Journal*, 114(493), F22–F49.

Drzeniek Hanouz, M., El Diwany, S. and Yousef, T. (eds.) (2007) *The Arab World Competitiveness Report 2007: Sustaining the Growth Momentum*, The World Economic Forum, [online] available at: <http://www.weforum.org/en/initiatives/gcp/Arab%20World%20Competitiveness%20Report/index.htm> [accessed 10 September 2010].

Dyer, P. and Yousef, T. (2007) Will the Current Oil Boom Solve the Employment Crisis in the Middle East? in: *Arab World Competitiveness Report 2007*, [online] available at: <http://www.weforum.org/en/initiatives/gcp/Arab%20World%20Competitiveness%20Report/index.htm> [accessed 4 July 2009].

Easterly, W. and Levine, R. (2003) Tropics, Germs, and Crops: How Endowments Influence Economic Development, *Journal of Monetary Economics*, 50(1), pp. 3–39.

Ekelund, R. B., Hébert, R. F. and Tollison, R. D. (2002) An Economic Analysis of the Protestant Reformation, *Journal of Political Economy*, 110(3), pp. 646–672.

El-Affendi, A. (1998) Islamic Theology, in: Craig, E. (ed.) *Routledge Encyclopedia of Philosophy*, [online] available at: <http://www.muslimphilosophy.com/ip/rep/H009.htm> [accessed 5 September 2010].

Fakhry, M. (1998) Greek philosophy: impact on Islamic philosophy, in: Craig, E. (ed.) *Routledge Encyclopedia of Philosophy*, [online] available at: <http://www.muslimphilosophy.com/ip/rep/H011> [accessed 5 September 2010].

Fernández, R. (2008) Culture and Economics, in Durlauf, S. N. and Blume, L. E. (eds.) *The New Palgrave Dictionary of Economics*, 2nd edition, New York, Palgrave Macmillan, [online] available at: <http://www.dictionaryofeconomics.com/article?id=pde2008_E000282> [accessed 14 October 2009].

Fernández, R. and Fogli, A. (2007) Culture: An Empirical Investigation of Beliefs, Work, and Fertility, NBER Working Paper No. 11268.

Fischer, R. (1992) *Der Islam: Glaube und Gesellschaftssystem im Wandel der Zeiten. Eine Einführung*, Oberdorf, Edition Piscator.

Frankel, J. A. and Romer, D. (1999) Does Trade Cause Growth? *American Economic Review*, 89(3), pp. 379–399.

Gallup, J. L., Sachs, J. D. and Mellinger, A. D. (1998) Geography and Economic Development, in: Pleskovic, B. and Stiglitz, J. E. (eds.) *Annual World Bank Conference on Development Economics 1998*, Washington, DC., The World Bank, pp. 127–188.

Glaeser, E. L., La Porta, R., Lopez-De-Silanes, F. and Shleifer, A. (2004) Do Institutions Cause Growth? *Journal of Economic Growth*, 9(3), pp. 271–303.

Gorodnichenko, Y. and Roland, G. (2010) Culture, Institutions and the Wealth of Nations, Working Paper, online available at: <http://www.econ.berkeley.edu/~groland/pubs/gorrolCulturedraftv2-2010-05-07.pdf> [accessed 11 September 2010].

Grant, E. (1996) *The Foundations of Modern Science in the Middle Ages: their Religious, Institutional, and Intellectual Contexts*, Cambridge, New York, Cambridge University Press.

Greif, A. (1993) Contract Enforceability and Economic Institutions in Early Trade: the Maghribi Traders' Coalition, *American Economic Review*, 83(3), pp. 525–548.

Greif, A. (1994) Cultural Beliefs and the Organization of Society: A Historical and Theoretical Reflection on Collectivist and Individualist Societies, *Journal of Political Economy*, 102(5), pp. 912–950.

Greif, A. (2005) Commitment, Coercion, and Markets: The Nature and Dynamics of Institutions Supporting Exchange, in: Ménard, C. and Shirley M. (eds.) *Handbook of New Institutional Economics*, Dordrecht, Springer, pp. 727–786.

Greif, A. (2006) *Institutions and the Path to the Modern Economy: Lessons from Medieval Trade*, Cambridge, Cambridge University Press.

Guiso, L., Sapienza, P. and Zingales, L. (2003) People's Opium? Religion and Economic Attitudes, *Journal of Monetary Economics*, 50(1), pp. 225–282.

Guiso, L., Sapienza, P. and Zingales, L. (2006) Does Culture Affect Economic Outcomes? *Journal of Economic Perspectives*, 20(2), pp. 23–48.

Guralnik, S. (1975) Science and the Ante-Bellum American College, *Memoires of the American Philosophical Society*, 109(60), Philadelphia, American Philosophical Society.

Guriev, S. (2004) Red Tape and Corruption, *Journal of Development Economics*, 73(2), pp. 489–504.

Hagemann, H., Erber, G. and Seiter, S. (1998) *Zukunftsperspektiven Deutschlands im internationalen Wettbewerb: Industriepolitische Implikationen der neuen Wachstumstheorie*, Berlin, Heidelberg, Physica.

Hakura, D. S. (2004) Growth in the Middle East and North Africa, IMF Working Paper 04/56.

Hall, R. E. and Jones, C. I. (1999) Why Do Some Countries Produce So Much More Output Per Worker Than Others? *The Quarterly Journal of Economics*, 114(1), pp. 83–116.

Halm, H. (2006) Die Araber: Von der vorislamischen Zeit bis zur Gegenwart, 2nd edition, Munich, C.H. Beck.

Harrison, L. E. and Huntington, S. P. (eds.) (2000) *Culture Matters: How Values Shape Human Progress*, New York, Basic Books.

Hedlund, S. (2001) Property Without Rights: Dimensions of Russian Privatization, *Europe-Asia Studies*, 53(2), pp. 213–237.

Hedlund, S. (2005) *Russian Path Dependence*, Abingdon, Oxon, Routledge.

Heston, A., Summers, R. and Aten, B. (2006) Penn World Table Version 6.2, Center for International Comparisons of Production, Income and Prices at the University of Pennsylvania, [online] available at: <http://pwt.econ.upenn.edu/php_site/pwt_index.php> [accessed 14 October 2009].

Hodgson, G. M. (2006) What are Institutions? *Journal of Economic Issues*, March, 40(1), pp. 1–25.

Hodgson, G. M. (ed.) (2007) *The Evolution of Economic Institutions*, Cheltenham, Massachusetts, Edward Elgar Publishing.

Hofstede, G. H. (1997) *Culture's Consequences: Comparing Values, Behaviors, Institutions and Organizations Across Nations*, Thousand Oaks, London, Sage Publications.

Huff, T. E. (2003) *The Rise of Early Modern Science: Islam, China, and the West*, 2nd edition, Cambridge, New York, Cambridge University Press.

Hye, M. A. (2004) Ash'arism, in: Sharif, M. M. (ed.) *A History of Muslim Philosophy*, 1(3), [online] available at: <http://www.muslimphilosophy.com/hmp/14.htm> [Accessed 06 September 2010].

Iannaccone, L. R. (1998) Introduction to the Economics of Religion, *Journal of Economic Literature*, 36(3), pp. 1465–1495.

Inglehart, R., Basánez, M., Díez-Medrano, J., Halman, L. and Luijkx, R. (eds.) (2004) *Human Beliefs and Values: a Cross-cultural Sourcebook based on the 1999-2002 Values Surveys*, Coyoacán, Buenos Aires, Siglo XXI Editores.

Inglehart, R. and Welzel, C. (2005) *Modernization, Cultural Change, and Democracy: The Human Development Sequence*, Cambridge, Cambridge University Press.

Islam, N. (2003) What have we Learnt from the Convergence Debate? *Journal of Economic Surveys*, 17(3), pp. 309–363.

Issawi, C. (1995) *The Middle East Economy: Decline and Recovery*, Princeton, Markus Wiener Publishers.

Jacob, M. C. (1997) *Scientific Culture and the Making of the Industrial West*, New York, Oxford, Oxford University Press.

Jaggers, K. and Marshall, M. G. (2007) *Polity IV Project: Political Regime Characteristics and Transitions, 1800–2007, Dataset User's Manual*, Polity IV Project, Center for Global Policy, George Mason University, Polity IV data, [online] available at: <http://www.systemicpeace.org/polity/polity4.htm> [accessed 14 October 2009].

Kaufmann, D., Kraay, A. and Zoido-Lobatón, P. (2002) Governance Matters II – Updated Indicators for 2000/01, The World Bank, Policy Research Working Paper No. 2772.

Kaufmann, D., Kraay, A. and Mastruzzi, M. (2009) Governance Matters VIII: Aggregate and Individual Governance Indicators 1996–2008, The World Bank, Policy Research Working Paper No. 4978.

Kerekes, C. B. and Williamson, C. R. (2008) Unveiling de Soto's Mystery: Property Rights, Capital Formation, and Development, *Journal of Institutional Economics*, 4(3), pp. 299–325.

Knack, S. and Keefer, P. (1997) Does Social Capital Have an Economic Payoff? A Cross-Country Investigation, *The Quarterly Journal of Economics*, 112(4), pp. 1251–1288.

Knowles, S. and Weatherston, C. (2006) Informal Institutions and Cross-Country Income Differences, CREDIT Research Paper No. 06/06, University of Nottingham.

Kuran, T. (2003) The Islamic Commercial Crisis: Institutional Roots of Economic Underdevelopment in the Middle East, USC Centre for Law, Economics & Organization, Research Paper No. C01–12.

Kuran, T. (2004a) Why the Middle East is Economically Underdeveloped: Historical Mechanisms of Institutional Stagnation, *Journal of Economic Perspectives*, 18(3), pp. 71–90.

Kuran, T. (2004b) *Islam and Mammon: The Economic Predicaments of Islamism*, Princeton, Princeton University Press.

Kuran, T. (2008) Institutional Causes of Economic Underdevelopment in the Middle East: a Historical Perspective, in: Kornai, J., Mátyás, L. and Roland, G. (eds.) *Institutional Change and Economic Behaviour*, Houndmills, New York, Palgrave Macmillan, pp. 64–76.

La Porta, R., Lopez-De-Silanes, F., Pop-Eleches, C. and Shleifer, A. (2004) Judicial Checks and Balances, *Journal of Political Economy*, 112(2), pp. 445–470.

La Porta, R., Lopez-De-Silanes, F., Shleifer, A. and Vishny, R. W. (1997) Trust in Large Organizations, *American Economic Review*, 87(2), pp. 333–338.

La Porta, R., Lopez-De-Silanes, F., Shleifer, A. and Vishny, R. W. (1999) The Quality of Government, *The Journal of Law, Economics, and Organization*, 15(1), pp. 222–279.

Landes, D. (1998) *The Wealth and Poverty of Nations*, New York, W. W. Norton.

Lawson, T. (1987) The Relative / Absolute Nature of Knowledge and Economic Analysis, *The Economic Journal*, December, 97(388), pp. 951–970.

Lewis, B. (1970) The Arabs in Eclipse, in: Cipolla C. M. (ed.) *The Economic Decline of Empires*, London, Routledge, pp. 102–120.

Lewis, B. (2002) *What Went Wrong? The Clash Between Islam and Modernity in the Middle East*, London, Weidenfeld & Nicolson.

Lindberg, D. C. (1992) *The Beginnings of Western Science*, Chicago, University of Chicago Press.

Lipsey, R. G., Carlaw, K. I. and Bekar, C. T. (2005) *Economic Transformations: General Purpose Technologies and Long Term Economic Growth*. Oxford and New York, Oxford University Press.

Mankiw, N. G., Romer, D. and Weil, D. N. (1992) A Contribution to the Empirics of Economic Growth, *The Quarterly Journal of Economics*, 107(2), pp. 407–437.

Mauro, P. (1995) Corruption and Growth, *The Quarterly Journal of Economics*, 110(3), pp. 681–712.

McEvedy, C. and Jones, R. (1978) *Atlas of World Population History*, London, Penguin Books.

Miller, T. and Holmes, K. R. (2009) *2009 Index of Economic Freedom*, Washington, DC, The Heritage Foundation.

Mokyr, J. (2002) *The Gifts of Athena: Historical Origins of the Knowledge Economy*, Princeton, Princeton University Press.

Murray, M. P. (2006) Avoiding Invalid Instruments and Coping With Weak Instruments, *Journal of Economic Perspectives*, 20(4), pp. 111–132.

Noland, M. (2003) Religion, Culture, and Economic Performance, KDI School Working Paper Series, Working Paper 03-13.

Norris, P. and Inglehart, R. (2004) *Sacred and Secular: Religion and Politics Worldwide*, Cambridge, Cambridge University Press.

North, D. C. (1990) *Institutions, Institutional Change and Economic Performance*, Cambridge, Cambridge University Press.

North, D. C. (2005) *Understanding the Process of Economic Change*, Princeton, NY, Princeton University Press.

North, D. C. and Thomas, R. P. (1973) *The Rise of The Western World: A New Economic History*, Cambridge, Cambridge University Press.

Olson, M. (1982) *The Rise and Decline of Nations: Economic Growth, Stagflation, and Social Rigidities*, New Haven, London, Yale University Press.

Parker, P. M. (1997) *National Cultures of the World: A Statistical Reference*, Westport, Greenwood Press.

Persson, T. and Tabellini, G. (2006) Democracy and Development: The Devil in the Details, *American Economic Review*, 96(2), pp. 319–324.

Persson, T. and Tabellini, G. (2008) The Growth Effect of Democracy: Is it Heterogeneous and How Can it be Estimated? In: Helpman, E. (ed.) *Institutions and Economic Performance*, Cambridge, MA, Harvard University Press, pp. 544–585.

Persson, T. and Tabellini, G. (2009) Democratic Capital: The Nexus of Political and Economic Change, *American Economic Journal: Macroeconomics*, 1(2), pp. 88–126.

Platteau, J.-P. (2000) *Institutions, Social Norms, and Economic Development*. London, Routledge.

Platteau, J.-P. (2008) Religion, Politics, and Development: Lessons from the Lands of Islam, Economic Research Forum, Working Paper Series, Working Paper No. 434.

Pomeranz, K. (2001) *The Great Divergence: China, Europe, and the Making of the Modern World Economy*, Princeton, Oxford, Princeton University Press.

Porta, P. L. and Scazzieri, R. (1997) Towards an economic theory of international civil society: Trust, trade and open government, *Structural Change and Economic Dynamics*, 8(1), pp. 5–28.

Przeworski, A. (2004) Geography vs. Institutions Revisited: Were Fortunes Reversed? New York University, mimeo.

Putnam, R. D. (1993) *Making Democracy Work: Civic Traditions in Modern Italy*, Princeton, Princeton University Press.

Quah, D. T. (1996) Empirics for economic growth and convergence, *European Economic Review*, 40(6), pp. 1353–1375.

Reichart, S. (2005) *Zum Konvergenzprozess der mittel- und osteuropäischen EU-Beitrittsländer*, Hohenheimer Volkswirtschaftliche Schriften, Frankfurt am Main, Peter Lang.

Rodrik, D. (2000) Institutions for High-Quality Growth: What they are and how to Acquire them, *Studies in Comparative International Development*, 35(3), pp. 3–31.

Rodrik, D. (ed.) (2003) *In Search of Prosperity*, Princeton, Princeton University Press.

Rodrik, D. (2007) *One Economics, Many Recipes: Globalization, Institutions, and Economic Growth*, Princeton, NY, Princeton University Press.

Rodrik, D., Subramanian, A. and Trebbi, F. (2004) Institutions Rule: The Primacy of Institutions Over Geography and Integration in Economic Development, *Journal of Economic Growth*, 9(2), pp. 131–165.

Roland, G. (2005) Understanding Institutional Change: Fast-Moving and Slow-Moving Institutions, paper presented at the Conference of Endogenous Institutional Change, Social Science History Institute, Stanford University, also published in *Studies in Comparative International Development*, 2004, 38(4), pp. 109–131.

Sabra, A. I. (1994) Science and Philosophy in Medieval Islamic Theology: the Evidence of the Fourteenth Century, *Zeitschrift für Geschichte der Arabisch-Islamischen Wissenschaften*, 9, pp. 1–42.

Sachs, J. D. (2003) Institutions Don't Rule: Direct Effects of Geography on Per Capita Income, Working Paper No. 9490, Cambridge, MA, National Bureau of Economic Research.

Sachs, J. D. and Warner, A. (1995) Economic Reform and the Process of Global Integration, *Brookings Papers on Economic Activity*, 26(1995-1), pp. 1–118.

Sala-i-Martin, X. (1996) The Classical Approach to Convergence Analysis, *The Economic Journal*, 106(437), pp. 1019–1036.

Sala-i-Martin, X. and Artadi, E. V. (2003) Economic Growth and Investment in the Arab World, in: Cornelius, P. K. and Schwab, K. (eds.) *The Arab World Competitiveness Report 2002–2003*, New York, Oxford, Oxford University Press.

Schumann, J. (2005) Reichtum, Opfer und Steuern in jüdischen, christlichen, islamischen und buddhistischen Quellen, in: Göcke, M. and Kooths, S. (eds.) *Entscheidungsorientierte Volkswirtschaftslehre: Festschrift für Gustav Dieckheuer*, Frankfurt am Main, Peter Lang.

Schumann, J. (2007) Zur Geschichte christlicher und islamischer Zinsverbote, in: Hagemann, H. (ed.) *Studien zur Entwicklung der ökonomischen Theorie XXI: Ökonomie und Religion*, Berlin, Duncker & Humblot.

Shatzmiller, M. (2001) Islamic Institutions and Property Rights: The Case of the 'Public Good' Waqf, *Journal of the Economic and Social History of the Orient*, 44(1), pp. 44–74.

Sheikh, M. S. (1982) *Islamic Philosophy*, London, The Octagon Press.

Smith, A. (1759) *The Theory of Moral Sentiments*, London, A. Miller.

Stock, J. H. and Watson, M. W. (2003) *Introduction to Econometrics*, Boston, Addison Wesley.

Tabellini, G. (2005) Culture and Institutions: Economic Development in the Regions of Europe, CESifo Working Paper No. 1492, forthcoming in *Journal of the European Economic Association*.

Tabellini, G. (2008a) Institutions and Culture, *Journal of the European Economic Association*, 6(2–3), pp. 255–294.

Tabellini, G. (2008b) The Scope of Cooperation: Values and Incentives, *The Quarterly Journal of Economics*, 123(3), pp. 905–950.

Temple, J. (1999) The New Growth Evidence, *Journal of Economic Literature*, 37(1), pp. 112–156.

Temple, J. and Johnson, P. A. (1998) Social Capability and Economic Growth, *The Quarterly Journal of Economics*, 113(3), pp. 965–990.

Tierney, B. (1982) *Religion, Law and the Growth of Constitutional Thought,* pp. 1150–1650, Cambridge, Cambridge University Press.

Tripp, C. (2006) *Islam and the Moral Economy: The Challenge of Capitalism*, Cambridge, Cambridge University Press.

United Nations Development Program (UNDP) (2002) *The Arab Human Development Report 2002: Creating Opportunities for Future Generations*, New York, United Nations Publications.

United Nations Development Program (UNDP) (2003) *The Arab Human Development Report 2003:Building a Knowledge Society*, New York, United Nations Publications.

United Nations Population Fund (UNFPA) (2003) The Arab Population, in: Cornelius, P. K. and Schwab, K. (eds.) *The Arab World Competitiveness Report 2002–2003*, New York, Oxford, Oxford University Press.

Weber, M. (2002) *The Protestant Ethic and the Spirit of Capitalism*, New York and London, Routledge (originally published as two separate essays, 1904–1905).

Williamson, C. R. (2009) Informal Institutions Rule: Institutional Arrangements and Economic Performance, *Public Choice*, 139(3–4), pp. 371–387.

Williamson, C. R. and Kerekes, C. B. (2009) Securing Private Property: The Relative Importance of Formal versus Informal Institutions, Appalachian State University, mimeo.

Williamson, O. E. (2000) The New Institutional Economics: Taking Stock, Looking Ahead, *Journal of Economic Literature*, 38(3), pp. 595–613.

Wooldridge, J. M. (2003) *Introductory Econometrics*, Mason, Ohio, South-Western.

WORLD AND EUROPEAN VALUES SURVEYS FOUR WAVE INTEGRATED DATA FILE, 1981–2004, v.20060423, 2006, The World Values Survey Association, [online] available at: <www.worldvaluessurvey.org> [accessed 14 October 2009], and European Values Study Foundation, [online] available at: <www.europeanvalues.nl> [accessed 14 October 2009].

World Bank (2008) *Middle East and North Africa 2008 Economic Developments and Prospects: Regional Integration for Global Competitiveness*, Washington, DC, The World Bank, [online] available at: <http://siteresources.worldbank.org/INTMENA/Resources/2008MENA-EDP-full.pdf> [accessed 06 September 2010].

Yousef, T. M. (2004) Development, Growth and Policy Reform in the Middle East and North Africa since 1950, *Journal of Economic Perspectives*, 18(3), pp. 91–116.

Zweynert, J. and Goldschmidt, N. (2006) The Two Transitions in Central and Eastern Europe as Processes of Institutional Transplantation, *Journal of Economic Issues*, December, XL(4), pp. 895–919.

Data sources

Freedom House, Freedom in the World Comparative and Historical Data 2009, [online] available at: <http://www.freedomhouse.org/template.cfm?page=439> [accessed 21 March 2010].

Hall, R. E. and Jones, C. I. (1999) Why Do Some Countries Produce So Much More Output Per Worker Than Others?, *The Quarterly Journal of Economics*, 114(1), pp. 83–116, data [online] available at: <http://elsa.berkely.edu/~chad/datasets.html> [accessed 27 October 2009].

Heston, A., Summers, R. and Aten, B. (2006) Penn World Table Version 6.2, Center for International Comparisons of Production, Income and Prices at the University of Pennsylvania, [online] available at: <http://pwt.econ.upenn.edu/php_site/pwt_index.php> [accessed 14 October 2009].

Kaufmann, D., Kraay, A. and Mastruzzi, M. (2009) Governance Matters VIII: Aggregate and Individual Governance Indicators 1996–2008, version wigidataset [computer file], [online] available at: <http://info.worldbank.org/governance/wgi/index.asp> [accessed 8 August 2009].

La Porta, R., Lopez-De-Silanes, F., Shleifer, A. and Vishny, R. W. (1999) The Quality of Government, *The Journal of Law, Economics, and Organization*, 15(1), pp. 222–279, data [online] available at: <http://mba.tuck.dartmouth.edu/pages/faculty/rafael.laporta/publications.html> [accessed 27 October 2009].

Marshall, M. G., Jaggers, K. and Gurr, T. R. (2007) *Polity IV Project: Political Regime Characteristics and Transitions, 1800–2009*, version p4v2007 [Computer File], [online] available at: <http://www.systemicpeace.org/ polity/polity4.htm> [accessed 2 July 2009].

Miller, T. and Holmes, K.R. (2009) *2009 Index of Economic Freedom*, The Heritage Foundation & The Wall Street Journal, [online] available at: <http://www.heritage.org/index/> [accessed 10 March 2010].

Parker, P. M. (1997) *National Cultures of the World: A Statistical Reference*, Westport, Greenwood Press, data [online] available at: <http://faculty.insead.edu/parker/resume/personal.htm> [accessed 27 October 2009].

Sachs, J. D. (2003) Institutions Don't Rule: Direct Effects of Geography on Per Capita Income, Working Paper No. 9490, Cambridge, MA, National Bureau of Economic Research, data [online] available at: <http://www.earth.columbia.edu/articles/view/1040> [accessed 27 October 2009].

UNCTAD GlobStat Database, World Investment Report 2008: Transnational Corporations and the Infrastructure Challenge, Major FDI indicators, [online] available at: <http://www.unctad.org/en/docs/wir2008_en.pdf> and <http://www.unctad.org/Templates/Page.asp?intItemID=1584&lang=1> [accessed 17 July 2009].

WORLD AND EUROPEAN VALUES SURVEYS FOUR WAVE INTEGRATED DATA FILE, 1981–2004, v.20060423, 2006, The World Values Survey Association, [online] available at: <www.worldvaluessurvey.org> [accessed 14 October 2009], and European Values Study Foundation, [online] available at: <www.europeanvalues.nl> [accessed 14 October 2009].

World Bank (2009), World Development Indicators (WDI) Online database, [online] available at: <http://data.worldbank.org/> [accessed 2 July 2009].

Appendix A

Derivation of the equilibrium wage (pp. 51-53):

To show: $V_c^u + \alpha$ is not worthwhile (lifetime utility unemployed cheater + gain from cheating in one period).

Agent will not cheat if: $V_h \geq \alpha + V_c^u$ (2.20)

Utility functions:

Employed honest agent:

$$V_h = W^* + \delta(1-\xi)V_h + \xi V_h^u \tag{2.21}$$

Unemployed agent; i=h: honest; i=c: cheater:

$$V_i^u = \delta h_i V_h + \delta(1-h_i)(\eta + V_i^u) \qquad i = h,c \tag{2.22}$$

Dissolve (2.21) for V_h^u:

$$V_h^u = \frac{V_h - W^* - \delta(1-\xi)V_h}{\xi}$$

$$V_h^u = \frac{V_h\{1-\delta(1-\xi)\} - W^*}{\xi}$$

$$V_h^u = \frac{V_h\Sigma - W^*}{\xi} \qquad \text{with: } \Sigma = 1-\delta(1-\xi) \tag{2.23}$$

From (2.22); setting i=h:

$$V_h^u = \delta h_h V_h + \delta(1-h_h)(\eta + V_h^u) \tag{2.24}$$

Dissolve (2.22) with i=h for V_h^u:

$$V_h^u = \delta h_h V_h + [(\delta - \delta h_h)(\eta + V_h^u)]$$

$$V_h^u = \delta h_h V_h + [\delta\eta + \delta V_h^u - \delta h_h \eta - \delta h_h V_h^u]$$

$$V_h^u - \delta V_h^u + \delta h_h V_h^u = \delta h_h V_h + \delta\eta - \delta h_h \eta$$

$$V_h^u (1 - \delta(1 - h_h)) = \delta h_h V_h + \delta(1 - h_h)\eta$$

$$V_h^u (1 - \delta(1 - h_h)) = \delta h_h V_h + \delta(\eta - h_h \eta) = \delta h_h V_h + \delta(1 - h_h)\eta$$

$$V_h^u = \frac{\delta h_h V_h}{1 - \delta(1 - h_h)} + \frac{\delta(1 - h_h)\eta}{1 - \delta(1 - h_h)}$$

$$V_h^u = \delta H_h V_h + \delta P_h \eta \tag{2.25}$$

with $H_i = \frac{h_i}{[1 - \delta(1 - h_i)]}$

$P_i = \frac{1 - h_i}{1 - \delta(1 - h_i)}$ i=h;c

Similarly; setting i=c in (2.22):

$$V_c^u = \delta h_c V_h + \delta(1 - h_c)(\eta + V_c^u)$$

$$V_c^u = \delta H_c V_h + \delta P_c \eta \tag{2.26}$$

Equalizing (2.23) and (2.25):

$$\frac{V_h \Sigma - W^*}{\xi} = \delta H_h V_h + \delta P_h \eta$$

$$V_h \Sigma - W^* = \delta H_h V_h \xi + \delta P_h \eta \xi$$

$$V_h \Sigma = \delta H_h V_h \xi + \delta P_h \eta \xi + W^*$$

$$V_h \Sigma - \delta H_h V_h \xi = \delta P_h \eta \xi + W^*$$

$$V_h (\Sigma - \delta H_h \xi) = \delta P_h \eta \xi + W^*$$

$$V_h = \frac{\delta P_h \eta \xi + W^*}{\Sigma - \delta H_h \xi} \tag{2.27}$$

Remember:

$$\Rightarrow V_h \geq \alpha + V_c^u \tag{2.20}$$

Insert (2.26) into (2.20):

$$V_h \geq \alpha + \delta H_c V_h + \delta P_c \eta$$

$$V_h - \delta H_c V_h \geq \alpha + \delta P_c \eta$$

$$V_h (1 - \delta H_c) \geq \alpha + \delta P_c \eta$$

$$V_h \geq \frac{\alpha + \delta P_c \eta}{1 - \delta H_c} \tag{2.28}$$

Insert (2.27) into (2.28):

$$\frac{\delta P_h \eta \xi + W^*}{\Sigma - \delta H_h \xi} \geq \frac{\alpha + \delta P_c \eta}{1 - \delta H_c} \tag{2.29}$$

$$\delta P_h \eta \xi + W^* \geq \frac{\alpha + \delta P_c \eta}{1 - \delta H_c} (\Sigma - \delta H_h \xi)$$

$$W^* \geq \frac{\alpha + \delta P_c \eta}{1 - \delta H_c} (\Sigma - \delta H_h \xi) - \delta P_h \eta \xi$$

$$W^* \geq (\Sigma - \delta H_h \xi) \left[\frac{\alpha}{1 - \delta H_c} + \frac{\delta P_c \eta}{1 - \eta H_c} \right] - \delta P_h \eta \xi$$

$$W^* \geq \frac{\alpha (\Sigma - \delta H_h \xi)}{1 - \delta H_c} + \frac{\delta P_c \eta (\Sigma - \delta H_h \xi)}{1 - \delta H_c} - \delta P_h \eta \xi$$

$$W^* \geq \frac{\alpha (\Sigma - \delta H_h \xi)}{1 - \delta H_c} + \delta \eta \left(\frac{P_c (\Sigma - \delta H_h \xi)}{1 - \delta H_c} - P_h \xi \right) \tag{2.30}$$

$$W^* = w(\delta, h_h, h_c, \xi, \eta, \alpha) \triangleright \eta \tag{2.31}$$

Appendix B

World Bank country group classification

High-income OECD members:

Australia; Austria; Belgium; Canada; Czech Republic; Denmark; Finland; France; Germany; Greece; Hungary; Iceland; Ireland; Italy; Japan; Korea, Rep.; Luxembourg; Netherlands; New Zealand; Norway; Poland; Portugal; Slovak Republic; Slovenia; Spain; Sweden; Switzerland; United Kingdom; United States

High-income non-OECD economies

Andorra; Aruba; Bahamas, The; Bahrain; Barbados; Bermuda; Brunei Darussalam; Cayman Islands; Channel Islands; Croatia; Cyprus; Estonia; Equatorial Guinea; Faeroe Islands; French Polynesia; Gibraltar; Greenland; Guam; Hong Kong SAR; Isle of Man; Israel; Kuwait; Latvia; Liechtenstein; Macao SAR; Malta; Monaco; Netherlands Antilles; New Caledonia; Northern Mariana Islands; Oman; Puerto Rico; Qatar; San Marino; Saudi Arabia; Singapore; Trinidad and Tobago; Turks and Caicos Islands; UAE; Virgin Islands (US)

Middle East and North Africa

Algeria; Djibouti; Egypt, Arab Rep.; Iran, Islamic Rep.; Iraq; Jordan; Lebanon; Libya; Morocco; Syrian, Arab Rep.; Tunisia; West Bank and Gaza; Yemen, Rep.

Euro area

Austria; Belgium; Cyprus; Finland; France; Germany; Greece; Ireland; Italy; Luxembourg; Malta; Netherlands; Portugal; Slovak Republic; Slovenia; Spain

East Asia and Pacific

American Samoa; Cambodia; China; Fiji; Indonesia; Kiribati; Korea, Dem. Rep.; Lao PDR; Malaysia; Marshall Islands; Micronesia, Fed. Sts; Mongolia; Myanmar; Palau; Papua New Guinea; Philippines; Samoa; Solomon Islands; Thailand; Timor-Leste; Tuvalu; Tonga; Vanuatu; Vietnam

Europe and Central Asia

Albania; Armenia; Azerbaijan; Belarus; Bosnia and Herzegovina; Bulgaria; Georgia; Kazakhstan; Kosovo; Kyrgyz Republic; Lithuania; Macedonia, FYR; Moldova; Montenegro; Romania; Russian Federation; Serbia; Tajikistan; Turkey; Turkmenistan; Ukraine; Uzbekistan

Latin America and the Caribbean

Antigua and Barbuda; Argentina; Belize; Bolivia; Brazil; Chile; Colombia; Costa Rica; Cuba; Dominica; Dominican Republic; Ecuador; El Salvador; Grenada; Guatemala; Guyana; Haiti; Honduras; Jamaica; Mexico; Nicaragua; Panama; Paraguay; Peru; St. Kitts and Nevis; St. Lucia; St. Vincent and the Grenadines; Suriname; Uruguay; Venezuela; RB

South Asia

Afghanistan; Bangladesh; Bhutan; India; Maldives; Nepal; Pakistan; Sri Lanka

Sub-Saharan Africa

Angola; Benin; Botswana; Burkina Faso; Burundi; Cameroon; Cape Verde; Central African Republic; Chad; Comoros; Congo, Dem. Rep.; Congo, Rep.; Côte d'Ivoire; Eritrea; Ethiopia; Gabon; Gambia, The; Ghana; Guinea; Guinea-Bissau; Kenya; Lesotho; Liberia; Madagascar; Malawi; Mali; Mauritania; Mauritius; Mayotte; Mozambique; Namibia; Niger; Nigeria; Rwanda; São Tomé and

Principe; Senegal; Seychelles; Sierra Leone; Somalia; South Africa; Sudan; Swaziland; Tanzania; Togo; Uganda; Zambia; Zimbabwe

RPLA: Djibouti; Egypt; Jordan; Lebanon; Morocco; Tunisia; West Bank and Gaza

RRLA: Algeria; Iran; Iraq; Syria; Yemen;

RRLI: Bahrain; Kuwait; Libya; Oman; Qatar; Saudi Arabia; the UAE

World Bank classification, data accessed September 20, 2010, [online] at: <http://data.worldbank.org/about/country-classifications/country-and-lending-groups>.

HOHENHEIMER VOLKSWIRTSCHAFTLICHE SCHRIFTEN

Band 1 Walter Deffaa: Anonymisierte Befragungen mit zufallsverschlüsselten Antworten. Die Randomized-Response-Technik (RRT). Methodische Grundlagen, Modelle und Anwendungen. 1982.

Band 2 Thomas Michael Baum: Staatsverschuldung und Stabilisierungspolitik in der Demokratie. Zur neoinstitutionalistischen Kritik der keynesianischen Fiskalpolitik. 1982.

Band 3 Klaus Schröter: Die wettbewerbspolitische Behandlung der leitungsgebundenen Energiewirtschaft. Dargestellt am Beispiel der Fernwärmewirtschaft der Bundesrepublik Deutschland. 1986.

Band 4 Hugo Mann: Theorie und Politik der Steuerreform in der Demokratie. 1987.

Band 5 Max Christoph Wewel: Intervallarithmetische Dependenzanalyse in der Ökonometrie. Ein konjekturaler Ansatz. 1987.

Band 6 Heinrich Pascher: Die U.S.-amerikanische Deregulation Policy im Luftverkehrs- und Bankenbereich. 1987.

Band 7 Harald Lob: Die Entwicklung der französischen Wettbewerbspolitik bis zur Verordnung Nr. 86-1243 vom 01. Dezember 1986. Eine exemplarische Untersuchung der Erfassung der Behinderungsstrategie auf der Grundlage des Konzepts eines wirksamen Wettbewerbs. 1988.

Band 8 Ulrich Kirschner: Die Erfassung der Nachfragemacht von Handelsunternehmen. Eine Analyse der ökonomischen Beurteilungskriterien und der wettbewerbsrechtlichen Instrumente im Bereich der Verhaltenskontrolle.1988.

Band 9 Friedhelm Herb: Marktwirtschaftliche Innovationspolitik. 1988.

Band 10 Claus Schnabel: Zur ökonomischen Analyse der Gewerkschaften in der Bundesrepublik Deutschland. Theoretische und empirische Untersuchungen von Mitgliederentwicklung, Verhalten und Einfluß auf wirtschaftliche Größen. 1989.

Band 11 Jan B. Rittaler: Industrial Concentration and the Chicago School of Antitrust Analysis. A Critical Evaluation on the Basis of Effective Competition. 1989.

Band 12 Thomas Märtz: Interessengruppen und Gruppeninteressen in der Demokratie. Zur Theorie des Rent-Seeking. 1990.

Band 13 Andreas Maurer: Statistische Verfahren zur Ermittlung von oligopolistischen Strukturen. 1990.

Band 14 Peter Mendler: Zur ökonomischen und politisch-institutionellen Analyse öffentlicher Kredithilfen. 1992.

Band 15 Heinrich J. Engelke: Die Interpretation der Rundfunkfreiheit des Grundgesetzes: Eine Analyse aus ökonomischer Sicht. 1992.

Band 16 Thomas Fischer: Staat, Recht und Verfassung im Denken von Walter Eucken. Zu den staats- und rechtstheoretischen Grundlagen einer wirtschaftsordnungspolitischen Konzeption. 1993.

Band 17 Stefan Elßer: Innovationswettbewerb. Determinanten und Unternehmensverhalten. 1993.

Band 18 Reinhard Scharff: Regionalpolitik und regionale Entwicklungspotentiale. Eine kritische Analyse. 1993.

Band 19 Karin Beckmann: Probleme der Regionalpolitik im Zuge der Vollendung des Europäischen Binnenmarktes. Eine ökonomische Analyse. 1995.

Band 20 Bernd Nolte: Engpaßfaktoren der Innovation und Innovationsinfrastruktur. Eine theoretische und empirische Analyse für ländliche Wirtschaftsräume in Baden-Württemberg. 1996.

Band 21 Klaus-Rainer Brintzinger: Die Nationalökonomie an den Universitäten Freiburg, Heidelberg und Tübingen 1918 - 1945. Eine institutionenhistorische, vergleichende Studie der wirtschaftswissenschaftlichen Fakultäten und Abteilungen südwestdeutscher Universitäten. 1996.

Band 22 Steffen Binder: Die Idee der Konsumentensouveränität in der Wettbewerbstheorie. Teleokratische vs. nomokratische Auffassung. 1996.

Band 23 Alexander Burger: Deregulierungspotentiale in der Gesetzlichen Rentenversicherung. Reformnotwendigkeiten versus Reformmöglichkeiten. 1996.

Band 24 Burkhard Scherer: Regionale Entwicklungspolitik. Konzeption einer dezentralisierten und integrierten Regionalpolitik. 1997.

Band 25 Frauke Wolf: Lorenzkurvendisparität. Neuere Entwicklungen, Erweiterungen und Anwendungen. 1997.

Band 26 Hans Pitlik: Politische Ökonomie des Föderalismus. Föderative Kompetenzverteilung im Lichte der konstitutionellen Ökonomik. 1997.

Band 27 Stephan Seiter: Der Beitrag Nicholas Kaldors zur Neuen Wachstumstheorie. Eine vergleichende Studie vor dem Hintergrund der Debatte über den Verdoorn-Zusammenhang. 1997.

Band 28 André Schmidt: Ordnungspolitische Perspektiven der europäischen Integration im Spannungsfeld von Wettbewerbs- und Industriepolitik. 1998.

Band 29 Bernd Blessin: Innovations- und Umweltmanagement in kleinen und mittleren Unternehmen. Eine theoretische und empirische Analyse. 1998.

Band 30 Oliver Letzgus: Die Ökonomie internationalen Umweltschutzes. 1999.

Band 31 Claudia Hafner: Systemwettbewerb versus Harmonisierung in Europa. Am Beispiel des Arbeitsmarktes. 1999.

Band 32 Jürgen Kulle: Ökonomie der Musikindustrie. Eine Analyse der körperlichen und unkörperlichen Musikverwertung mit Hilfe von Tonträgern und Netzen. 1998.

Band 33 Michael Ganske: Intertemporale Aspekte von Staatsverschuldung und Außenhandel. 1999.

Band 34 Margit Ströbele: Die Deregulierungswirkungen der europäischen Integration. Das Beispiel der Sondermärkte. 1999.

Band 35 Marion Benesch: Devisenmarktinterventionen in Theorie und Praxis. Eine umfassende Analyse ihrer Zielsetzungen, Wirkungsweisen und wirtschaftspolitischen Bedeutung. 1999.

Band 36 Torsten Gruber: Unterschiedliche geldpolitische Transmissionsmechanismen und Stabilitätskulturen als mögliche Ursachen geldpolitischer Spannungen in der Europäischen Währungsunion. 2000.

Band 37 Bertram Melzig-Thiel: Arbeit in der Informationsgesellschaft. Chancen und Risiken neuer Informations- und Kommunikationstechnologien für die Beschäftigung. 2000.

Band 38 Annette Fritz: Die Entsorgungswirtschaft im Spannungsfeld zwischen Abfallpolitik und Kartellrecht. Eine industrieökonomische Branchenstudie. 2001.

Band 39 Harald Strotmann: Arbeitsplatzdynamik in der baden-württembergischen Industrie. Eine Analyse mit amtlichen Betriebspaneldaten. 2002.

Band 40 Dietrich Benner: Qualitätsungewißheit bei Gütern mit Vertrauenseigenschaften. Entwicklung und Anwendung eines entscheidungstheoretisch fundierten Analyserahmens. 2002.

Band 41 Jürgen M. Schechler: Sozialkapital und Netzwerkökonomik. 2002.

Band 42 Kay-Uwe May: Haushaltskonsolidierung durch Ausgabekürzungen. Restriktionen und Strategien. 2002.

Band 43 Peter Kühnl: Der Wechselkurs als Zwischenziel der Geldpolitik im Aufholprozess. Die monetärkeynesianische Entwicklungsstrategie der Berliner Schule vor dem Hintergrund der makroökonomischen Entwicklung ausgewählter Länder Mittel- und Osteuropas. 2003.

Band 44 Steffen Wirth: Nichtparametrische Analyse von Bildungsertragsraten. Neuere Entwicklungen und Anwendungen. 2003.

Band 45 Bernhard Holwegler: Innovation, Diffusion und Beschäftigung. Die ökonomische Theorie der Technologiediffusion und ihr Beitrag zur Erklärung technologischer Arbeitslosigkeit. 2003.

Band 46 Guntram R. M. Hepperle: Zukunftsorientierte Industriepolitik. Möglichkeiten und Grenzen. 2004.

Band 47 Udo Vullhorst: Stabilisierungspolitik bei supranationaler Geldpolitik und nationaler Fiskalpolitik. Eine spieltheoretische Betrachung. 2004.

Band 48 Matthias Rösch: Die Bedeutung von Investivlöhnen und Gewinnbeteiligungen für Einkommensverteilung und Beschäftigung. 2004.

Band 49 Michael Bubik: Erfolgskriterien für Unternehmenszusammenschlüsse. Eine theoretische und exemplarische Analyse. 2005.

Band 50 Jörg Weltin: Internationale Unternehmensbesteuerung. Allokation der Besteuerungsrechte unter veränderten Rahmenbedingungen. 2005.

Band 51 Susanne Reichart: Zum Konvergenzprozess der mittel- und osteuropäischen EU-Beitrittsländer. 2005.

Band 52 Daniel Hartmann: Geldpolitik und Beschäftigung. Die geldpolitische Strategie der Federal Reserve: Vorbild oder Auslaufmodell? 2005.

Band 53 Marc Peter Radke: Explaining Financial Crises. A Cyclical Approach. 2005.

Band 54 Katja Hölsch: Umverteilungseffekte in Europa. Eine Analyse für ausgewählte Länder. 2006.

Band 55 Ulrike Lehr: Contingent Valuation Daten und Bayes'sche Verfahren. Ein Vorschlag zur Verbesserung von Umweltbewertung und Nutzentransfer. 2006.

Band 56 Jutta Maute: Hyperinflation, Currency Board, and Bust. The Case of Argentina. 2006.

Band 57 Michael Knittel: Geldpolitik und Stabilität des Bankensystems. Das Liquiditätsproblem aus Sicht der Theoriegeschichte und der gegenwärtigen Finanzmarktentwicklung. 2007.

Band 58 Oliver Frör: Rationality Concepts in Environmental Valuation. 2007.

Band 59 Jochen Gert Arend Wiegmann: Produktivitätsentwicklung in Deutschland. 2008.

Band 60 Nicola Meier: China – The New Developmental State? An Empirical Analysis of the Automotive Industry. 2009.

Band 61 Carsten H. Wander: Logistik und Wettbewerb. Zur Rolle logistischer (Re-)Organisation in einer wettbewerbsbasierten Marktwirtschaft. 2009.

Band 62 Sven Wydra: Produktions- und Beschäftigungseffekte neuer Technologien. Am Beispiel der Biotechnologie. 2010.

Band 63 Andreas Schaal: Die Relevanz von Venture Capital für Innovation und Beschäftigung. Theoretische Klärung und empirische Analyse. 2010

Band 64 Sybille Sobczak: Geldpolitik und Vermögensmärkte. Volkswirtschaftliche Bedeutung von und geldpolitische Reaktion auf Asset Price Bubbles. 2010

Band 65 Constanze Dobler: The Impact of Formal and Informal Institutions on Economic Growth. A Case Study on the MENA Region. 2011.

www.peterlang.de

www.ingramcontent.com/pod-product-compliance
Ingram Content Group UK Ltd.
Pitfield, Milton Keynes, MK11 3LW, UK
UKHW021832100926
8556IPUK00004B/286

9 783631 616161